MW01135898

THE
YOGA
OF
SELF PERFECTION

*Based on Sri Aurobindo's
Synthesis of Yoga*

M.P. PANDIT

PUBLISHER:
LOTUS LIGHT PUBLICATIONS
P.O. Box 2
Wilmot, WI 53192 U.S.A.

First U.S.A. edition September 21, 1983

These talks complete the series based on Sri Aurobindo's Synthesis of Yoga

Published by Lotus Light Publications
by arrangement with Sri M. P. Pandit

Cover Design: Paul Simpson

ISBN 0-941524-20-5

Library of Congress Catalog Card Number 83-081299

CONTENTS

1

THE PRINCIPLE OF THE INTEGRAL YOGA

In the series of talks that we started some two years ago at *Peace* in Auroville, on *The Synthesis of Yoga* by Sri Aurobindo, we covered the Yoga of Works and the Yoga of Knowledge and then we took up the Way of Love, the Yoga of Devotion. There was an interruption thereafter because we felt that it was necessary to have a grounding in the Teachings of the Mother before we could study with full benefit the last part of *The Synthesis*, the Yoga of Self-Perfection.

Sri Aurobindo enumerates the main principles of Karma Yoga, Jnana Yoga and Bhakti Yoga and then proceeds to develop his own Yoga of Self-Perfection, not indeed discarding the benefits of the different lines of yoga, studied so far, but assimilating and utilising them for larger ends. He seeks to pull out yoga from the hermitages and special retreats into the open so that yoga can be a way of life itself and be utilised to develop life to its optimum. And that is why he calls his Integral Yoga the Yoga of Self-Perfection. In all lines of yoga that we have studied, one power, one faculty, that is prominent in the system, is taken up, developed and utilised as a spring-board to delve into the spirit. It may be one power or a group of powers. For instance, in Hatha Yoga, which in some form or the other is today highly popular in the West and also in some parts of the East, the practicians seize upon the body and the life-energy: they attach great importance to the physical body and have evolved certain exercises and postures of the limbs, which are called *āsanas*, by which the physical energies are brought together, and the body is gradually accustomed to longer periods of immobility so that it can function as a foundation for the yogic edifice. When the body is trained to hold itself for considerable periods in an immobile status, all the energies that are gathered start rising in potency. They acquire greater effectivity and power. After that is done, the Hathayogin concentrates upon the life-force, the breath. With the aid of Pranayama, the regulation and elongation of breath, control is acquired over the life-force and the nervous energies, and both the physical energies and the life-energies are gathered, controlled, and regulated. They are thereafter directed into that centre of the physical body where the life-energy is involved. The spot, where this nature-energy is concentrated, is at the base of the spine. It is called the Kundalini. When the physical and the life energies are poured and directed to smite this centre, the Kundalini is awakened, and it shoots up through the various centres of energy in the body, opening new channels of activity in those centres. It then goes on climbing upwards till it goes above the brain and meets what is known as Shiva or the silent, static Consciousness. The rationale is that when the nature-energy succeeds in linking itself with the divine Energy above, there is a liberation of consciousness. Man is no longer held as a slave to the lower nature; he breathes the freedom of the higher Nature. This is Hatha Yoga.

Raja Yoga concentrates upon the mind, the mental energy. After a few preliminary exercises of purification and self-discipline, for that ultimately is the meaning of Yama and Niyama spoken of by Patanjali, the Rajayogin proceeds with the aid of

Asanas and Pranayama to acquire sufficient hold over the bodily and life-functions so that he can exercise control over the mental activity. It has been found that by acquiring mastery over the movements of breath, the life-force, the mind can be brought to a silent status, the thought-activity controlled and by further steps of discipline like meditation and concentration, the mental energies are released into the quietude of Samadhi or trance. The mental apparatus is entirely detached from outer nature, quietened and stilled so that in its silence, in its immobility, the inner Self, the Atman reflects itself as in a limpid lake. That is the aim of Raja Yoga: liberation through the mind.

In each of these lines of Yoga, one power is taken up. The Hatha Yoga can be called the psycho-physical system, the Raja Yoga the psychological and spiritual system, and then there is the famous triple path, the path of knowledge, the path of works, the path of devotion, normally associated together. In the path of knowledge the aim is to fix upon the faculties of knowledge, purify them, gain control over them by discrimination, by rejection of what is wrong and by acceptance of what is right so that the thought-mind, the discursive mind with which we are familiar, is trained to develop a spiritual awareness, a spiritual outlook, a spiritual reference and gradually convert itself into a spiritual centre of thinking. As it grows the mind gets liberated into a spiritual dimension.

Similarly with Karma Yoga, the yoga of works: the dynamic will is seized and it is trained to consecrate itself, to offer itself to the Supreme Lord, the Master of Works. In this process of surrender and disinterested exertion the will gets transformed and is

elevated to a status where it can unite with the Will
of the Lord.

In the yoga of love or the path of devotion,
it is the heart's emotions, the capacities of the heart
for identification with others, for loving, that are used.
These capacities are taken hold of and directed to
flow upwards rather than outwards. The heart-centre
is systematically tapped and the very texture of the
emotional being is subjected to a spiritual culture with
the result that the whole of the emotional being around
the soul ultimately melts into love and adoration of
the Divine.

But it is also a fact that though one may start
at any point, start with any power that is prominent,
or can be conveniently seized upon, all power is one:
ultimately whatever the power one cultivates, whatever
the power one exploits, each power reveals itself to
be one with the other powers. For instance, the power
of knowledge as it develops, also reveals itself to be
the spring-board behind the impulse for dedication
and disinterested work. It also reveals itself as the
motive-force for love of God, for unless one knows
that the Divine is the Supreme, that the Divine is the
Lord and Master, spontaneous love cannot spring up.
So also, if one starts with love, as love develops, knowledge dawns that the One who is worshipped, the
One who is adored, is the Lord of all, not ours
alone. So each power, as it develops, enters into
the territories, mind-made territories, of other powers
and that is because all power is power of the soul.
Every power in life derives from the soul. This gives
rise to the possibility of having a yoga which is not
concerned with one power alone, with the liberation
of one part alone, but a kind of synthesized yoga

which combines all methods and makes the liberation as extensive, as wide and as high as possible.

It is not that such attempts have not been made before. There is, for instance, the Yoga of the Tantra. The Tantriks have seized upon the truth that all life moves between two ends—soul and nature, Purusha and Shakti—and they have attempted to embrace life from one end to the other. They do not take only one power, but seek to include all the powers by extending their vision from one end to the other. In their practice, they also seize upon the different motive-forces that make Nature exert herself, and give them their full value. They raise desires, emotions, activities, to a certain higher level, give them diviner values and allow them their due role in the workings of yoga. Not only do the Tantriks attempt to take up the whole of Nature without making the distinction of high and low and turn it Godward, but they also seek to derive the utmost value from life. Not merely liberation, but a full exploitation of the resources of life. Not *mukti* alone, but also *bhukti*, cosmic enjoyment, is a legitimate claim of a divinised nature. Tantra has been in existence for centuries. Whatever the deformations that may have taken place in its practice, the Tantra Yoga in its conception is a grand attempt at synthesis.

The synthesis of the present age on which Sri Aurobindo has worked is still larger. It combines, as one would expect, the best of all yogas, not in a kind of artificial unity, but in a living synthesis. As he puts it so graphically, this yoga, the yoga of self-perfection, the Integral Yoga, is called the Purna Yoga because it covers the whole of life. The liberation that it envisages is a liberation for all the parts of man. This synthesis starts with the method of the Vedanta in order to reach the aim of the Tantra. As Sri Aurobindo explains, in the Tantra they take hold of the shakti, nature-power, and try to arrive at the divine soul in its fullness through a manipulation and utilisation of the shakti. In the Vedanta they start with the soul, the self, not with the shakti, not with nature. But in Vedanta once they arrive at the self, they rest in the self. Here once one starts with the self, the inner Purusha, one makes that the centre of the movement to arrive at a higher Consciousness that enables one to realise the aim of the Tantra which is to take up all nature and raise it to a diviner level. If one were to start with nature in the beginning itself it would be risky, because very often one tends to get bogged down in the processes—the glittering processes of nature—and miss the aim altogether. If one establishes oneself in the soul-consciousness first, arrives at a certain freedom, liberation in the soul-centre, gets sufficiently detached, acquires a certain mastery over nature, then from that poise it *is* possible to extend the rule of the soul, the rule of the inner being more and more in life, bring the external and the lower nature under control, subject it to the process of purification and elevation and ultimately arrive at a state of liberation which includes not only the liberation of the soul, but also the liberation of nature from ignorance and false-hood. Released from falsehood, Prakriti becomes Shakti. And Shakti is nothing else but Shiva himself, the Lord as Nature; she is revealed not as something different from the Lord, but a poise of the Lord.

Another difference between the tantric synthesis and the synthesis of which Sri Aurobindo speaks is that one starts in the Tantra from below. All attempt is first directed towards the awakening of the lower centres. In the process all the lower energies are set in motion. One first comes into contact with the restless nature which is ignited into activity. And then follows a laborious process of going up step by step. But in Sri Aurobindo's synthesis one starts with the soul in the mind, the spirit as embodied in the mind. One opens those levels to the higher Shakti, the higher Consciousness and once it is received, it is the Yoga-Shakti that moves step by step, opening up various areas, various regions of consciousness and being. One starts at a safe level; instead of starting from the bottom one starts at the top where one is more conscious, where things are more under control. Man being a mental being, it is very natural for him to start in the mind. When one knows better, is better aware, one can control better. The process is of surrender, a self-surrender at all points. Not the self-surrender of the *bhakta* who surrenders only in the heart, nor of the *jnānin* who exposes only his mental summits, but from all points at which one is conscious; one directs one's will to surrender at each level of the being. One knows and recognises that this vast endeavour cannot be done by one's own effort. One opens oneself to the higher Shakti, to the Divine Power and makes an effort to consistently keep open every part of oneself to the action of the descending Force, and allows oneself to be possessed by the Divine.

The third feature is an enlargement of the object of yoga. In the traditional lines of yoga including the yoga of the Tantra of which we have been speaking, the whole effort is directed towards the liberation of the individual. But here it is recognised that individual liberation is a first and partial result. Man does not live by himself alone. Whether he likes it or not, he is part of the cosmos. The Divine that is in him is also there in others, and his own liberation, his own perfection can never be complete, can never be whole, unless that liberation, that perfection is worked out at least to a certain extent in those around him. So this dimension of the universal, the aspect of cosmic realisation, the cosmic problem is a speciality of this synthesis. It is recognised that man is part of the universe, and if he is to be whole, the universe also has to participate. He has also to contribute to the total evolution of the universe. And here comes in the conception and the practice of the collective yoga, the aim being the perfection of life, and a divinisation of life. No life can be perfected or divinised in its solitary greatness because one *has* to receive impacts, currents from outside, from above, from below, from around. And unless those levels around oneself are also raised and subjected to purification, and an environment is created by which there is a growing perfection in a collectivity, however small it may be, no individual perfection or liberation is safe. This is another aspect of the synthesis. Freedom from ego, freedom from ignorance, possession of one's nature by the Divine Consciousness,—this goes on step by step in the individual, enlarges itself to cover larger and larger areas in the course of its own self-affirmation. No realisation is worth its name unless it can stand the scrutiny of tests, unless it can meet life face to face and prove itself equal to the demands made upon it. And this is where a gradual evolution of a gnostic self comes in, a collectivity of seekers of Yoga who build a milieu, a realm where this common ideal of liberation and perfection in the Divine, possession by the Divine, is practised, each one helping the other, the collectivity helping the individual and the individual contributing to the collectivity.

It is not easy to start at all points at once. One starts in this yoga also, as in other yogas, at' the point where one is strong. My strong point may be the heart, I may have a larger capacity to extend myself, to love others, to unite with the feelings of others. I start with the way of love. You may be an intellectual and start with the mind. Another may be a dynamic worker who does not get satisfaction in the contemplative way of life; he starts where he feels he is fitted. We recognize that all these parts, all these powers, converge after a certain time, each strengthens and nourishes the others. They are so many tributaries that join into a mighty river and carry the soul onwards. This possibility, rather this certainty, that all these powers are going to unite at some point is always kept in mind. Things do not happen logically, step by step. One may start with the mind and suddenly there may be an opening in the heart; it is not kept waiting till the mind is developed. It is taken up on the way, joined to the mental effort; and here comes in the element of integrality. The whole system with its entire reservoir of power is treated as one unit. The starting points may vary, but after a time the energies of nature join at different points and become one. These, in short, are the main features which distinguish the new synthesis—the Yoga of Self-Perfection.

(From Questions and Answers)

What he means is the spirit in the mind or the soul in the mind. We recognise that the Divine embodies itself in the mind as the mental Purusha. And we start there, not at the level of the reasoning mind

or at the level of the thought-mind. We shall not
get bogged down in the processes of analysis. If we do
so we shall become expert logicians, but not necessarily
yogins. But if, from the beginning we lay stress upon
the soul-element in the mind, concentrate on mind in
the place where it is hooked to the Divine, where it
naturally opens to the higher levels, where it does
not insist on mentalising experiences, that will be the
right way to start at the mental level. That is what
Sri Aurobindo means when he says 'a spirit embodied
in mind.' We start from there. It is not easy. All of us
have to start from the level where we are. The aim
is to arrive at a level or layer in the mind which is
comparatively free from these involvements and use
that as a spring-board for developing the consciousness,
for opening the being to receive the higher influx.

*   *

It is the mental consciousness. It is the mental
awareness with which we approach the heart or the
life-energy. We are essentially mental beings, so it is
through the mind that we are aware. What is the
motive-force of my working? How far are my emotions
and feelings pure? This approach is, you may say, of
the awakened or the enlightened mental. So whether
you start through works or through love or through
knowledge, the approach is from a layer of the mind
comparatively purer, nearer the soul, than the ratio-
cinative mind.

Q.: *How to control thought?*

A.: The one effective way is to intensify our
interest in what we want. Supposing we want to
realise the Divine, then the interest must be intense,
so developed that the mind naturally flows in that
direction. What normally happens is that only a part

of ourselves is attracted to the ideal, and when we sit for meditation or contemplation, that part is indeed looking towards what it wants, but the rest of the mind has its own interests, its own attractions, its own habits. They all engulf us and we feel restless, we feel the invasion of thoughts, but if our main interest is widened, established as the strongest point, thoughts cannot disturb. To take an example: we are reading a good story or something that has appeared in the newspaper that is of absorbing interest; at that time there may be a musical party going on, or a radio blaring at your neighbour's, children playing— all factors that normally distract our minds. Still the mind goes on reading, because we are interested. So it has been said, 'Create an interest, intensify that interest, make that interest a capital interest, then other distractions die down.' In a word, aspiration and sincerity are needed.

Secondly, thoughts are always there. It is not that they come more when we sit for concentration or meditation. We are normally extrovert, thinking of something or the other. A hundred thoughts are simultaneously going on, but we are not aware of them for our interest is held by one thing. When we close our eyes and sit, we suddenly become aware that these thoughts are there. The thoughts have not come specially because we are meditating. Meditation and concentration are occasions to study what these thoughts are and what they reveal. They come because something in us wants to think of them. They reveal our nature. Vivekananda says that we can utilise these thoughts to study our nature, to find out our weak points and our strong points and take appropriate action. Once we start doing so, they dwindle.

2

THE INTEGRAL PERFECTION

I have in my possession a few unpublished selections from the Mother's talks to a few individuals, and I thought that before we took up our subject of *Integral Perfection*, we could spend a little time over them. They are notes taken down by disciples and afterwards read out to the Mother and approved by her. They were not actually written by her:

In ancient times, the disciple had to undergo severe tests to prove his readiness for initiation. Here in the Ashram we do not follow that method. Apparently there is no test, no trial. But if you see the truth, you will find that here it is much more difficult. There the disciple knew that he was undergoing a period of trial and after he had passed through some outward tests, he was taken in. But here, you have to face life and you are watched at every moment. It is not only your outer actions that count. Each and every thought and inner movement is seen, every reaction is noticed. It is not what you do in the solitude of the forest, but what you do in the thick of the battle of life that is important. Are you ready to submit yourself to such tests? Are you ready to change yourself completely? You will have to throw out your ideas, values, interests and opinions. Everything will have to be learnt anew. If you are ready for all this, then take the plunge. Otherwise, don't try to step in.

*   *

Flies, mosquitoes and other insects are the forma-tions of the Asura. The Asura does not create, he only gives the form. In the vital world you find monsters, very ugly and formidable. They are repre-sented in physical form by these numerous creatures. Some of them actually look like monsters while some may take very good shapes. The Asura may appear as a dazzling light, and unless you can go behind it and see the reality, you may take it to be the divine Light.

*   *

In the beginning of creation, even before the birth of the gods, four Asuras were born of Aditi. Two of them have changed. One has not made up his mind, and the fourth one has decided to fight against the Divine. He knows very well that he cannot succeed, but he insists that he should be destroyed. He knows that his time is almost finished, therefore he is trying to bring as much destruction upon earth as he can. He does not get disappointed or depressed by defeat. He becomes more violent. He knows me and is obliged to inform me about all his plans beforehand. There is no disease from which I have not suffered. I have taken all the diseases upon my body to see their course and to have knowledge of them by experience in the physical, so that I may be able to work upon them. But as my physical has no fear and it responds to the higher pressure, it is easier for me to get rid of them.

*   *

The whole thing is based on the wrong idea that all men are equal, so they must get the same variety and quantity of things. It is not true. While giving your rejected fruit to the servant, you should not think that he is mean and so he deserves all that is bad.

If you give with this idea, you will be insulting humanity. The insult will be in you and it will do harm to you. You must be able to see from the point of economy in the world; certain things are good for some and other things are good for some others. I have seen with my own eyes how people take out what you would call the most dirty things from the gutter and put them straight into the mouth. Well, they don't get cholera, they don't die. They have a strength that you don't have. If you keep them on boiled water and the best of your food, they will get sick. You can give them good things, but do not deprive of them of their strength. In comparison to what they eat, the rejected things that you give them are luxuries for them. If you give them with the idea that you are giving them things the poor 'I' is unable to take and they have the strength to assimilate, then where is the insult? You will be doing them great harm, if you accustom them to your so-called higher standard of living and deprive them of their strength and immunity without giving them the means to keep to it. For sometimes you may provide them with better things, but afterwards they will not have the things of your standard and you will have made them incapable of living within their means. Either raise their standard fully and give them the capacity to earn more and be able to maintain the standard or let them keep their standard and teach them to improve matters within their means.

*   *

If you have to exercise authority, have authority on yourself first. If you cannot keep discipline amongst the children, don't beat them or shout at them or get agitated. That is not permissible. Bring down calm and peace from above and under their pressure things will improve.

*   *

The question of life after death seems to be so stupid and meaningless. It presumes that there are two distinct compartments of life divided by death. In fact, it is not so. There is only one life and it continues. After death it is the same life without any change. Only it is minus the physical body. Otherwise, in all other respects, it is the same. If you are only the body and nothing else, then it could be said that life ceases as soon as the body drops down. But even the cats and dogs are not merely a body. They also have their vital. I have known dogs that used to go out from their body consciously. There was a dog of Theon who, when I was in meditation, used to rise out of his body and come to me and poke his cold vital nose into me to inform me that it was time to come out of meditation. I would come down and find his body under the staircase lying in a deep sleep.

When you die, the psychic may go for a repose into the psychic world. But the life of the vital continues in the same way for a very long time. Only you lose the fortress that affords protection, I mean the body. When you are in the body, when the vital goes in some dangerous places, it can always rush back to the body for protection. But once you are without a body, you are at the mercy of each and every passing force, unless of course you have the divine protection. That is why leaving the body will not solve any of your problems. If at all, it will only increase them by taking away the protection of the body.

*   *

The evolution of creation has reached up to man, the highest that can be reached by the mind. Then there is the creation of the Asura: insects, worms and the like belong to this replica of the beings of the vital world.

The third is the creation of the gods and angels. They are the "birds"—swan represents the soul.

*   *

To each one here power, light and strength are given as much as one can take and even more. It is given for transforming the person. When you take all that and use it for your personal ends and for the so-called human love, it is dishonesty, it is a crime of the first order. You must use everything for the purpose for which it is given. Otherwise you commit a crime. I am not speaking merely of the physical things. All the inner things that I am giving you all the time, all the strength, light and energy of life that are being poured into you are meant for the service of the Divine, for the sake of transforming you.

The more people are greedy, the more I give them, if they are satisfied with physical things only, they can have them. But it is not good for them. I like to give to those who do not ask.

*   *

The question was, "When I report to you about the doings of others, does it mean that I complain against them, and is it right to do that?"

It all depends upon your attitude. If you report a matter with a spirit of vengeance against someone or to show your superiority, or with any other personal motive, then it is absolutely wrong and you should not do that. But the true way is that you should be

like a mirror and reflect faithfully whatever you see.
Don't give your personal colouring and be quite dis-
passionate. If there is something wrong in the mirror
itself, then I can correct it. But you must try to see
that your mirror does not distort the picture.

*   *

We spoke last time of perfection as the aim of life,
at any rate, the aim of awakened life. Now what
exactly is the content of that perfection? In the progress
of humanity this perfection has been attempted in two
dimensions. One, what we would call a mundane perfection which involves a progressive harmonising of
the qualities and functions of Nature, improving the
qualities of the mind, raising up the level of motives,
desires and activities, ensuring the evolution of the
society in which the individual plays his due part,
the society contributing to the development of the
individual concerned and a culturing, an external
culturing of education, art, aesthesis and delight,—all
going to build up a giant edifice of external civilisation. Age after age things have improved, human
effort is put in to make things more elegant, to make
the best of the time and the opportunities offered to
man to build up something like a perfect external man.
This may be called the objective perfection.

Side by side, there is a religious perfection where
stress is laid not so much on the external life, external
consciousness, external edifices, but on developing the
inner faculties, which are not normally operative in
day-to-day life, those faculties which are recognised
on all hands as desirable, as contributing to harmony,
unity, love, benevolence. These qualities are deliberately nurtured, say with the help of ethics, morality,
religion, scriptures, in every possible way to build the

2

highest type of man, the saint, the sage, the mystic. As we observe, a saint is one in whom the heart is highly developed and from whom compassion, kindliness, love emanate spontaneously. He embraces larger and larger segments of humanity. A sage is one whose mind is specially cultured, subjected to the working of the higher light of knowledge; he is one who has cultivated and naturalised a wider outlook, whose vision includes the whole cosmos and who can see beyond his immediate individual interests and not only see but shape his conduct in terms of his new perspective. He is the seer, one who sees beyond, beyond the normal range to which the pragmatic man is accustomed. There is the mystic who has, as a result of religious practices or other kinds of discipline,—you may call it yoga,—the facility to enter into a realm of experience which does not lend itself to be scrutinised by intellectual reason but is nevertheless true. And wherever these mystic experiences have occurred, there is a common underlying basis, there are certain features that are common, they can always be corroborated. Even today the mystic experiences of a thousand years ago can always be evoked and verified in one's consciousness, if one adopts the means therefor. These are some of the representative specimens of the religious type of perfection. But by and large they aim at going beyond this world.

The mundane perfectionist has this earth as his field. But those who perfect themselves in the religious way, the spiritual way, so far have their eye fixed elsewhere, above this earth, but not here. Either of these modes of perfection is limited. One shuts itself within this narrow fragment of the universe called the earth, the other shifts its gaze from the field in front and looks elsewhere for perfection to be attained and enjoyed. But the integral perfection of which we speak here is of a different type. We start with the principle, with the truth, that all life is a secret yoga. We are not aware of it, but there is continuous purposeful movement in Nature at every level, each thing leading to something.

On the level of mind, there is continuous progression of the faculty of thought, each layer of the mind is built up based upon the previous attempts. The mind of the average man of today is quite different from that of the man, say two hundred years ago. That is because Nature has traversed great areas in the course of her evolution and developed more and more mental ranges of the earth-consciousness. So too the life-region. So also the body. Everywhere whether it is the body or the life or the mind, the fundamental power is trained not only to organise and perfect itself within that formula, but to exceed it. The body really comes into its own vibrant movement only when the life-consciousness is established in it and fused with the body. Similarly, life-energy becomes more meaningful and chooses the right direction when it is informed by the mental consciousness. At each level Nature pushes, takes ages, but still throughout there is a nisus, an impulse, a push given to the evolving consciousness to grow from grade to grade, acquire full control over each grade, to transcend that grade. And the ultimate aim obviously, after having arrived at our stage of mind, is to go beyond mind.

And what is beyond mind? It is generally agreed that it is a form of Spirit. We may call it by different names, but it is a power of the Spirit that is seeking expression in higher and higher forms of the mind and the mind also seeks to develop new forms of its activity by invoking, pulling down new faculties of the Spirit. It seeks to grow into the Truth, into the Spirit. And there is a continuous coercion if man is not voluntarily co-operative. There is a coercion of the lower members to lay themselves open and grow into the higher term.

With the arrival of man, this movement takes on a new character. Man becomes conscious and takes up the direction of the effort. He wants to telescope the process, to expedite the result. He is impatient and puts in an effort and that effort is twofold. One is the personal endeavour to rise. Sri Aurobindo speaks of the triple labour of aspiration for what one wants, rejection of what is contra, of what is hostile to what one seeks, and surrender. Surrender is the laying open of more and more of the being to the Truth which one wishes to embody, to the Truth that is invoked. But with all that one does there is a limit to personal effort. The most that we have succeeded in reaching so far is a kind of spiritualisation of mind. The mind has agreed to give up its confinement to the intellectual or logical confines. It has put on the character of the higher mind, of the quality of the spirit which is free. It has accepted the leadership in many cases of the spiritual being. But there it stops.

The next step after one arrives at this limit is to invoke, summon an aid, a help from higher Powers beyond the spiritual range. And these Powers above the mind, above the spiritual mind, come from sources which are much higher, from the sources in the Divine. In a word, our human nature has not only got to be perfect within the human limits, but it has to be liberated into the dimension of a divine nature.

3

PSYCHOLOGY OF SELF-PERFECTION

When we were speaking of the quality of perfection that is the aim of this path, we concluded that the entire human nature is to be transmuted into terms of a divine nature. Each term in which human nature functions has its own appropriate term in divine nature, in the supernature, and to transform progressively every bit of human nature into its divine equivalent is, in short, the aim of integral transformation. In the Indian tradition there is what is called "liberation into like nature"—*sādṛśya mukti*; that is the seeker aims at achieving a kind of liberation by which he puts on the precise nature of the deity or the godhead who is the object of his realization.

If, for instance, the ideal is Krishna, the devotee aims at achieving a liberation in which love, delight, heroism are the achievements. If it is Shiva, he tries to arrive at an acme of peace, of detachment, of silence. In short, there are different aspects of the Divine which lend themselves to be realised and each person chooses the aspect of the Divine that he wants to grow into. That is called *sādṛśya mukti*. There are three or four kinds of liberation but we need not go into them now.

Let us return to this idea of "liberation into like nature". Human nature is complex and we aim not at achieving liberation in certain aspects but in all the aspects of the Divine in manifestation. That is where there is a complexity, there is a comprehensiveness and we have to see what are the elements that are to participate in this transformation.

The present day psychology that concerns itself
with this subject is concerned with the mind alone.
How the mind functions, how the mind receives sensa-
tions and perceptions, how it organizes them into cognition, how it reacts, how it develops the higher faculties
—that is what it is concerned with. Modern psychology
is essentially a science of the mind; it starts with the
mind and ends with the mind. Even where the psychology is based upon the fact of matter, the mind also is
recognized as the fine fruit of matter. One doesn't go
very far this way; only that part of nature which
responds to a material pull, which can be cultivated
with the base of matter, enters into consideration. But
human nature is so vast, so complex that there are
areas and faculties which are not based upon matter,
which refuse to be grasped in the net of the mind. They
also claim their share in the transmutation. A psychology of the Integral Yoga has to take into consideration
all these elements. The present psychology, with which
modern science is familiar, has little use for knowledge
with a spiritual foundation. But for us nothing is valid
until we recognize its base in the spirit.

Even to begin with, the knowledge that we recognize is psychological knowledge, but based upon a
spiritual foundation. We start from the spiritual foundation and look upon all the other parts of the being
as so many poises, self-projections, postures of the Spirit.
According to this philosophy, it is the Spirit that is
paramount, it is the Soul that is the first reality. It
uses mind, life and body. It may take a stand in mind
primarily and you have the phenomena of the spiritual
mind, knowledge being arrived at through the spiritual
mind. When the Spirit takes its poise in life, one is apt
to believe and perceive and even experience that the

whole reality of the world is in life. You are familiar
with the philosophy of Bergson,—*Elan vital*. For him it
was an unchallenged experience. The soul in him poised
itself in the life-force and wherever he looked he recognized the exterior of the life-force and he failed to see
that behind the life-force was the *chit-tapas*, the consciousness-force of the Spirit.

So also, when the Spirit bases itself upon the body
that gives rise to the science called materialism, where
they say matter is the only reality. Everything is traced
to matter. But what is matter and how does matter
come into being?

After analysis, and further analysis, you perceive
that there is the essence of the Spirit, there is the Soul,
there is the divine Spirit which takes its poise at different
levels of its self-manifestation. That, after all, is the
definition of the Spirit. What is Spirit? Spirit is the
essence of a thing. There is a gross form—you dissolve
that form; there is a subtle form which is visible to the
subtle sight—you dissolve even that subtle form; there
is a causal form which can be perceived by the causal
eye—you dissolve even the causal form. Then, what
remains is the core of the thing, the essence, the spirit.
So everything has something in its essence and that is
the spirit. The integral psychology takes its base upon
this fact that all life, all nature, all movement derives
its origin from the spirit—not from mind alone, not
from matter alone. Whether it is mind or life or matter,
they all derive their reality, their credibility—to use a
modern term—from the spirit that ensouls them. Spirit
is the essential matter.

To put it in another way, it is the Spirit turned
towards manifestation that translates itself as Sat-chit-
ananda—Existence, Consciousness, Bliss. These three

terms also can manifest themselves singly. Some may realize in their consciousness only the Sat aspect; they see only an Existence. For them nothing else is real. Movement is temporary, illusory, forms come and go but something remains. This Existence is the sole Reality, the prime Reality. This experience is based upon realization of the Sat aspect of Sat-chit-ananda in the universe.

Similarly there are some, especially those who believe in the Tantras - the Shakta Tantras - who see nothing except a Consciousness-Force, a Chit. Everything is a product of Consciousness, and a Consciousness with its Force is the origin, the sustainer and the destroyer of the universe. So wherever they look it is the Shakti, the Consciousness-Force. They are also right, but only to an extent. They realize only the Consciousness-Force, the Chit aspect of the triple Reality in the universe.

Then there are those who see, who are prepared by their evolution to experience only the Delight aspect of the universe. To put it very bluntly they are the hedonists who seek only pleasure, only joy, who measure the value of life in terms of the pleasure and joy it can yield. Even they are not wrong; they also have their truth to sustain them. Their soul or their being responds to the manifestation of the Delight, the Ananda aspect of the Sat-chit-ananda. There are so many levels of realization, each one not cancelling the other, but— from an integral view—complementing the other, making up the whole.

There is also, Sri Aurobindo points out, the possibility of the supermind, the supramental consciousness manifesting itself and being realized as the primal Reality of this universe. We have seen that one can realize any of the three Supernals as the sole Reality in life; similarly, the fourth status, the status of truth-consciousness can also be realized when it is organized in the earth consciousness and becomes manifest as a living force, as the truth of the universe. The characteristics of that realization would be complete knowledge accompanied by an unfailing will—a self-effectuating will always going with knowledge, knowledge being effortless and will being spontaneous.

It is not that the character of the evolution of the whole earth is going to change with the manifestation of the supramental consciousness. This change will be for those who have opened themselves to the action of the supramental consciousness, who are surrendered to the Purusha on the supramental plane. It will be for them individually or for an aggregation of such individuals, what Sri Aurobindo calls the "gnostic community". Their evolution will proceed from light to greater light, from knowledge to greater knowledge, from perfection to greater perfection. Their way will not lie through disintegration and destruction but through construction and integration.

There seems to be a good deal of misunderstanding on this point. It is not that the nature of evolution all over the world will change overnight. The change will be true in the case of those in whom the supramental consciousness is at work, those who open themselves to it. Even there, there are two levels of the functioning of the supramental consciousness. At the lower level, which is much higher than the highest that we are able to reach at present, the stress is on diversity, but a diversity constantly harking back to unity. There is a multiplicity of manifestations but each unit, each line of manifestation, each diversity, points to unity. But on the higher levels of the supermind, it is unity and the unitary feeling that predominates but a unity

subserved by a diversity. Unity is not absolute; it is
seconded by diversity.

So the whole supramental plane, the worlds of the
supermind are not functioning on one wavelength so to
speak. Sri Aurobindo describes two or three levels of
the supermind, but here he speaks of two levels—the
lower level and the higher level. The higher level is
where the unitary sense is predominant and the lower
level where the stress is on diversity.

Another factor that we have to keep in mind is
that the divine soul, the purusha can take different
poises on different levels of manifestation and according
as he takes his poise, identifies himself with that particular principle, he becomes the Purusha of that plane.
If the purusha takes his normal standing in the mind,
you may say the governing principle in that person is
the mental purusha; he gains through knowledge, he
progresses through knowledge, he derives his life
experience through knowledge. It is the soul or the
purusha poised in the mind that directs his whole life-
movement.

Similarly, the purusha may take his stand at the
emotional level, in the heart. Such a person is pre-may
dominately a man of emotions, capable of love, of
compassion, of kindness. So also the purusha may take
his stand at the life-level, the level of the dynamic
life-force. This we call the active man, the rajasic
man who achieves things. Then there is the purusha
who takes his stand in matter. He is slow moving,
lethargic, stationary, unprogressive but with a solidity
about him. All these are different levels, and looked at
from the point of view of evolution, they are all progressive levels. The purusha poises himself step by step,
draws the experience of each level, enriches himself

with the optimum experience he can have at each level and then crosses over to the next.

This is the way of evolution. He does not seek to bypass or put away from him the experience of the intermediate levels and go straight from the material poise to, say, the mental poise.

The other day we were discussing the colloquy of Agastya with Indra. When the Rishi wanted to storm through the levels of the spiritual mind without establishing his consciousness at each proper level—in other words without paying the proper due to the gods of each plane—when he wanted to shoot straight up, a number of sentinels stood in his way and Indra himself denied entry to him. He had to plead, he had to accept to play his rightful role, pay his debt to the custodian of each level since he had chosen the path of evolution, the path of the Aryan which is to ascend the hill of existence step by step. It was out of question for him to bypass or to soar, leaving untrod a number of steps. They have to be covered and the normal way of evolution is to exhaust the possibilities of each level of creation, assimilate the best, and after that to ascend to the next level.

This is where the doctrine of rebirth comes in. It is not possible for the soul to evolve across the whole gamut of existence in one life. A series of lives are precisely designed to enable the soul, the purusha, to assimilate the experience of each level, plan his next adventure and so embody himself in his next birth that he takes his rightful poise in the principle which is his next by right. As the purusha progresses step by step, his power over nature also increases.

At the beginning, when he is on the level of the material principle, he is a slave of material nature. As he advances, as he ascends, he gets a little more detached, he learns to stand above certain movements of nature to begin with and ultimately he arrives at a point where he is not a slave of nature but he becomes the witness of nature and afterwards he becomes the lord of nature. That is how what is *prakriti* when the purusha is in the material plane, reveals herself as *māyā* when the purusha detaches himself, holds himself in a witness position and watches things that are going on. Maya is the power of cunning, skill, weaving a number of finites out of the one Infinite, stretches of time out of the Eternal. When the purusha becomes the lord of nature, she reveals herself to be none else than his shakti, his power, himself as power.

Shakti, Maya and Prakriti—these are the three roles or poises of nature according to the grade reached by the soul.

As long as the purusha enjoys that relation with nature in the higher hemisphere, the *parārdha* as it is called, which is based essentially on the principles of Sat, Chit and Ananda and the supermind, the relation is one of divine nature. But once the soul, the being crosses the line demarcating the higher hemisphere and the lower hemisphere and enters into the realm of mind, it is in the domain of ignorance culminating in the world of falsehood. It is this lower hemisphere that has to be transformed, subjected to the pressure of transmutation by the soul, the purusha.

If this is true of the universal purusha, it is equally true of man, who is the microcosm. In man also all the seven worlds—the Sat-chit-ananda, the supermind, matter, life and mind of the universe are projected. They are mini-worlds which are reproduced in his system in their essence. Each one of us is an epitome of the universe. We have got centres which are, so to say, the spring-buttons of those particular worlds, levels of consciousness. Each one has to be opened up, exposed to the force of evolution, opened to the action of the higher Force and cultured so that each one comes to its highest and allows itself to be integrated with the next higher one. And the process by which these different levels of consciousness in us are developed consciously is called yoga. You may call it psychology, para-psychology, yogic psychology or whatever you like, but it is a willed development of consciousness, a planned linking of the developed consciousness with the external instruments, and a regulation of the movements of the outer instruments in accord with the level of consciousness attained within.

That is the function of yoga—to build from imperfection to perfection. The Brihadaranyaka Upanishad gives a splendid description when it speaks of the progressing or moving of this evolution from non-being to being, from darkness to light, from death to immortality. That sums up in one prayer the whole aim of this yoga —to move from imperfection to perfection, to reveal the divine Presence in matter, the divine Force in life-energy, the divine Mind, the supermind, the supramental faculty of knowledge, in our own mind, to reveal the transcendent Divine in our individual being. If that is on the side of the soul, the purusha, the prakriti, as we said, has to be lifted, explored, cultured, purified, subjected to the light of the soul till it stands out as only an executive mode of shakti. And shakti is not only a power of God, a power of the Lord, but, as we have seen, it is the Lord himself as power. That is the meaning when Sri Aurobindo writes consciousness-force. It does not mean force of consciousness; it means

consciousness as force. Force is not a quality of consciousness, force is not one of the faculties of consciousness; it is consciousness functioning as force, consciousness throwing itself as force.

(*From Questions and Answers*)

Q.: *What would be the difference in the evolution between
the supramental being and a normal realized being?*

A.: One can realize either the Sat aspect or the
Chit aspect or the Ananda aspect without undergoing
complete transformation of nature. It is not necessary
to be transformed. The human being transformed into
supernature is not indispensable for realizing the
Sat-chit-ananda. Sat-chit-ananda as a principle is there
on every plane of existence. Even in matter there is Sat,
there is Chit, there is Ananda. Without bothering to
evolve yourself, to ascend the stair of evolution, you can
withdraw and concentrate upon the ananda aspect or
the existence aspect at the material level, realize the
Divine in that aspect, enter into what is called *jada
samādhi*—the inner trance—and stop there. You have
realized at that level, without transforming anything
beyond it, the Divine at that level. But you have not
transformed your nature. In other words, you have found
liberation into the ananda or into the chit aspect organized at that level of your being.

That is why you see many sadhus or yogis who are
very crude in their minds and their habits, but they
vibrate with a high consciousness. They are not transformed. Whatever they do externally, their soul state
is not touched; they are established. That is why
Sri Aurobindo says that without ascending the stair of
evolution it is possible for any being to drop back, and

since the Divine is at every level, to realize him in any aspect at that level.

It is only if you want to realize the truth-consciousness, the supramental consciousness, that the transformation is necessary. Otherwise, if any part of you is left untapped, unexplored, unexposed, the truth-consciousness cannot function there. What will function will be the normal nature-consciousness. The truth-consciousness demands that where it is to manifest and function, that part must be transformed. And that can happen in the conjunction of the emerging truth consciousness or the supermind from below and the descending force of the truth-consciousness from above.

*　　　　　*

The supramental consciousness is the organization of all the three levels, the three higher principles of Existence, Consciousness and Bliss manifesting in a harmonized way. So all the three are there and when you realize the truth-consciousness you realize all those three, rendered in terms of truth-consciousness ready to manifest. Sat and Chit and Ananda can very well remain in their states without being manifest. The supermind plane is where those three principles are organized and marshalled to move into manifestation. That is the speciality of it. The realization of that fourth state is something unique which you cannot have even by directly realizing the higher states of Sat-chit-ananda.

Yes, they have overshot, or they have contented themselves in realizing the spirit at lower levels. That is why they have missed the secret of existence. Here where the manifestation is organized at its source, where is what Sri Aurobindo calls the "Real Idea", where everything is predetermined, is the fount of creation. So if you go there, you realize the truth of creation, you realize the truth of manifestation, your nature is changed into supernature. You can't go there unless your nature is already changed into supernature, but that's another matter.

Q. : *Does the realization of maya as shakti come with the supernature ?*

A. : It comes even before. Even at the level of spiritual mind one can realize maya as shakti. It depends upon the poise of the soul. As long as you are in a witness state it is maya; when you are in the state of the overseer, lord, that becomes your shakti.

Sri Aurobindo speaks, in the second chapter of the second volume of *The Life Divine* of Brahman, Ishwara and Purusha. Corresponding to Brahman is maya, to Ishwara is shakti, to Purusha is prakriti. This is in the universal context.

4

THE PERFECTION OF
THE MENTAL BEING (I)

It goes without saying that for this perfection to be possible, there has to be a complete reversal of the relation which governs the movements of our life, the relation of our soul with mind, life and body. At present, as a rule, the king is subject to his ministers. The soul is involved and subject to mind, life and body which are to be the souls' instruments. The soul is deep within and the little bit of it that is active in our mind, life and body has to subscribe to the law of these principles of being.

This has to change. The soul must assert itself and we must educate ourselves in such a way that the soul can exert its will, find its expression and act through the mind, through the life-force and through the body. This is a complete change and a reversal of what has been going on all along in the evolution of nature. The existing powers have to be dethroned and the veiled monarch brought out and restored to the position which is his due.

The first step is to find our true being. Normally we mistake our ego-self for our true being. But the true being is our higher purusha, not the lower purusha who is identified with the ego, involved and lost in the rounds of nature. The ego itself is not the purusha, not the being. The death of ego does not mean the death of individuality. The ego is one thing; the being is another. The ego is a formation of Nature to centralize the various contacts and impacts in the flux of

3

life, to give a sense of stability, a point from which to
act. This has been slowly evolved by Nature. It is not
the being; it is an instrument, an instrumental point
of nature on which the soul may base itself and
function. But once this purpose of centralization of
contacts, of action and reaction is fulfilled, then it is
time that the ego falls off. The central point has to
change its character and the outer crust of ego has to
fall so that the real being within comes forward and
occupies that seat. The ego is a psuedo-self, the false
self; Sri Aurobindo would call it the desire-self. This
desire-self, the ego-self has to be replaced by the true
being, the higher purusha.

And who is the higher purusha of whom we can
become conscious? When we as human beings want to
know what our true being is, we become conscious of
ourselves as mental beings—mental because we think,
become aware only through our minds, understand
only through thought. Our contact with everything is
through the mind. Nothing is true to us unless it is
mentally rendered in our consciousness or to our being.
This makes man essentially a mental being—I say
essentially because there are other poises of being to
which we shall come later. So we may say that our
higher purusha is the being functioning in the mind.
The being itself is not the mind. The mental being,
what is called the *manomaya puruṣa*, is not the mind.
The mind is an instrument, just as the body is not
myself. It is I to whom this body belongs; I am one,
the body is another. Similarly, the mental being, the
manomaya puruṣa is one and the mind is another. The
mind is a formation of nature—nature as mental nature.
It provides the basis, the stuff, the field for the true
being to function at that level. This becoming con-

scious of the mental being, the higher purusha, is the
first step towards the changing of one's relation with
nature.

When this mental being of which we become
conscious tries to survey the situation, learn the truth
about itself, there are three intuitive perceptions that
are possible—one after another. The moment we try
to observe as mental beings from the level of the mind
what is going on—what is this nature, what is life, and
so on—we find a poise of detachment. Things go on
moving, the mental being observes. It takes the poise
of the witness, it is the *sākṣi*—one who observes, who
sees, who watches. That is the first poise of which we
become conscious.

Next, as it goes on observing, the mental being
becomes aware of the large area of actions open to it,
which is greater and vaster than the normal physical
range to which one limits oneself when one is not awakened. This is the second perception. The third is that it
is not limited only to the body, to the life action, or even
to the process of thinking. It becomes aware of a higher
dimension or a depth which is spiritual, which adds
a new element. This becoming aware of the spiritual
element, opening to it and putting on that spiritual
character, absorbing the spiritual vibrations, is the third
intuitive perception.

These are successive steps which we normally
experience when we observe ourselves. No doubt, once
we separate from nature there is always the possibility
—and it happens almost every time—that we come
back to the usual rhythm of nature when we come to
action. In the beginning, at any rate, it is only when
we are not involved in action, when we keep ourselves
separate from nature that all this knowledge, all this

wisdom is there. The moment we come back into the field of action we are once again involved in nature.

You would ask, is there no difference? Sri Aurobindo says, there is. Once that separation has been achieved, that experience makes a radical difference in the rest of the life. We always know, even when fully involved—again, thrust into it—that it is not our true position. We always remember that freedom of separation, that transcendence over involvement and there is always an attempt—conscious or half-conscious or subconscious—to swing back into that poise in which we are away from nature. This experience repeated again and again, consciously dug in, creates new grooves through which the mental being learns to hold itself separate from involvement in nature.

We spoke of the experience of the true being, the true purusha in the mind. It is also possible to feel that being as poised, as organized on the life plane. As on the mental plane, as in the mind, so in life. We feel that all the energies of life are flowing from us and we run with them. It is not thought that appears important, but it is the dynamic force of life with which we are completely identified and lost. Here also, it is possible for the purusha, for the being to withdraw and separate itself from the current of life-force and act as a witness, then assume control, and then enlarge its sphere.

It is equally possible for the higher purusha, higher being to feel its poise in the physical body. We feel that this body is our self, everything is involved in the body. This is called the *annamaya puruṣa*. The being poised in mind is the *manomaya puruṣa*, poised in the life-force is the *prāṇamaya*, and the one poised in the physical body, the material sheath is the *annamaya*. So

whichever the purusha, whatever the poise in which we
awake to our true being, the necessity is to draw back, to
create a separation initially between that nature and the
corresponding being. Once the separation is achieved
and confirmed, then we have to assume mastery. Once
the mastery is established, thereafter a new direction, a
new swing of movement training the nature to function
differently is the next step.

We spoke of life being and the physical being—
physical purusha and life purusha—in order to throw
light on the other aspects of the situation, but man is
essentially a mental being. To him even his life, even
his body is true, vivid only through his mind. A
sensation in the body is not true unless the mind renders
that impulse at the sensational level. If the mind is in
trance—which is very rare—or if the mind is knocked
out or unconscious—which is more likely—then any
stroke given to the body will have no effect on us. We
do not feel it because it is the mind that renders all
experience true. Man is essentially a mental being,
and any change that we want to effect in our life necessarily starts with the mind. We are thinking beings,
beings poised in the mind, and it is but natural that our
action for change should start with the mind.

There are two ways in which the mind sets about
this work of self-perfection. The first step is to withdraw
from nature, to hold back. As we withdraw, there are
two possibilities. One is to completely disengage ourselves from nature, refuse to give sanction to nature,
and in this process bring about a stop to the whole
process. This is the Sankhyan position, which we discussed before. That is one way. The second is that as
we awake to the inner realities, moving away from
external preoccupations and involvements, the vision

widens. A larger consciousness, a wider being sucks into itself our inward-looking mental being. The mental being loses interest, without attempting to do so, and gets more and more absorbed in its own inner self. That way, also, there is a departure from nature. One way is a complete cessation—not only from involvement in nature, but from its existence as a conscious purusha in the world. The second is a kind of emergence in a higher reality.

But these don't solve the problem; the problem is one of perfection. Our goal is not to withdraw from nature, leaving nature to itself and either end our lives as self-rapt souls or souls merged in the *līlā* of Brahman, but to communicate the knowledge, the consciousness gained to the outer being, to re-mould and reshape the external nature in terms of the inner gains. That takes us to the next step—once the separation has been effected, thereafter how to acquire mastery over nature in order to perfect it.

(From Questions & Answers)

Each soul is given freedom of choice by the Divine as to whether it will continue in slavery to nature or it will withdraw from nature and end in a vast blankness or merge in the Absolute, or it will work on nature and manifest the Divine in it. This step of refusing the sanction, withdrawing the consent is usually the first step. Whatever your goal, the first step has to be that because ninety per cent of our movements in nature are of ignorance. So until this character is changed, the soul or the soul as poised in the mind, has necessarily to say "No; it is not going to be, I am not going to sanction this movement". By this persistent practice, nature loses its impulse to turn in those old ways, and slowly you learn to function in such a way that part of nature goes in the right direction, though a part may still survive in the old ways. Thereafter, you allow the right movements but withhold the sanction for the wrong movements. This is a constantly changing process, but the withholding of sanction applies to movements of ignorance, movements that tie you down.

Philosophically, according to the Sankhya, even if it is a right movement, you have to deny your sanction because the fact that the nature is in movement is itself wrong. It is antagonistic to the bliss of the soul. But that is a theoretical position which need not concern us.

This is again a question of free will functioning as a part of determinism. There is a great Divine Will. The imperative, the order to all the souls that go out originally is to manifest the Divine. But each soul is given freedom to decide how it will manifest the Divine, to what extent it will manifest, or to say at some time, "I am tired of it and I don't want to do it". The Divine Will allows that. That is the essence of it.

We may say, again, that even what one is going to decide is determined, so the fact is that even the sense of freedom is a machinery for working out the Divine Will. To put it in another way, provision is made in the divine scheme for tired souls to drop off. God is also human.

Q.: *What is meant by the 'left hand path'?*

A.: The terms left hand path and right hand path have many connotations. The right hand path, you may say, is the path of the purusha, the soul, the path of knowledge, the path of concentrating on the development of consciousness alone, leaving everything else. The left hand path is to accept nature, to progress

through nature and not away from nature. Whatever
is supposed to obstruct your progress, you take hold
of it, subject it to the process of purification, orientation, and force it to yield to your will. That is the
original idea. So, for instance, the world is supposed
to be a snare, life in the world, sex, is supposed to be
a net. Now you don't run away from all these things,
you take the problems as they come and try your
best, sincerely, to utilize them for further progress. It
has its advantages, it has its dangers, it has its self-
deceptive scope. But by and large, the original idea
behind the left hand path is greater, vaster in scope
than the narrow right hand idea.

Today the left hand path has fallen into disrepute
because it is nature which has pulled down man and
he serves nature. So instead of man riding over nature,
it is nature which is riding over man. That is why it is
discouraged. Otherwise, where the left hand path is
practiced in its purity the emphasis is on the integral
character of experience. You reject nothing that God
has created, you give full value to everything that is
a part of the creation. It may take long, but it is not
a narrow path. It is a large, wide, and comprehensive
path. You must have the patience, and more than
patience you must have the sincerity to see truth as
it is.

So much so that for those who are sincere, it is
said that even in the sex experience, the action of the
light shows where one is sincere or insincere to the
path. If it is gross, if it brings down your consciousness,
if it clouds your being, if it takes you an inch nearer
the animal, it has failed. If it has given you a lift over
the normal hum-drum round of life and makes you
float in some bliss, in some joy which opens out larger

horizons in the mind and the being, opens up the springs of love and kindliness and benevolence, it has served its purpose. That is possible. But this is a theoretical discussion; in our yoga these things are not normally permissible.

Q.: *In other yogas they may reject all thought, but in this yoga how do you detach yourself from the highest level of rational mind?*

A.: As you progress, the mind puts on the character of the soul. The gulf between nature and soul lessens. And you impose the character of your soul on the nature. For instance, the character of knowledge, the character of pure discrimination, the character of aesthesis of the mental being is imposed on mental nature. So when mental nature starts functioning, it doesn't react in the normal way to impacts from outside, but through the values and power stamped upon it by the mental being.

5

THE PERFECTION OF
THE MENTAL BEING (II)

Last time we spoke about the subject of purification of the mind. We were discussing how man becomes aware of his purusha, the central being, reflecting itself at different levels of nature. His poise is now in the mind, *manomaya-puruṣa*, now in life-force, *prāṇamaya puruṣa*, now in the physical body, *annamaya puruṣa* or the material being. These are all simultaneous positions taken by the soul on the different principles of existence, and common to them all,—as long as we live in ignorance—is one factor that the soul or the purusha is a slave, subject to nature. We said that the first step towards liberation from this slavery to nature is to withdraw our consciousness, our awareness, our mental being from the activities of nature. Once we start doing it systematically, as a discipline, we become aware that our purusha, our soul or central being is no more involved in the activities of nature, but he is witnessing all that goes on from a position aloof. He is the *sākṣi*, the witness.

In certain yogas, this itself is considered to be a liberation. But actually, it is only the first step towards disinvolvement from nature and acquiring a positive poise in our effort upwards. When we observe things as a witness, we see that nature goes on—though we are not involved in it—with her movements, and we find that our external personality gets involved. Whether inwardly we approve of it or not, by habit, by stress of circumstances the determinations of nature are stronger than the self-willings of our being.

If we observe still further the determinations and the movements of nature, the being finds that these movements of nature are really dependent upon the sanction of the purusha. Unless the sanction is there, the movement cannot go on. Once we become aware of this hold on nature, that whatever may have been the impetus given so far by karma or by habit, fresh determinations can form themselves only with this sanction, we get a foot-hold, we start getting mastery over nature. Gradually, by accepting or refusing to give sanction, we get nature under our control. Thus one starts as witness, *sākṣi*, then realizes the sanctioner, the upholder, *bhartṛ*, and culminates in the master of nature, *īśvara*. This is the usual process of liberating oneself from nature, and when the object is not only liberation from nature but even to acquire mastery over nature, there comes the third step: after attaining the sanction-poise we develop the master-poise.

If one observes that there is scope for free-will in the determinations of nature, it is not wrong. But even the free will that most of us feel, the freedom to choose, the sense of freedom, that also turns out to be a part of nature's machinery. Providence has designed nature in such a way that its own decisions, its own determinations can be presented to us as if it is we who decide. Actually, the choice that is given to us is limited. It is partly determined by the past events—what has happened in the past creates certain habitual movements, grooves, tendencies—what we call *samskāras*—and they all incline us in a certain direction. Nature also assembles the circumstances in such a manner that we are obliged to decide in a particular way.

These are true determinations of nature which the soul or the being has to take account of, and this con-

tinues to be so as long as we accept to live and function
in the triple formula of ignorance—ignorance of the
body, ignorance of the life, ignorance of the mind. In
our awakened moments we have some perception that
while all this may be-true in our day-to-day life, somewhere in our being there is the point of real control.
If we can touch there, we can overrule the determinations of nature. But that point of control does not belong
to the mind; it is outside the mental range, in the realm
of the spirit, the spiritual consciousness, or something
higher than the mind, the realms of the supermind.
Only when we go deep into the spirit or high above
and cross the mental border, do we get to the real
possibility of exercising control over nature. Even those
who do not admit the necessity of achieving the supermind and are content to develop their spiritual consciousness to the utmost, feel the freedom of the central
being reflected in the spirit and they do exercise it.
Yogis, sadhaks and seekers who have found a lodging
in the spirit gain control over nature to a certain extent.
More control comes when they are completely identified with the spirit, but this identity with the spirit—
in traditional yogas—takes place only in conditions of
trance, and in such conditions activity is not possible.
So they rule out the possibility of practical control over
all movements of nature as long as one stays in the body
which is subject to the rule of ignorance.

The situation changes if we make an effort of ascent
into the higher levels of consciousness. If we go beyond
the highest levels of the mind and get into the supramental poise—just as we are now poised in the mind,
the life and the body—, if by yoga we gain access to
the gnostic levels, the level of truth-consciousness of
which Sri Aurobindo speaks, and build up some kind

of identity with that consciousness, we become free. We become *svarāt*, no longer slave to nature. But even there the whole difficulty in proceeding is due to the ignorance and the shadow of ignorance which sticks to us for a long time. We function, we know only through the mind and the mind knows only in fragments. Mind never has the knowledge, mind has to seek knowledge, mind has to piece together knowledge. Mind is never the knower, mind cannot know nature, mind is not the *jnātā*. The way out is to develop the mind, to draw up the mind into the *vijnāna*, the supermind. When our habitual poise in the mind as the *manomaya puruṣa* yields to a new poise in the *vijnānamaya puruṣa*, in the supermind, then we have the knowledge. Knowledge gives the power and power gives the control.

But this cannot come about unless we force nature to change radically. From top to toe, centuries of past habits govern our external nature. Step to step, element by element, our nature has to be forced to change. There is a natural nexus formed at the ego point between the mind, the life-force and the physical body. There all is focussed, centered in the ego. Any action, any reaction has to proceed in this pattern. This has to be changed. All our systems of ethics, discipline, religion, aim at modifying, putting on brakes over this working but what is needed is an uprooting of this nexus that has formed around the ego and lifting up of nature into a totally new dimension.

In the present mixed and confused action of nature, each part conflicts with the other—what the mind wants the life-force is not ready for, what the life-force wants to do the mind is not ready to sanction, and in what both want the body does not co-operate. Now this internal conflict, giving rise to a mixed and confused nature, has to be corrected. And the first step towards this correction is purification—a psychological purification slowly untying the knot of ego, asking ourselves at every moment, in every situation whether what we are going to decide is being influenced by the ego or by the truth of the situation, whether it is convenient to the ego or not. This psychological discipline has to be practised, leading gradually to a conversion of the instruments of nature—mind, life, heart, emotions, body—into a higher order of functioning. The present order is tied to lower nature but the direction has to be changed. That is what Sri Aurobindo gives in a small formula: first there is purification, *śuddhi*; when the *śuddhi* proceeds sufficiently there is *mukti*, liberation from ego; from liberation we achieve a certain perfection of nature, with the aid of the gnostic consciousness, *siddhi*. But *siddhi* is not the end. It leads to an uncaused bliss. The culmination of the supermind is in *ānanda*; even as all creation starts in *ānanda*, it ends or culminates in *ānanda*. That is *bhukti*, enjoyment—thus, *śuddhi*, *mukti*, *siddhi*, *bhukti*.

But all these remain empty phrases till we grow out of our limited, narrow individuality. As long as we think we are separate from others—"I am only this mind and this body and this life and this soul and this heart"—we are incomplete creatures. Our individual center remains, but it has to be extended. Unless we extend our consciousness, it is impossible to bring about a change in nature. It is also impossible to rise even to the overmental levels, let alone to the gnostic levels. At present our life is characterised by a sort of mutual seizing. Each one considers himself separate from others, the whole world is foreign to him and with whatever little strength he has got he tries to appropriate whatever is possible for himself. Gradually, however, nature teaches him to expand and he learns to expand only because he stands to gain more. He extends his interests, he builds up a family, clan and so on. His interests become larger and he adds to his sense of possession the sense of sympathy, co-operation, leading ultimately to harmony.

But these are all processes of nature. The true universalisation can come only when we strike out from the soul level. When we mentally conceive of everything as one it remains a mental formula. There has to be a practical change in our day-to-day relations which can come only when we tackle the problem at the soul level. We must feel at the soul level, the psychic level, that we are one with others. We embrace the whole of the universe in our consciousness. The true unity, the universal feeling and consciousness can be built only through the soul. Otherwise nature has its own way of upsetting whatever balance we arrive at, whatever synthesis we arrive at through our mind.

The three gunas—*rajas*, *tamas* and *sattva*—in their operation tend to upset all balancings and we can never be sure of our stabilized experience of universalisation. But if we base ourselves on the soul level, then whatever little we gain is a permanent gain. As this universalization of individuality proceeds and we get away from the operation of the gunas of nature, we put on the higher nature of the supramental being. The individual becomes the *samrāt*, the master. It is out of question that such an individual can exist in himself or for himself alone. It is a universal and a global consciousness that flows through whoever is open, whoever is identified in soul with it and whatever help is needed elsewhere, whatever vibrations are needed to heal or to uplift will flow without so much as an outer knowledge and an outer sanction from the person concerned. For the individual the whole universe becomes his empire and gnostic consciousness, delight, power and will flow through him over the rest of humanity.

(From Questions & Answers)

Q.: How would you describe the relation of the soul values to the higher ethical values?

A.: Ethical values do not contradict soul values. But situations may arise where an action that one is called upon to do may appear, to an ignorant mind, to be unethical. But for one who does not function from the ego level, acts only in obedience to a higher will, there is no choice. The man-made laws of ethics, made for a different grade of humanity, do not govern his conduct. That is why the Indian tradition gives the man of spiritual liberation the freedom of the *parivrājaka*, a wanderer of the spirit who is not bound by laws of the society. It is quibbling to say that those who have no rule of morality to subscribe to will be immoral. It is foreign to their nature, it is below their dignity to do things which are immoral. They don't desist from doing things because that would be immoral, but because it does not come in their line of nature.

This is a very theoretical and hypothetical question which many raise. Those who have not risen above the need of observing ethics can't conceive of a situation when the ethics no longer apply. Ethics are meant to humanize the animal in man. Ethics are meant to subjugate tamas and rajas and bring man to the sattvic level where spiritual law can take possession. Otherwise, when Sri Krishna asks Arjuna to "take a holiday of fight", where is ethics there? Where is *ahimsā*—non-

violence—there? What function is Rudra—the destroyer—serving if nobody is to be hurt? There are
occasions when things have to be done whether they
appear ethical or not.

There is the famous question, which Gandhiji had
raised, that of euthanasia. A cow was suffering incur-
ably and the doctors said the cow couldn't live. The
question was whether the cow was to prolong its agony
or could it be put to sleep? There was a controversy in
the *Harijan*—I was a student at that time. I don't
remember what Gandhiji did afterwards.

He allowed it to be put to sleep.

Now, Sri Aurobindo's approach is different. He says
in such case it is not so much the pity for the animal
that moves you as your nervous inability to stand the
sight of the suffering. So it is your great consideration
for yourself that makes you think you are relieving
the animal from suffering. But, he asks, what does
the soul of the animal feel about it? Could it not be
that the soul has chosen intense suffering in order to
do its round in evolution more quickly? One has to
ask the soul, and till one has the knowledge of what
the soul wants, one has no right to take away the life.
For all that we know, the soul may be still sticking to
life in spite of the pain. The will to life is there at all levels.

*Q.: There were recent cases like that involving human
patients.*

A.: But were the patients consulted?

*Q.: Apparently they were so far gone that they couldn't
be consulted.*

A.: The only thing to do would be to do nothing;
leave it to nature.

I remember that in some cases the Mother asked
medicine to be stopped so that things could happen

4

according to the wishes of the soul, without interference from the human end. But then there are the doctors who are convinced that there is no possibility of cure or help. When the soul really wants to go, it doesn't consult doctors or lawyers. It just leaves.

6

THE INSTRUMENTS OF THE SPIRIT

I have a few more tidbits from the Mother which have
not been published so far. One was told to a worker:
It is only the Mahasaraswati aspect who can look after
you. It is she who looks after each detail. Sri Aurobindo
has said that she does not forgive unless you try to
change yourself.

*   *

India is not the earth, rivers and mountains of
this land. Neither is it a collective name for the inhabi-
tants of this country. India is a living being—as much
living as, say, Shiva. All the countries have their own
spirit. For example, although Austria has become part
of Germany, still they are quite separate and the spirit
of Austria is in agony. India is like a goddess; if she
likes, she can manifest in human form.

*   *

About colour prejudice, from the aesthetic point of
view I can say that the brown colour is better than the
white, but it quite absurd and foolish to think that
anybody is better or worse simply because of his colour.
The African Negro thinks that his colour is the most
beautiful of all; the Japanese think that people of their
colour are superior to any colour. Colour prejudice is
a low thing. It indicates a very low consciousness a
consciousness just emerging from the inconscient. It is
not an idea, it is not a feeling—it is something still
lower than that. When you think in terms of colour
prejudice, your own psychic laughs at your foolishness.
It knows that it has lived in white, brown, yellow, red,

black, all sorts of bodies. When you get this kind of feeling, bring it before your consciousness and it will disappear.

*   *

Fear is hidden consent. When you are afraid of something it means that you are afraid of this possibility and thus you strengthen its hands. It can be said that it is a subconscient consent. Fear can be overcome in many ways. The ways of courage, faith and knowledge are some of them.

*   *   *

Coming back to our theme, the instruments of the spirit. Considering from the point of view of purification, we recognise that our soul, our self can function through certain God-given instruments. They are the mind, the emotions, the life-force, the body. And these, in the nature of things, involved as they are in the movement of progressive evolution starting from the inconscient, are seeds of impurity which vitiate our living and act as barriers in our attempt to change ourselves. All disciplines propose a number of measures for purifying these instruments. In the Indian tradition, particularly, they speak of eliminating activities, movements which bring in any kind of impurity and they propose a number of inhibitions through religious taboos, ethical and moral rules and so on. They go on eliminating as far as possible areas of activity where these movements are supposed to be inevitable, and ultimately they confine themselves only to those movements which they think have relevance to divine life or godly life. Going a little further, when they have sufficiently narrowed down their range of movements, they seek to merge in Brahman, in the Pure Consciousness, and stick to that poise leaving the body to run its course.

So the net result is that they leave the field of life to its own imperfections, leaving it as incapable of purity, and withdraw into themselves so that they can share the innate purity of the soul.

This is clearly not the solution for a seeker who aims at a divine manifestation in life, at a whole-sided perfection of himself. He is not satisfied with any kind of spiritual quietism to promote purity. He aims also at a divine kinetism. He would like to express something of what he has gained within himself in terms of purity, of harmony, of love and so on in his actions, in his daily life. He would combine both quietism and kinetism at appropriate junctures. He would make these complementaries instead of opposites, and aim at total purity. His object in striving for total purity is not to observe the laws of ethical perfection. A spiritual seeker is not normally attracted by the normal kinds of temptations with which ethical laws and rules deal. He does not need a manual of ethics to behave himself, provided he is sincere. He knows what promotes Godward growth and what stands against it. Whatever religions or ethics or canons of morality may say, his standards are different. Anything that leads away from the unity of the soul, from the closeness of his being with the Divine, anything that could interfere with the working of a divine guidance, he shuns.

The question may be asked, what is the necessity of perfection at all? Indeed, there would be no need for measures for perfection if we were sufficiently pure in our instrumental being. But as it is, things are not that way. There are two kinds of impurity which stick to us right from the beginning. One is the fact that evolution —of which we are products—starts from the base in the inconscient, in nescience, unconsciousness. That shadow goes on vitiating our upward efforts, pulling us constantly down, through a shadow over our being, however high we may reach on the mental peaks. This is an incapacity due to the origin of our evolution in the inconscient. The second is due to the process of our evolution.

We have seen that in evolution one principle after another goes on establishing itself, drawing upon the previous principle already established, and as the edifice comes up from the physical to the life, from the life to the mind, from the mind to the spiritual, we see that there is an interconnection, an interdependence between these different formations of the evolutionary spirit. The lower form of consciousness acts as a drag on what has been evolved taking its place higher in the ladder, with the result that there is a constant mixture of movements. Whatever the life-force may want to do, there is constantly the dragging weight of the physical body, the limiting walls of the material sheath. Similarly, however clearly the mind may like to think, discriminate and reason out, there is always the mixture—known and unknown—of one's own desires, likes and dislikes, formed habits from the past.

Thus, none of our instruments functions at its optimum or with its characteristic quality unimpaired. In the functioning of every instrument there is an influence and a mixture from the other instrumental parts. Thus comes in the necessity of elimination of impurities and cultivation of purification.

To take an instance, it is said that the basis of life is delight, the aim of life also is delight. If that is so, every contact and impact in life should give rise to reactions of delight, of *ānanda*. Instead of that, we have varying reactions—at times the reaction of pleasure, at times the reaction of suffering, pain, shock, shrinking.

Why? It is because we have our own desires which make us inclined in particular directions, seek experiences of a particular kind and avoid the other experiences. This impulsion by desire, from below or from within, vitiates our contacts and receptions from outside and what should be a constant response of delight to the contacts of life is turned into an unpredictable reaction. If, by some measure of purification, we can isolate and eliminate this element of desire, there would be nothing to interfere with every movement of life evoking from us a reaction of *ānanda*.

As our instrumental being stands today, we have the physical body which has its own roots in the inconscient, *tamas*, obscurity. It is enlivened by a life-force which imparts its character to the body and in the process takes on something of the grossness of the physical body which it activates. There is the realm or region of emotion, what we may call the heart, and above that, in distinction to the gross physical body, there is the inner instrument, the *antah-karaṇa* as they call it. It consists of *buddhi*, the intellect with will, the ego, the sense mind and the heart. All these four are based upon the stuff of consciousness which we call *citta*, basic stuff of consciousness. From the activities of this *citta*, or the activities thrown up by the unpurified *citta*, arises the desire-soul, the desire being which is quite different from and in fact it covers up our true soul, our true being, the psychic being. It is this desire-soul that mixes with every movement of ours and spoils things.

Now this *citta* is largely subconscient. Only a part of it do we know through the ideas, thoughts and emotions that come up. The bulk of it is below the surface. It goes on forming itself; it is not a ready-made stuff. Each thought that we think, each emotion that we feel, sends down a current which is absorbed and kept in the bank of *citta*, and all these impressions remain in our subconscient *citta*. They come up at the most inconvenient moments. They come up in dreams, they come when we are trying to build something opposite—as if to remind us that they are there stored in our own subconscient. They need to be eliminated before the opposite elements are formed.

The contents of this subconscient basic stuff are passive and active—passive when they are simply being received, active when things come up as a reaction or in response to a call from the mind for something in the memory to come up. This is the passive and the active content of the *citta*. Both together form what is called memory, and it is this memory of all that we have been doing in the past, memory of things going on in our environs, a deep memory of what we have done in earlier births that together incline our nature in a particular direction. This is how habits are formed. Our habits are not eternal things, they are products of movements stored in our *citta*. In other words, our habits are formed by ourselves. That is how what is formed may be unformed, dissolved. This is indirect opposition to the belief that nature cannot change. After all, what is nature? The strength of nature is in its ability to hold to a thing rigidly, repeat things. This comes by the force or the strength of this memory, *citta*.

Similarly, our emotions also rise from the movement of this *citta*—*cittavrtti*, as Patanjali says. The movements of this basic stuff of consciousness throw up our emotions. The desire-soul is a product of all these movements and it conceals and covers the psychic being.

We spoke of life-force, prana activating the body, supporting the mind in its movement. But this life-force, again, is not pure. It is always influenced by our desire mind. The desire mind gives it an orientation. This is what Sri Aurobindo calls the nervous reaction of the psychic prana. Not life-force pure, not the physical pure, not even mind pure, but a movement in us which is more or less a nervous action of the life-force under the influence of desire. This is a major culprit in our deviations.

Sri Aurobindo illustrates how a pure emotion, which borrows directly from the soul—like love—wanting to give oneself, wanting to arrive at a union of consciousness with another, is quickly turned by this desire life-force and mixed up with the desire of the body, what is called lust. Even if one starts on the pure level of love in its purity, very soon this kind of pull from desire through nervous action links up the higher emotion with the physical desire and love is debased into lust. This happens in almost all cases of higher feelings, higher emotions—they are deformed. This is inevitable as long as desire and its sustainer, ego, are active in the system.

Even in the mind the action of this inmixture is marked, especially in the action of the sense mind. A hundred things may be there in front of us, but our sense mind through the senses always rushes to things where its desire draws it, where it is impelled by this desire life-force. Ultimately all these are traced to the activity of *citta*, not yet purified but dominated by desire and ego.

This is so as long as we confine our action to the surface mind, which is dominated by the desire mind. This external sense mind is a slave, but there is an inner sense mind, a subtle sense mind. Corresponding to each of our physical senses there is a subtler sense—an eye behind the physical eye, an ear behind the physical hearing, and so on. Now when this inner sense, the inner sense mind becomes active, the physical or the corporeal organs are no longer necessary. Things go straight; there is a direct contact. This results in phenomena like clairvoyance where we begin to see things which are even beyond the physical range of sight; clairaudience where we begin to hear things from afar; we enter into the minds of others—telepathy; we put our will over others—hypnotism. All these start taking place when something of the inner mind, the subtler mind, awakes and moves into action.

Just as there is the inner sense mind corresponding to the physical sense mind, similarly corresponding to the outer *buddhi*—the intelligent will—there is an inner *buddhi* which is a power of knowledge and will. And this *buddhi* functions in three grades. The first is that part of the intellect-will which gives the understanding with which we are familiar. The sense mind may go and get the report and the *buddhi* then coordinates things, reasons out and gives us some sort of a working understanding of things. The second is the operation of selective reason without being influenced by interested interpretations. This *buddhi* is, we can say, almost pragmatic because it seeks to find out the truth of things with a view to using them in life. It is not so much concerned with the pure knowledge of things, but knowledge as related to life—free from the errors of sense mind. And then there is the activity of the higher reason which seeks for pure knowledge irrespective of its utility in practical life. These are the three grades of *buddhi*: first, that which contributes understanding of things, second is a reasoning of things to get practical knowledge, and third is the activity of the higher reason which seeks only for pure knowledge, irrespective of other considerations.

This *buddhi*, whether inner or outer, functions around our ego, as related to our ego. In some it may not be the vital ego, but a mental ego—our own line of thinking, our own ideas and preferences. But the *buddhi* itself is not an independent organ. It is an intermediary between *manas*, our sense mind, and higher up, the Truth Mind. It is a channel. As we succeed in releasing the roots of *buddhi* from the sense mind, from desire and ego, and setting it free to function on its own, there is also a positive side by which it is slowly drawn upwards into the action of the Truth Mind. As it extends its range and opens itself to the direct action of the Truth Mind, the character of *buddhi* itself changes. It becomes a spontaneous operation of discrimination and organisation on the mental level, of a knowledge that proceeds from the level of truth. This subject of transition of the *buddhi* from the sense mind to the Truth Mind and the Supermind will form an independent topic for one of our further'sessions.

(From Questions and Answers)

Q.: *In hathayoga, is there a purification of prāṇa?*

A.: In Hathayoga there is really a purification of the physical body and that part of prana which is involved in the body. It is Rajayoga that purifies the bulk of prana—prana on its own level and what is connected with the mind. For instance, man being a mental being, a good deal of his prana or life-force is connected with his mind or it pours itself into his mind. With an animal it does not happen that way—it pours itself more into the physical. The Hathayoga and the Rajayoga together give a total discipline of purification of this prana so that it is free from the lower inmixtures. But the higher imperfection remains: mental errors, confusing and misdirecting the prana.

So a total perfection or a total purification involves action on all the levels and it is neither Hathayoga or Rajayoga but really an Integral yoga that can completely purify and perfect the prana.

Q.: And how are prāṇa and citta related?

A.: You can say that prana is the feeder to *citta*. *Citta* is a constantly developing proposition; it receives through the mind, it receives through prana also. So from both sides it goes on receiving and forming itself.

Q.: How can one fit clairvoyance into the yoga?

A.: These things have no special place in our yoga, but they are not taboo either. They are incidental. If I am brilliant, that is something; it is a gain. It is neither a special qualification nor a disqualification; it shows a development of the mind. Similarly, clairvoyance shows an opening and a development of the subtle sight. It can be made use of for one's expression in life manifestation of God in life, though as one's spiritual consciousness develops, it is the Divine that uses all these openings. One does not need to cultivate these movements in the belief that they are necessary.

Q.: If one has clairvoyance, should one not use this power for any purpose which is not spiritual?

A.: What is not spiritual? It comes to that. If all life is yoga, every activity can be made spiritual. But here again is the same question: whether a spiritual man will be immoral. He doesn't think of it. He is not moral because of morality, but because it is just out of his line. Similarly, if the faculty of clairvoyance is there or opens out in anyone, he will not seek to pry into what is going on in somebody's mind. But if there is a need to know, it functions spontaneously. If I need to know what is the solution to a particular problem—say, an intellectual problem—it just flashes before me. Or if I want to know why so and so, who has gone from here has not come back and I am concerned, it is certainly permissible to project may subtle sight and see what has happened.

All these things are all right when you function from a centre of reference which is spiritual. Even otherwise, even if a rogue uses these things, there is nothing wrong. They are faculties of nature.

7

PURIFICATION—THE LOWER MENTALITY

In one of our earlier sessions we had discussed the role of renunciation and purification in yoga. Sri Aurobindo sums up their roles in a picturesque language: if renunciation is the left arm, purification is the right arm of the yoga of knowledge. Renunciation is a negative element; it is not enough that you renounce things. Even if you renounce riches, relations or attachments, all that you do is to dispossess yourself. Even with the utmost sincerity—taking for granted that what you renounce outwardly, externally, you do not cultivate internally by dwelling upon it through your mind and senses, assuming that the renunciation is true and entire, it is still a negative step. No edifice is built—especially a spiritual one—on negative bricks. The negative elements remove certain obstructions, cut knots that tie us down to lower nature, but this has to be followed up by more positive elements, the most important of which is purification. Unless we purify our nature, purify our mind, heart, life energies and even the physical system, it is idle to expect that the higher consciousness or the deeper consciousness can, for any length of time dwell in us much less function.

Purification is not a process of just one or two steps. Man is a multiple being. He is not mind alone or heart alone or soul alone. As we have seen, he is made up of a number of principles of existence, a number of formations each of which expresses its apposite principle. So part by part, limb by limb, we have to build up the purification. We will now deal with the purification of the lower mind. We have not one mind; there is the lower mind covering the action of the sense mind, the sense mind leads into the receptive mind and the active sense mind; then there is the mind, *manas*, that coordinates the reports of the senses and comes to its own conclusions; reason comes along, thought begins to form. This operation of mental energy based upon sense data may be called the lower mentality. This has to be purified, but is it possible to purify one limb entirely and then next go to another? Man is an organic being, so what happens in one part naturally affects the other parts. Even if you succeed in purifying one part—say, the heart for instance—by vigorous discipline based upon ethics or religion, or supposing you purify your mind which decides things, it is not unusual to be suddenly invaded by impulses and rushes from the vital. You become uncentered by invasions from outside. That is because the doors are open in other parts of the being. So in a sense no purification of one part can be perfect unless all the other parts are also purified. It is not a logical process of going from one part to another, but laying stress upon one part that is most open, that gives you the lead and simultaneously extending that purificatory movement to other parts in a subsidiary way. What is done, what is worked out in one part has always to be done in the context of the various other parts of the being. There is no such thing as purification of this part first and of that part next, though for purposes of our understanding we go step by step.

We are dealing with the purification of an instrument which is the most important for man. Man is a mental being and in spite of the fact that he lives in a body which is activated by a life-force, it is ultimately the mind that decides what the man is. It is the functioning of the mind that decides the level at which he lives. How the body is put to use, how the life energy is made to work depends upon the poise of his mind, the development of his mind. Therefore, for man at least, mind is the first instrument that should be taken up for purification.

Mind, as we have seen, is an inner instrument. It is called in Sanskrit the *antaḥ-karaṇa*, the inner instrument. The inner instrument consists of *buddhi*, that is intelligence and will or intelligent will, thereafter come the mind, the senses, the sense mind—active and passive —and so on. Now, this inner instrument with which we function is, if we observe dispassionately, at the mercy of what Sri Aurobindo calls the psychic prana, life-force acting as the vehicle of desire. This force does not function only on the vital level; it has a mental colouring. The desire may originate from anywhere in the vital or the life energies, but it succeeds in getting the assent of the mind. It gets a psychological colour and infects the working of the whole system through the mind. You can call it the psychological prana if you like, to make it more specific. It is that which brings about the vitation in the whole working.

If something comes before me, for instance, do I look at it purely from the point of view of what it is, how it is made? The first reaction normally is, how will it be useful for me? Do I have it? Can I have it? My assessment of the thing, my reaction to the thing depends upon what part it can play in my life. There is, at bottom, the desire to possess. If I don't have possession of it, how can I get it? In some way or other we relate things that come before us to our desire-self, and this is the main point of vitiation. As there is a truth behind everything in God's creation, there is a truth here also, though the truth has been deformed and perverted in its expression. The principle behind this psychic prana is *bhoga*, enjoyment. Things are to be taken up and enjoyed; they call it *bhoga*. But what is the divine intention? *Bhoga* as a principle has to be accepted, even in yoga but is *bhoga* completely negative or an inferior principle? The form we have given to that principle is deformed. *Bhoga* proceeds right from the plane of Ananda. It is a divine delight that pours itself out in a million forms so that the Divine can enjoy itself in the form of another.

Only this morning I was reading in the 11th book of *Savitri* how in the infinity the first whisperings of this innocent delight are accompanied by an enamoured laughter at the prospect of discovery, of seeking, of touching, to the rhythm of which the worlds come into existence. The very birth of the universe and the worlds are an outcome of an impulse originating in the Divine Being to put out things from himself in order that he can have a relation. Where there is only one there is no enjoyment, there is only a self-absorption. So something in the Divine is moved to put out things; the One becomes many, the One becomes a million and the One starts having relations, discovering itself through various obstructions, through various channels. It discovers and establishes contact, gets union and has the joy of recognition and union. This joy of discovery, joy of enjoyment, of the delight of the Divine by the Divine and for the Divine is the true principle of *bhoga* that underlies the action of the psychic prana.

Where, then, does the deformation come? The deformation comes with the ego; it is the companion of desire. Because there is a personal desire we miss the cosmic enjoyment. Like air, like ether, the enjoyment is spread out all over the universe. We seek to appropriate

5

things to ourselves individually, we fragment things and there we cut across the scheme of God.

Look at a person who has a developed consciousness, whose consciousness has gotten free from these bonds of self-appropriation. Anything that he sees, anything that appeals to him brings joy to his face; his face becomes radiant. When he sees children he laughs—he doesn't think of whether they are his children or others'. It is just the innocence of the child which brings laughter and joy bubbling up in him. To that extent his consciousness is not involved in the grossness of life, the movement is not mixed. It is to demarcate, expel and eliminate this element of desire, this self-appropriating desire from the psychic prana which runs throughout the mind, the vital and the body that the purificatory discipline is intended. We miss the divine *bhoga* because we seek to personalise, to appropriate individually what is meant for the Divine.

It is to demarcate, expel and eliminate this element of desire, this self-appropriating desire from the psychic prana which runs throughout the mind, the vital and the body that the purificatory discipline is intended. We miss the divine *bhoga* because we seek to personalise, to appropriate individually what is meant for the Divine.

And how do we get out of this desire? It is easy to say "don't desire", but desire itself is a big word. There is a divine desire, there is a creative desire, and there is a human desire. We are at the moment speaking of human desire. This human desire has to be got rid of, narrowed down till it is dissipated completely by acquiring control over our physical and psychic prana. After all, what moves the desire? Behind desire there is a will; the will functions through desire. For the divine desire also there is a divine will. There is one cosmic will which functions through the instrumentation of desire. The first step in this purification is to get control over this desire. Normally what happens is that the physical desires something. Generally the physical body desires only creature comforts, physical pleasures, security and such things. At a higher level the life force extends the field of its desire—it has ambition, it wants aggrandisement; it is not satisfied with only physical pleasures, it wants a vital pleasure of domination, of control, of ruling over many, satisfaction of its wishes and imaginations. The vital desire it is that really dominates the human being. Though the Upanishads say that mind is the leader of the life and body normally, in our day-to-day life it is the vital, the desire linked to the life-force that is the ruler. That colours our thinking and mind is at the mercy of every vital invasion.

This desire at the vital level has to be first got hold of and the rules have to be reversed so that instead of the vital dominating over the mind, precipitating the mind into whatever direction it chooses, it is the mind that must stand aloof, the mind must decide in what way the vital shall function, in what direction the vital energies shall move. For that, even in small matters the mind should be cultivated, the mental will—to put more definitely—must be strengthened. In all matters once we decide to do a thing, that must be given a full operation, whatever the inclinations of the body, whatever the inclinations of the vital being. What the mind has decided must be enforced. That way new grooves are formed by which in any situation the mind emerges first and has a look at the situation and we know to what extent we have to take interest in a thing, in what way we should deal with the situation. Otherwise nature rushes through the vital desires to vitiate every situation and the mind is just a follower.

We spoke of the sense mind, those senses which are impelled in the direction of objects. In each case they are impelled by desire. There is the emotional mind, where we have so many emotions, feelings and the like which give habitual responses, again governed by desire. By habit it is decided that such contacts are helpful, enjoyable, such other contacts are unpleasant. And the emotional mind goes on giving standard responses, but that is not the final truth. Is what is pleasant always good, and what is unpleasant always harmful? The moment we grow in our consciousness, in our understanding, we rather see that the opposite is true—that what is normally very pleasant is rarely good and what we normally seek to avoid has some virtues in it, has some contributive elements in it. That is why the Upanishad speaks of *śreyas* and *preyas*, the good and the pleasant, what is spiritually good and what is not.

We can revise, we can change our responses by putting pressure upon our desire-being. If we once recognise that we are prisoners of habitual movements, then it is possible to begin to change our response. For instance, when we go to a play, a drama on the stage, the response to a scene of suffering is one of rapt interest. When a similar situation of suffering arises in our own life, our response would be different. How is that? It is because in the theatre we are not personally involved, we are not personally affected; we function at a different level in taking the sap of things, the *rasa*. There even grief and hurt yield a certain *rasa*. It has an effect of catharsis when we see a tragedy and something in us responds and reacts to the situation. We are able to get out of the normal grooves of reaction of unhappiness on seeing suffering.

That shows that suffering has a part to play in the

evolution of the soul. Very often, Sri Aurobindo points out, the soul in its evolution chooses suffering in order to progress by the hard way and the quicker way. It is like exercise in physical culture, where if we do only light exercises which don't pull our muscles it takes time to build up the body. But if we make a habit of choosing the harder exercises where initially we get some pain and it is more exacting, then we build up our muscles sooner. So, the soul may choose the way of suffering in order to progress more rapidly. The outer human mind does not know it and it tries at times to remedy the situation by committing suicide, not knowing that the suffering is the soul's choice. Even if being tired or being misdirected by hostile forces, one commits suicide, in the next birth the soul is likely to choose the same kind of circumstances because it has been tricked, it has been denied its choice.

This is by the way. The point is that it is possible to change our reactions to things once we get away from the interfering desire, and this desire is shot through and through by our psychic prana, which influences everything from the physical body right up to the mind. Even our thoughts are subconsciously coloured and pulled here and there by the course of desire.

We have a passive sense mind and an active dynamising mind. Now, it is the passive part of the sense mind that is at the mercy of all contacts from outside. It reacts to anything that comes and impinges upon it. If we take care to separate the desire element in our prana from the operation of this sense mind, the sense mind becomes indifferent to many contacts and impacts; it will not react. It will not run after things that are likely to give pleasure; it will not unless we consciously impel it to do so. Corresponding to this passive part of the sensational mind there is the dynamic part which exerts itself to get things. Now if the usual desire is not there, if it has been purified and we have taught ourselves not to seek things for our own enjoyment, for our own *bhoga* but for the divine, for the larger self, then the very nature of the functioning of this impulsive mind undergoes a change. It weighs, it judges before it goes into action.

Everywhere—right from the lowest strata of mind to the reasoning mind—there is this intermiscence of psychic prana and desire. Even in the physical desire there is this psychological desire mixed up, because man is essentially a psychological being. Whatever work he does, whatever emotions he expresses, whatever thoughts he thinks, behind all is the influence of the psychic prana. We begin by sedulously watching our movements, rejecting at every step things that are moved by desire; unless we start in a small way it is impossible to expect that we will be in a position to eliminate desire from our being. May be we are very charitable when it concerns ourselves and say that, after all, these are innocent desires. A desire may be innocent, but it is a hundred such innocent desires that activate and build up a body of desire in us.

The Mother used to say that there are people who imagine they can tell small falsehoods, and when it really came to a test they would speak only the truth. However, once the habit is formed of reacting with a lie even in small matters, it develops to the point that one lies for the sake of lying. We are very familiar with people joking and saying it is just for the fun of it. Nobody gains, but the lower vital enjoys it. To tell a lie, to be cunning, to cheat, to deceive—all these are expressions of one particular part of the lower vital. It becomes so much a habit that even when one does not stand to gain anything, one goes on indulging in it just for the pleasure of it.

This is why Sri Aurobindo and Mother vehemently object to gossip. We know how when each item of gossip is taken up for scrutiny and we trace it to its source we find there is a big zero. Things develop, they gather volume from mouth to mouth. The Asura uses this gossipping mentality to deflect the human consciousness towards an anti-divine goal. Once the wall of goodwill, benevolence, charity and understanding is broken by such activities of the lower vital as gossip and scandal mongering, the door is open to the entry of the hostile forces which denude the persons who talk and the persons who hear, of the least element of goodwill, without which no divine life is possible.

Everywhere there is this desire. Even in gossip there is a desire to condemn somebody, to put down somebody so that, in effect, one rises above. One has a feeling of satisfaction that he is superior, the other inferior. Whether others believe that he is superior or not is another matter—they ultimately believe that both are inferior—but the havoc is done. This personal desire to show off, to aggrandise at the expense of others has been at the centre of the havoc on every plane—material plane, mental plane etc. "My ideas, my ideology, my teaching, my guru are the best, truth is my monopoly". Everywhere there is this desire for superiority. It expresses itself on a hundred levels, in a hundred forms.

These are the areas where we have to apply the torch of purification. We have to take a torch and hunt for these lairs of desire in every part of our being. That is the first self-discipline. We have to be severe to ourselves and charitable to others. And this purification of the lower mentality is ultimately fruitful depending upon the support it receives from the purification of the higher mind or the higher mentality. We have to start at the lower end, no doubt, but we have to support our action in the lower regions by light from above, by help from the higher regions. That is where the purification of the higher *buddhi* comes in. Before we start purifying we must know what is to be purified, we must learn to discriminate good things from the bad in ourselves. It is only when that window in our thought mind is open, when discrimination starts functioning naturally and spontaneously, that we are guided to put our finger on the right spot. This will be the subject of our next session—purification of the higher mentality.

As we said, no purification anywhere can be complete without purification everywhere, but we have to start somewhere. For man it is easiest to start at the level where he is and that is the level of the lower mentality. We have seen the area to be cleared, but one needs a light and that light he can get from his *buddhi*, intelligence, understanding, because man is essentially led by his understanding, however much it may be coloured by desire.

(From Questions & Answers)

Q.: What is pleasant and what is good?—that itself is a big question.

A.: For a man whose consciousness is rooted below in creature comforts—greed for food, sex, comfortable life—certain things are pleasant. He feels they are good and he looks for them. For a man who has developed a little higher consciousness, he finds these things are dissipating, they sap his energies, they kill his time and he does not have a sense of development, of progress. For him they are not good. So what is normally pleasant turns out to be bad for the higher growth of the human consciousness. Everything has to be decided according to the level of consciousness where one dwells. What happens with most of the seekers is they know a thing is bad, wrong, but still they can't resist, they say 'just this one time.' When it is shown and the consciousness appreciates that a thing is bad and one still goes after it, it is rank insincerity. And where there is insincerity there can't be spiritual progress.

This inability to distinguish automatically between what is good and what is not good is rooted in our vital desire. It is the ego, the desire-soul that decides what is good for it from its own standards. The true judgment, the true assessment of things can come only from the true soul, the psychic being or the purified mind which is open to the influence and the light of the soul. And the mind cannot be open to the light of the soul unless it is purified of its dross of desires at every level. Desire is the main source of conflict and the intention of purification is to get rid of this deformation imposed by the ego, to thin out slowly the entity called the desire soul so that the true being, the true centre, the psychic being gradually comes forward and displaces the frontal ego and begins to function as the leader of the journey of our life.

*   *

Desire is different from need, though the lower vital and the mind given to the vital interpret things to their own advantage. They always take every desire to be a true need. The ability to distinguish between need and desire can come only by a sustained action of purification. Desire is desire on whatever level it functions. For instance, a crude man who has desire for food wants to eat; if you give anything to a child it wants to put it in its mouth. These are crude desires implanted by nature. Someone who is a little more developed doesn't care

so much for such a desire as to get admiration from
people, acquire control and influence over people. That
is the vital desire. And then at the mental level one has,
say, a greed for books. The Mother once said that greed
is at the root of tumour. When some one died from tumour in the brain I got intrigued as to how it happened.
The man was not an intellectual, not a scholar; his brain
could have no greed. I asked the Mother how the tumour
had to come to his brain. She said he had ambition—
ambition to become a guru and that kind of thing. Greed
comes when we try to acquire a thing of which we have
no true need. Greed may be at any level; there may even
be greed for spiritual progress—they want to storm the
kingdom of heaven by violence, they do austerities, they
do many things. Even spiritual wealth, spiritual progress can be gobbled up by the lower vital. Anything is
fair enough; even spiritual gains are prostituted by the
lower desire if it has not been got rid of. It lurks in so
many forms and it keeps its individuality intact.

*   *

You have to develop discrimination and for that
there has to be sincerity; each one knows where one is
sincere and not sincere. There is not a dunce who does
not know it. Everyone knows. There is something of a
divine element in each person which points its finger,
"this is right, this is not right for you". One may pre-
tend not to hear, one may say it is superstition, but
everyone knows where he is sincere and where he is
not. Unless there is this sincerity, discrimination can't
function.

8

PURIFICATION—INTELLIGENCE AND WILL (I)

We considered last time the process of purification of the lower inner instrument, the lower *antaḥ-karaṇa*, and today we are to study the purification of the intelligence and the *buddhi*. We have already seen the distinction between mind and *buddhi*. Mind, consists of several minds. There is the sense mind, the mind that depends upon the data brought by the senses, mentalises the data and reacts from the nervous level. That is the sensational mind. Depending upon it, close to it, is the thinking mind— not the thought mind proper, but the mind that thinks along the lines of the sense mind. Above it is the reasoning mind, which, if it chooses, can be aloof, detached from the sense operations of the mind or it can allow itself to be infected, influenced and let into deviation by the force of desire. Buddhi is something still higher. It is a combination of will and the thinking mind—the will that gives the impulse to the thinking mind.

It is these higher echelons of the mind and the *buddhi* that are now to be purified after the lower levels of the *antaḥ-karaṇa,* the inner instrumentation, have been dealt with. What is called in the Indian terminology, *manas,* is the sense mind; usually the mind of an average man is the *manas*. He does not think for the sake of thinking, he does not think out ideas. He just reacts to events, to impacts, to contacts; things fall upon him and he reacts. The whole operation of his mind is ninety percent confined to that. It is said, Nature thinks, man does not think, he is thought. But at a level where man still has a

certain independence and can think out ideas, give
exercise to the mind and judge things on his own without
depending upon sense contact, that is the beginning of
the mind proper.

In the normal *manas* there are two elements. One is
of the physical nerves; one sees an object or thinks there
is the object, and on an impulse from the nervous being
the sense faculty is put out. When it comes back there is a
mental-nervous operation. The report that has been
brought is interpreted rightly or wrongly to suit the
governing motive or desire of the moment, and a mental
colouring is given to it. These are the two elements of
manas.

Now, for purification man has first to disengage his
thought from this sense mentality. He may be conscious,
indeed, that there is a layer of the mind which reacts
naturally and spontaneously to sense contacts. But before
he absorbs those experiences and allow them to influence
or cloud his thinking, he has to draw the line. A gulf has
to be created, a barrier erected before the sense impressions, the movements of the sense mind can rush into
the mind proper. The thought has to be guarded and for
this, a self-observation, a relentless discipline of observing
one's thoughts is necessary. How far are they disinterested, how far do they seek knowledge for its own sake,
and how far do they interpret things in such a way that
they can be made to serve the ego, the desires? There
is no pure action. This impurity, this intermiscence of
the lower elements in the thought range has first to be
arrested. And the first step towards it in an awakened
man, one who has awakened to the necessity of going
beyond the sense mind, is reflection. He has to reflect,
time and again—not necessarily only in periods of meditation or solitude, but even otherwise. One faculty

must be always active, reflecting upon things, just as one may be busy with many things but feelings go on flowing and exerting themselves. Similarly, there must be an automatic functioning of the reflective apparatus, especially in him who seeks the truth. He has to study the nature of the movements that go on. As soon as a thought rises on the mental horizon there must be an instant reflection—what is it, from where does it come and why does it come? Is it something which may have been thought yesterday, or a thought that has crossed, or something in dream that has given rise to this thought, or is it somebody in the environment who may be thinking along those lines and that thought has entered into the mind, or is it due to some desire, some impurity that it has come? One does not think all this step by step. It is the operation of a moment. There is something that nature has implanted in man and unless he deceives himself, unless he tries to hide from himself, there is an immediate perception that this thought is related to this desire of this movement. Of course, there are times when things are ambiguous and one has to give closer scrutiny to find out what is their true nature. That is another matter. Normally, when one speaks of reflection in this context it is a spontaneous and automatic reflection which acts unless one is too much involved in the mud of desire.

The *buddhi* part, the part that has will in it and decides that this shall be so and this shall not be so, is a little separate. The reflective element is not to be confused with the *buddhi*. Reflection is at the thought level, the higher or the purer or the disinterested thought; it is in that range that the reflection starts. It is just possible that even when one knows by reflection that a thing is wrong, one may lack the will to follow it up. There comes the deficiency of will in the *buddhi*. It is not enough to have knowledge, not enough to know that a thing is wrong; one must also have the will in the *buddhi* to back up this conviction and exert itself on the rest of the being to desist from that movement. So, the *buddhi* which is largely the will part of the intelligence comes after reflection.

Ultimately, what is this *buddhi?* It is, truly, an instrument of the soul. The soul has so many instruments, but *buddhi* is one of its closest instruments. Through it the soul awakes to nature. Unless our *buddhi* is alert, the awakening of the soul cannot be felt in our nature. It is through the *buddhi* that the soul reaches its awareness, awakening, its own will to our being, to our nature. The understanding of the *buddhi* also is caused by a wave from the soul. When it is a right understanding it is the soul within that is responsible, and it is again through the instrumentation of the *buddhi* that the soul takes possession of nature. Instead of the soul being involved in nature, as the soul awakes, it is through the instrumentality of *buddhi*, awakened intelligence, that the soul exercises its power over nature. The aim is to build up through the *buddihi* a full possession of nature and a complete mastery over nature. Soul and nature have got different poises at different levels of evolution. At the normal level of human life, it is nature which has the upper hand, the soul is involved, the soul is forgotten, soul is a slave. As we wake up, as our consciousness develops, as we take appropriate means of self-discipline the soul gathers itself and witnesses nature. That is the relation of equality in which the soul does not inter- fere. But it goes on organising its detached position, non-involvement. Once it is sufficiently free, liberated from the hold of nature even as a witness, *sākṣi*, the soul takes a step higher and begins to assume lordship over nature. The soul becomes the master of nature and for all these steps to be taken, it is *buddhi* that is the instrument. It is through the exercise of *buddhi* that the soul gains ascendency over nature, takes the enjoyment of nature, the intended enjoyment for the Divine.

In spiritual life it is mostly is a rejection of nature. They all speak of rejection of nature—it is said you cannot change nature. The classic example given is of the dog's tail—twist it however much you will, it will go back to its curve. But that is a negative philosophy and it is not true either. It suits the escapists, those whose objective is only to escape from life, to cancel themselves from the scheme of evolution and merge into some Nirvana—either of a zero or of Brahman. Speaking of rejection of nature, it is enough for them that nature is put away and soul is separated, and in that scheme no action is permitted as part of spiritual life. Action has to be gone through to exhaust the accumulated *karma* perhaps, but action is a binding force. Whatever action is done, with whatever motive or no motive, it binds and forges *karma* which can be exhausted only with the falling of the body. So neither change of nature nor action from a new poise of nature is envisaged, much less practised in many of the lines of spiritual effort.

But in an integral path like this which seeks to perfect life, which knows that in essence there is no difference between nature and soul, that nature after all is a self-casting of the soul, a movement of the soul, this standpoint is not valid. We have to accept nature, change nature little by little and make it a willing instrument and a joyous channel for the flow of the dynamism of the soul. And for that purpose *buddhi* is the highest instrument that nature has given us. How are we going to purify this *buddhi*, this intelligence that is backed up by will?

The first thing is to exceed the limits of the sense mind. Normally when things come in our ken we see them, we hear them; but it is possible to take cognisance of things even without the operation of the sense faculties. Of all our sense faculties it is touch that is the most important, but below the human level—as in the trees and the animals—they come to know even without the sense of touch because their sense mind, the sense mentality takes a direct cognisance of things without having to function through these particular sense organs. Man has lost this capacity. He will recover it perhaps in different terms, but he has to cultivate the habit and discipline of exceeding the limits of the sense mind.

For instance, he can learn to exercise his thought faculty on its own, without being propped up by the sense data. He can learn to think and govern his life, develop the ethical part of his mind on its own, without depending upon the compulsions of sense life to teach him lessons. Similarly, the aesthetic part, the aesthetic faculties of his mind can be developed in their purity, without getting entangled in what the senses find appealing or repelling. These are starting points; we shall not take the sense data as the entire field and the sole cause and impulsion for the development of our mind. There is such a thing as thought mind proper, ethical mind proper, aesthic mind proper. These are to be developed for their own sake, to build up a total perfection. We should not have to depend upon proddings of sense experience to build these personalities.

Similarly, we have what is called the pragmatic mind. We are likely or prone to consider everything from the point of view of how far things are useful to us. In

American philosophy there is a movement initiated by
William James called the philosophy of pragmatism. He
says that any theory, any conception, any perception is
true or not true, depending solely upon how far it is
serviceable to life. If it can better your life, if it can
elighten your personal life, it is good. You accept it
and give it a positive mark; otherwise you reject it as
speculative, as mental, as imaginary. This tendency of
relating everything to its pragmatic value is a very
narrow view of things. There is this pragmatic mind
which, again, pulls the mind down to earth—earthly
needs, earthly benefits. This has to be replaced by what
we call the idea mind. There we think of things on their
own basis. A thought rises, a conception, an idea forms;
we consider it, how far it is true and why it is not true in
some cases, but we do not consider whether it will be
useful for this purpose or that. Things do not always have
a utilitarian aim. After all, the higher values of our
civilisation have been evolved not from the utilitarian
standpoint, though today in our material civilisation we
seek to judge with that barometer. But the ancients, or
leaders of civilisations older than ours, thought and moved
in different realms. They regarded truth for its own sake.
Of course there is a controversy as to whether you can
have art or truth for its own sake, but these are all
mental debates. The point is, it is a necessary part of
purification to disengage ourselves from the pragmatic
element in our mentality. We should cultivate an ideal
mind, but even when we cultivate the ideal mind it is
seen that in a hundred veiled forms there is the unknown
mixture of shootings from desire, from selfish motives.
Already there is some pre-judgment. Desire need not be
always a crude physical desire for food and drink. Desire
can be to entertain my pet notions, to infect others with

6

them, to get others to accept my philosophy of life. There is already a proclivity, a proneness to have certain ideas, certain truths, and when we speak of an ideal mind these subconscious tendencies, preferences, creep in. It is a part of purification to close the doors to the upsurge—known and unknown, seen and unseen—of these elements from the unpurified parts of the being.

As this purification, on these various levels of the forming mind—the aesthetic mind, the ethical mind, the thinking mind, the ideal mind—proceeds, whenever we have opportunity, whenever there is an occasion to build up these terraces of consciousness as we would say, there is a greater and greater detachment from involvement in the lower movements of the inner instrumentation and there is an increasing discovery of something that exists by itself. It does not care whether it serves the life needs or not. It has been there since before we were born, and it will be there after we shed the body. We become aware of this self-existent being in a very profound and solemn way, and this being casts its reflection in the aesthetic consciousness, ethical level of consciousness, knowledge level and will level. That is where things are in their purity. All the rest we can contribute—our technique, our methods of presentation—but basically they are reflections of a self-existent being. The being has intended them as so many spring-boards for manifestation into those relevant fields of human existence.

Again we come back to the necessity of giving free room and free scope for this emergence of the self-existent being into the consciousness. We have first to remove desire of all kinds from the being. The *buddhi* has to be lifted up from its involvement in our sense mind or reasoning mind or whatever kind of mind, as long as these minds are open to impurity. As we begin to eliminate desire consciously, we begin to feel an effortless detachment. With detachment there comes equality. The *buddhi* is not tossed about—as Arjuna says in the Gita—by the sense contacts. Whether the contacts are pleasant or unpleasant, the *buddhi* stays equal. There is an equanimity; it observes, it watches. This equality establishes a calm which nothing can destroy. Even if there is an apparent disturbance it is on the surface, very much like when we throw a stone in a pond of water. There is a movement but it settles down and once again there is a limpid surface of water.

(*From Questions & Answers*)

Q.: *How can you tell when the soul is awakening?*

A.: The soul has got certain characteristic qualities and these qualities express themselves through their powers. The soul, for instance, has the qualities of harmony, love, compassion, benevolence, beauty, wholeness, disinterested love, disinterested goodwill, a welling up kindliness and compassion, a going-out of oneself to identify with others, feel for others. When you look around you feel a unity with nature, you begin to feel love for everybody whether it is a person or a parrot. Your whole being gets flooded and you feel all the cares and troubles and anxieties of day-to-day life as in a picture; they don't affect you. You are always smiling—outwardly you may not smile, but there is a smile within. There is a revolution in the balance of nature. It may not be immediate, but the signs are unmistakable.

What may happen is that in the beginning this awakening may not come all at a time, but in parts. But unless you have taken steps to purify yourself, the emotional being seizes upon these manifestations of the soul and puts them to its own use. The vital seizes—unless it is purified and kept under check—upon these movements of expansion, movements of self-sacrifice, for its own aggrandisement: To gain command over others, to assemble others around itself. The original source of support and strength is a soul movement, but it has been seized and prostituted by the unpurified outer instrument—whether it is the emotional parts or the vital parts or the calculating mind.

In an atmosphere like this Ashram, everyone, without exception, has his moments when the soul is awake. He may begin to doubt the next moment and the smoke may cover it up, but still the atmosphere constantly presses upon him and the soul awakes. These are the characteristic signs—the flow of love, feeling of oneness and unity, and indentification with larger and larger sections of the environment, and a wide sense of purity. One can't think ill of others. If a thought harmful to others comes into the mind, one feels unclean as if one has soiled oneself. When that sensitivity is reached to the surface one can take it that the soul is awake and whatever the stupidities of the ignorant world outside, the soul will not be denied. Once the soul is awake it cannot be put back to sleep.

Q.: Where does citta enter into this scheme?

A.: *Citta* is the basic stuff of consciousness of the whole being. It is neutral. There is an area where there is no active force, there is no awakened thought. The *Citta* is the basic stuff on which the mind, the heart, the subliminal all draw upon. *Citta* is not mental conciousness.

*   *

Will is inalienable from the soul. The soul is the purusha and where there is the purusha there is the will, there is the *buddhi*. It is we who have to learn to invoke that *buddhi*, to activise it, to exercise it, to give it shape, to give it a personality. We have to develop it as we develop a physical muscle. We have to start exercising our will as a discipline even in small matters. After a time, without any special effort, the will exerts itself spontaneously. There is a subconscious will, an instinctive will. Once we develop the will consciously, that control goes down to the subconscient and even when we are attending to other things, this subconscient or unconscious will exerts itself. It is a matter of practice.

*   *

Usually the vital puts the will on its side. The will itself is neutral. If, at that time when the vital tries to put the will on its side, the mind puts the will on its own side, the mental will will prevail because the mind is a higher position. But often when the vital allies itself with the will, we like it, our desire-soul supports it. That is why it can get away with things. If the desire-soul is rejected or displaced by the true soul the problem does not arise.

9

PURIFICATION — INTELLIGENCE AND WILL (II)

We spoke of the purification of the lower instrumentation, *antaḥ-karaṇa*. We spoke of the purification of life desires, emotions and we arrived at a stage where we were considering the purification of *buddhi*, the intelligent will, the will which presides over the mental movements. This purification of *buddhi* consists of two phases. One is of detachment: the mind detaches itself from anything that is posed before the mental intelligence. It does not identify itself immediately, but takes care to step back for a moment. Having detached itself, it fronts the object with equality—without like or dislike, repulsion or attraction, waiting for the right reaction to come. This process of building up a spontaneous action of detachment and equality leads to a practical purification of the *buddhi*.

But this is not done in a day. We have to analyse the nature of *buddhi*, the functionings of *buddhi*, and know in what precise way these steps of purification are to be applied. If we consider the normal operations of our mental intelligence, we see that there is a movement or a type of activity which is habitual. To anything that comes by, it responds in a mechanical way, governed by the environmental tradition, habitual reactions, habitual thoughts and so on. We can even predict in precisely what way the *buddhi* is going to react to a particular situation based upon past experience, upon what happens elsewhere in the environment. We can call it the habitual movement.

Secondly, there is a bias in the *buddhi*, what we may call a pragmatic intellectuality. As each thing comes it before it, it evaluates from the point of view of how far is it going to be of use to itself—whether to arrive at a knowledge that it is seeking, or to derive some delight or whatever. It is a personal self-reference and its assessment of the object depends upon the pragmatic value that object has from this viewpoint. Here it is more the will rather than the thought element that is prominent, because it is the will that is concerned with the possible use or utilisation of a situation for its own interests. Thought is more concerned with the pursuit of knowledge for its own sake, but not so the will.

Then there is a third level of functioning and that is when the *buddhi* seeks the truth for its own sake. It is not influenced by its own needs, it is not swayed by the habitual or existing impressions or *samskāras* or trends. It is out to seek knowledge for its own sake, and that brings an objectivity. Here it is the element of knowledge that is prominent.

Thus there are three successive levels in the functioning of *buddhi*—the habitual level which is mechanical, the level of the pragmatic intellect dominated by the will, and still higher, the pursuit of self-existent truth dominated by knowledge. We have to analyse these three elements and then apply the process of purification on their respective levels.

We spoke of the element of will dominating in one grade, the element of knowledge dominating in another. This disparity between knowledge and will is, as we have observed on a number of occasions before, a characteristic feature of our mental ignorance. Where there is will, there is not enough knowledge to guide it; where there is knowledge the necessary will is lacking to effectuate that knowledge. This gulf between knowledge and will is healed only on the higher levels and it reaches a perfect indentity on the gnostic level, the supermind. Till then, there is a constant variation in the contribution of these two factors.

After we analyse the various components or the functions of *buddhi* and start disciplining it, we find that though the *buddhi* itself is constituted of knowledge and will, it never works at its optimum or in its purity. It is always in search of truth, it is never in possession of truth. To be in possession of truth is a sign of knowledge, the knowledge mind, but at the level of the *buddhi* of which we are speaking there is only a quest for knowledge. Knowledge is not in its possession. Even if we succeed in silencing the mind, in eliminating its restless movements and dartings after sense objects and feelings which excite its interests, we will find that *buddhi* can only reflect. And it reflects in parts. Ours is not an integral or a total *buddhi*. It functions, or it is alive in some parts here and there, some segments are obscure or not functioning. So the knowledge or whatever is reflected in our *buddhi* is a partial reflection. The reflections are piecemeal, and in interpreting the reflections there is always the pragmatic pull. Even if we believe that we are objective, there is always the subconscious bias, the subconscious pull to interpret to understand from the point of view of its possible utility in some sphere or other.

Granted that we process our mental intelligence on these lines, make of it as perfect an instrument as possible at our level, in our circumstances, still we suffer from two main limitations. Whatever the realisation of the mental intelligence it, is after all a mental realisation; it does not organise itself spontaneously or automatically in the rest of the being. It is at the level of intelligence that we realise certain truths and we know "All is Brahman", "Thou art Brahman", etc., but do they translate themselves in our actions, in our vision? They do not. The mind knows, certainly the enlightened *buddhi* knows that all life is one, that God is everywhere, that all are equal, equal in the Self. But it is a mental realisation. That is what the Mother means when she says that learning, knowledge learned from others are acquisitions; they are store-houses of information. Unless it becomes part of our consciousness and moulds our consciousness in the direction in which the truth points, it is not true knowledge, not true realisation.

We speak of transformation, we speak of supermind, of gnostic communities, do these concepts form an actual part of our day-to-day life? As long as they do not, they are mere theories for us. We speak of practical things and philosophical concepts. This is a legacy of the old world ignorance. One who is serious about arriving at a working purification of the *buddhi* must understand that the understandings of *buddhi*—even when it is purified—are largely mental realisations. Even when it is in a position, by discipline, by brilliance, to catch hold of a number of truths, not to lose itself in one truth but understand many truths, many aspects of the truth, it lacks the genius, the capacity to organise, to unify the truth. This also, the unification of truths, can come only on the gnostic level. Till then there will always be a stress on one truth at the expense of another, depending upon the trend of nature, upon the ideal one seeks for. So the entire coordination of knowledge and will and a complete unification of truths as a multiple expression of one Reality are possible and become a regular feature of life only at the gnostic level, when one realises the supramental consciousness.

The ancients discovered these constitutional incapacities of the *buddhi* to communicate the real spiritual experience and relate it to life; they decided in many of their philosophies that the best thing is to cultivate the *buddhi*, teach it detachment, enforce equality upon it, and then pressurise it to leap into a higher status of being, to turn its eyes away from the world and grow towards the heights, look upwards and pass into the realms of the higher consciousness. But this is only a way of shirking the problem. Certainly mental intelligence is not given so that it may be fused or it may disappear into higher realms of consciousness. It has to be raised to its optimum and transformed, enlightened into an effective power or projection of the gnostic *buddhi*, gnostic intelligence.

The kind of liberation that a seeker of the integral path should envisage is not to force the *buddhi*, the mental intelligence to disappear into the higher mind, but to lift the soul from the mental level to the higher level leading to the gnosis. Normally the soul of man, the mental being, is poised in the mentality. From there it has to be educated, lifted up gradually to higher levels. It does not mean that these lower are to be abandoned; they have to be cultured and the link maintained. The direction should be upwards with a constant turning back to integrate the levels that have been left behind.

The soul so lifted up passes through the illumined mental levels or the intuitive levels and it has to naturalise the action of these higher states of consciousness before it can hope to obtain a permanent lodging in the gnosis. For that a comprehensive purification is indispensable. Sri Aurobindo puts it pithily saying *śuddhi* is indispensable for *mukti*.

10

THE LIBERATION OF THE SPIRIT

Once the lower instrumentation has been subjected to the operation of purificatory processes, the emphasis on *śuddhi* shifts to the liberation of the soul. But liberation of the soul is not extinction of the soul. Liberation consists of two steps: one is rejection of the lower elements, things that hold it down and rejection of things that deform, discolour and detain the soul from its light. That is, in a word, to reject identification and involvement with lower nature. Once that is done, the second step that inevitably follows is assumption of higher nature. The way is not only a negative way. Once the negative purification and cleansing is done, the dispossession is over, thereafter follows the putting on of the character, acquiring the elements of higher nature—call it supernature, or divine nature. These have to be systematically aspired for, cultivated and made part of ourselves.

This double process of rejection of the lower and assumption of the higher involves a release from what Sri Aurobindo calls some master knots. The ordinary knots of ego and desire and senses in the lower instrumentation are ordinary knots which can be either loosened or cut by the ordinary ethical disciplines. But there are more subtle and more psychological knots which are not easily visible on the surface. They are the four master knots which bind the soul in a very subtle manner. They are the knot of desire, the knot of ego, the knot of dualities and the knot of the gunas. These are the four impediments that the Gita speaks of and Sri Aurobindo remarks

that it is a very capital description of the knots that
besiege the progress of the soul.

To eliminate these elements, the Mother does not
favour cutting of the knots but loosening them, untying
them dexterously, so that nothing is excised and the
being does not suffer any permanent shock. Ours is
an organic growth. Our knots have to be so loosened
that things become natural, without damage. For
instance, with ego and desire, we have to expand our
consciousness. As long as we are confined within our
limited range, as long as we imagine that we are separate beings living separately in the world and we need
to assert ourselves in that environment in order to have
our way, there is the desire to possess, desire to conquer,
there is the stress of ego to outshine, to aggrandise. But
once we realise that we are part of the universe and start
universalising our thoughts and feelings—in a word
become universal in soul—there is a great change.
There is no longer the old tension. A slow transmutation takes over and in 'that largeness of consciousness,
broadness of will, the hold of the ego dwindles. Desire
as such is shamed away from our vision. We cannot
think of having to acquire for ourselves what belongs to
others or what is not given to us. This universalising of
consciousness is the one antidote to dissolve desire and
ego.

These knots of desire are, again, double knots. There
is a knot in the instrumental being dominated by desire
in the senses, the emotions and the sense mind and there
is also an upper knot, an upper end to the knot in the
buddhi. It may originate at a lower level but the basic
support and the help to survive, to continue to prey upon
others comes from the foundation of *buddhi* in the mind.
The solution that has been proposed in many of the

traditions is that the *buddhi* should be simply refused indulgence in desire. It should be isolated and the mind opened to an impersonal reality, an impersonal peace and silence; the *buddhi* is released into it so that it no longer feels the pull of desire and loses interest. This is possible, but is that the intention?

The *buddhi* supports desire because there is a will in the *buddhi*. That will is not the human will but the will of the spirit, and the will of the spirit is to enjoy, to manifest, derive the delight of existence from all things. The deformation comes in the self-limitation of the individual. Man lives into the mould of ego, he thinks and feels in terms of a separative existence and the struggle starts. There is an interference with the operation of the supreme will and the human egoism and desire come into play as deforming factors.

The soulution is, instead of negativing the mental intelligence, to slowly displace its ego sense, its ego consciousness by a growing oneness with the universal being, with the transcendental divine. The individual should begin to downplay his identification with the egoistic formation and look more and more towards these meeting points with the universal being, as also the links with the transcendent. In that way the whole movement falls into its proper proportion and the ego turns out to be nothing more than a surface double. It is not that the individual is to be abolished. The individual has his truth. Even as the transcendental divinity, the universal or the cosmic spirit have their truth, so also has the individual. The transcendental Reality or the Divine creates the universe; the universal Divine is the same Divinity in another poise maintaining and keeping up the movement of the universe; the individual is the point of concentration through which the transcendent effectuates his purpose.

All the three are necessary. Simply because the ego deforms the individual, that does not detract from the intrinsic value of the individual. It is the deforming factors that have to be eliminated. The individual has a role; the individual is the key for the cosmic evolution. It is the individual involvement in the limitations of the mind that has to be remedied. The individual forfeits his right to function as a centre, as a natural centre of the Divine, because he gets mixed up with the limitations of the mind. This limitation has to be gradually eliminated. The sense of separate existence is the basis of human life in this world of ignorance.

All methods, all means that diminish this stress of separate existence are welcome. Some thinkers, approach this problem in a different way. The emphasise the reality or the truth of the higher, the greater claims of society on the individual, and go to the extreme of looking on the individual as a cell in collective existence and sacrificed the interest of the individual for the collectivity. That is an exaggeration. The truth is neither entirely in the individual nor entirely in the collectivity, but in a balanced function by which the individual looks upon himself as an articulate centre of the collectivity and the collectivity as a field for his growth, a field to which he has to contribute his best forthedivine manifestation.

This separativity of consciousness leads to a limitation of consciousness. The consciousness itself is large and one, but when we choose voluntarily or involuntarily to limit ourselves to this little body, this little mind, to what conerns us personally, practically, then our consciousness is limited. As the consciousness is limited, the knowledge is limited. As knowledge is limited, the vision is limited. The approach is limited. The approach being limited, actions suffer a handicap. This handicap, this defect in actions leads to a sense of sin. Sin is a certain inherent shortfall. It is not something inherited but can be traced to a limitation of consciousness, limitation of knowledge, which again derives directly from separativity in consciousness. So the sense of sin can be removed and it does fall away once we rise out of our scaffolding of this sense of separativity and egoism.

And it is only when this sense of sin, sense of defect, deficiency is put behind that one is able to breathe the true air of bliss, the true *ānanda*, experience the *ānanda* for which God has made this universe, and participate in it.

To sum up, it is the liberation from desire, liberation from ego, leading to oneness with the divinity around and above that leads to a liberation into delight.

(From Questions & Answers)

Q.: *The dissolution of the first two knots would seem to take care of a lot?*

A.: Yes, because the dualities originate in desire. The gunas form constituent parts of our nature. It is they that decide where we are going to lay stress, whether rajas, sattva or tamas. They too revolve round the knot of ego. Where the ego is not, or where the ego is weak, the gunas have no centre around which to organise themselves. So it is the desire and the ego that are the lynchpins. These four are the knots, though I suppose the knot of the gunas would be the last because it means liberation from nature herself.

Q.: *Don't the three gunas correspond to the triple soul force in Savitri?*

A.: No. You can say these three are the mechanical *buddhi*, the practical *buddhi* and the thought *buddhi*.

There (in Savitri) it is Inertia and Suffering, Force and Knowledge; the Mother of Sorrows taking care of falsehood, ignorance and pain, the Mother of Might working to put down evil, the Mother of Light radiating to dispel ignorance and bring knowledge. I don't think these correspond here; *buddhi* is only a part of the mind. It is an important part, but still a part of mind, and the soul is much bigger than the mind.

Q.: *How to distinguish between the soul and the mind?*

A.: After all, the mental purusha who conducts the operations of the mind is only a reflection of the soul. It is a fragmented reflection, an interfered reflection possibly, but when the soul directly influences the mind, necessarily the mental being begins to partake of the character of the soul. Oneness, harmony, inevitability of knowledge, self-evident intuition—all these let one know that the soul is active in the mind. The mind then doesn't think in segments; it thinks in whole.

So when the influence of the soul is active, on whichever level, it is unmistakable—as beauty and harmony in the aesthetic being, as uncalculating love in the emotional being, as uncaused peace and uniterrupted joy in the physical being, as pure knowledge and unerring perception in the mind. These are the obvious signs that the sun of the soul is shining on those regions.

Q.: *When you say the soul is released...*

A.: It is a way of putting things. The projection of the soul which is involved in the mind has to be released. All these beings are projections, as it were, of the soul. It is not that the soul is inert behind; the soul is active. The part of the soul which is reflected and involved in the mental consciousness has to be given a lift.

11

THE LIBERATION OF NATURE

We have been considering so far the liberation of the instruments, the liberation of the spirit. Now we take up the liberation of nature. All life is a series of interactions between nature—the experience presented by nature— and its acceptance by the soul or the self. The level on which this interaction takes place determines the quality of life. Normally nature, as we have seen, is constituted of three modes, the gunas. These three gunas, tamas, inertia, indolence, immobility; rajas, kinesis, drive, push; sattva, calm, order and control, enlightenment— these in their interaction constitute the action of nature and the continuous action of these three modes leads to a character of duality, opposites, characterising our relation with life: the opposites of pain and pleasure, good and bad, pleasant and unpleasant.

The aim before us, when we speak of the liberation of nature, is to achieve freedom from the action of the gunas, from the impact and the action of the dualities. That is what the Gita says, that is what all yogic tradition demands from us. But there are two kinds of liberation. The traditional conception of this liberation is that we withdraw from nature, keep aloof as far as possible from involvement, start with indifference and gradually detach ourselves, try not to participate in the play of the gunas, in the interaction of the dualities. Through this detachment we acquire a poise by which we can gradually merge either in the silence of Brahman or Bliss.

But this is an incomplete liberation. The true liberation of nature can arise only when we acquire mastery over the functioning of the gunas and the play of dualities. We have to acquire control over nature, exert our will upon nature, decide which guna is to negate which other guna, exercise our will to prevent ourselves from playing into the hands of either of the opposites or dualities. In other words, we must not only release the soul from the action of the three modes of nature upon it, but also uplift our soul or inner being so that it exerts its will element on nature to regulate the gunas and the play of dualities as it chooses.

Freedom is not an emptiness of the gunas. If we keep ourselves aloof we may arrive at a state of comparative emptiness of modes and gunas but that is not liberation. It is a superiority to the gunas that the Gita hints at and the integral yoga of Sri Aurobindo calls upon the seeker to achieve.

To come to more detail. Each of these qualities acts upon each of our levels of being, though broadly speaking we can say that tamas is a characteristic quality of our physical, material being, our material nature. Rajas, kinesis is characteristic of our life nature and sattva, calm enlightenment, is characteristic of the mind. But this is only for the sake of a clarification of concepts. Man is a multiple being with all parts interacting, interpenetrating each other. So the tamas not only acts in the physical, material nature making it inert, lazy, resistent to change, resistent to movement, but it also casts its shadow on the life-force, dragging it down, making it heavy. It also reaches the mind and prevents it from adventuring into new ideas, new dimensions of concepts, holds it back. It makes it stick to its opinions, hard concepts, resistent to new winds of change. Similarly with the emotions. We have got many old *samskāras*, we are accustomed to react to situations in a particular way by habit. It is the tamasic element in nature that recalls those past habits and pulls us back to the old grooves each time we want to give a different reaction. So also at the aesthetic level. At every level of our consciousness the role of tamas is to hold us back, to drag us down, to prevent an advance either upwards or forwards. That is, there is an inertia not only of the physical being but an inertia of force, an inertia of knowledge.

So also the rajas, which is supposed to be a vital quality. Though it is a characteristic quality of life-force, it is not confined to it. When the rajasic element drives the body, the material nature, the inertia is pushed back and the body shares in that impulse—may be a desire-ridden impulsion of life-force—and cooperates with it excellently. The body may appear to be restless till it acclimatises itself to the new temperature of rajas. The body learns to participate in the rajasic movement and that is how we can make a clean departure from the old habits of the physical body. We impose upon it something of the drive, the force of rajas from the life-level. So too in the mind. When the rajas acts in the mind, the mind is always eager to make more conquests, to know more things. The motive may be to acquire domination or some such; the mental movement is quickened.

So it is one of the tactics of the old yoga to learn to balance one preponderating quality with another. If we are traditionally tamasic, we learn to activise our rajasic nature and direct the rajasic force where tamas predominates. Now if rajas alone were to predominate, we would never know where we are going to be tomorrow. We lose control, we place ourselves under the control of the rajasic force. There comes in the sattva, the element or the quality of calm, equality, order and control. That element is not peculiar to the mind alone. As we practise the inner discipline we know that the life-force also, however impetuous it is, becomes self-gathered if we can impose upon it an order based upon a quiet and a calm undisturbed poise. The force does not spill itself immediately at the first provocation. It is gathered, waits for the signal. That is how the impulsive nature of the rajasic force is brought under control by the exercise of the sattvic guna. So too with the body. It may be too gross or too rajasic; if the sattvic element is increased, the whole metabolism of the physical body undergoes a change. It is by increasing or decreasing the play of these gunas in the body that changes in different kinds of functioning can be brought out.

Whether the modern scientists have got instruments to discover these changes I am not sure. They have devised instruments to measure heartbeats, brain vibrations when people go into meditation, into japa. But whether this manipulation of the qualities of the gunas and the resultant changes in the activities of the system—may be blood circulation, may be circulation of nerve force—can be measured is another subject.

Now for sake of clarification, we have spoken of these three gunas as if they are distinct. But nowhere can these gunas be seen to be acting in their independent roles, separate fields. There is always a mingling of gunas. In the same person, the nature of the mingling may vary from time to time, from situation to situation, from level to level of his growth. The one result of this mingling of the gunas is that there is always a multiple action calling forth a multiple attention. The very nature of life is that these gunas are in a state of disequilibrium. If all the gunas are in a state of equilibrium there is no movement. Who disturbed the original equilibrium and set the whole process going? The philosophers are not agreed. The Sankhyans and the other older philosophies differ on this point; it is not part of our philosophy because we do not consider that the whole creation started with the disturbance of the gunas. It is the Sankhyan position.

May be this disturbance of the gunas is one of the processes, at a lower level, at the level of Prakriti, earth-nature. The creation, in Sri Aurobindo's conception, starts on the gnostic level, the supramental level, with the Real-Idea.

Granted that we try the ethical discipline, the spiritual discipline so far developed, and bring about a balance and try to make the working of the gunas as perfect as possible, we achieve only a relative perfection. Our mind continues to be in the shadow of ignorance, the vital and the physical continue to be dragged down by the inconscient or the nescience. For each combination of the gunas that we overcome more combinations are presented to us.

The lynchpin of the action of the gunas is the ego, and the ego, as we have discussed so often, is of many kinds. There is an ego of the physical kind which gives the physical body the conviction that it is separate from others, that its own claims are superior to the claims of other parts of the being. The very solidity of the physical body, the claims of physical desires, physical hungers—all these are organised and articulated through the physical ego. So also, there is the ego of the life-force, the vital ego of which everybody knows. There is the mental ego that its own ideas are correct, its knowledge is true and everybody must conform to its pattern of thinking. And there are other egos—the ethical ego, even a spiritual ego. The point is that the ego is a very ubiquitous element, it presents itself in different forms on different

levels, and wherever it is, some touch of the guna is there.
The gunas function through the instrumentality of the
ego.

The way out of this octopus hold of ego is not by withdrawal. When we withdraw, the ego may get weak but
it continues. We have to transcend it, put it behind us,
put it below us and build up our true being, make it
an active being without functioning through the mould
of the ego. It is an ordinary notion that if the ego is not
there, no action is possible. But this again is an illusion
created by the ego. Actually, an action based upon ego
is a very limited and an imperfect action. If we can
manage to dissociate our action from its source in the
ego, from its cog in the desire motive, action ceases to be
personal. Action takes on the character of universal
nature and it becomes more dynamic, more liberating.
Action under the stamp of ego becomes a bondage;
action above or freed from the tentacles of ego is a liberative force. That is the first step.

As we advance in yoga, as we build up new tiers
of consciousness, we begin to see that the three gunas—
tamas, rajas and sattva—as they appear to us are not
the final qualities. They appear to us as they do because
they are reflections in our lower nature of ignorance, as
everything in our creation is a reflection or a projection
of something else in the higher nature. The three gunas
also are reflections or projections of truths in the Divine
Being above. Necessarily, when those truths are projected in our sphere they undergo a deformation, but their
truth continues to be there whether it is active here or
not. As we evolve in our consciousness, we see that what
is considered as a force of inertia, immobility, is truly a
refraction, a deformation of the force or quality of peace,
of solidity, immutability, of *śānti* in the Divine Being.

Similarly, rajas, the restless force is a transformation in
our terms of the divine will to achieve, to conquer, to
effectuate; sattva, the calm that we achieve, the equality
which we build up are pale reflections of light. The
prakāśa, of sattva is derived from *jyoti*, radiance—the
supreme light of knowledge, of consciousness in the
Divine Being. As we grow in our consciousness, these
very gunas begin to change their character. We realise
in our states of concentration or meditation or trance,
or in happy states of communion with the divine consciousness that behind these external appearances of the
gunas in ignorance, there are higher truths accessible to
us. But we cannot attain them as long as we are in the
mental ignorance. We have to go beyond the belt of
mind, the ignorant mind, and cross into the gnostic belt
for the ultimate pattern to emerge. Till then, intermittently, we see the increasing change of sattva, rajas and
tamas into their counterparts in the higher being, higher
nature. This reaches a high level of perfection only when
we attain to the gnostic level.

As the gunas are realised to be the counterparts
of higher truths in the divine being, the hold of the
dualities based upon these gunas is lessened. There is a
liberation from reaction to situations where these dualities present themselves. Here also, the discipline starts
first with a certain dispassion—a dispassion, say, for
pleasure, for happiness, for joy. Because we know that
where there is joy there is grief, where there is good there
is evil, we become indifferent. We start with a willed
dispassion. We do not take interest in responding to
these contacts, however pleasant they may appear.
Sri Aurobindo calls it a liberative dispassion. This leads
to a confirmed indifference, *udāsīna*; we sit above the
flow of these dualities, watching them, but without being

affected by them. So first comes dispassion, second is indifference and third is mastery. Whether the dualities that come are in the form of pleasure and pain, or good and evil, suffering and joy, there is a mastery in our reaction. We respond to the situation in the right way; pain does not make the usual impact of pain, pleasure does not make its normal impact. The soul draws the right *rasa*, sap of things from both. Here, too, as in the gunas, rejection is not liberation. Rejection of the dualities can only be a first step, it has to be proceeded upon—rejection, indifference, mastery. This is the formula for the liberation of nature, either in its aspect of the play of gunas or in its aspect of the play of dualities.

(From Questions & Answers)

Q.: *In whatever work we do the ego comes in bringing insincerity...*

A.: That is why the Gita says, and Sri Aurobindo also writes in his *Yoga of Divine Works* that every bit of work must be looked upon as an offering to the Lord. Ultimately it is not our work and our energies that we are pouring; it is his energies, his power that is working and we have to recognise that we are his chosen instruments and when we consecrate and offer that work to the Master of works, the glow that accompanies the performance of the work is much more liberative and joyous than any work that we do under the drive of desire.

These questions arise only to seekers, they are not relevant to those still in the rounds of ignorance. They have to be trained to make their desires more noble, less selfish. They have to be led through the gunas, Desire, yes, but a more noble desire, altruistic, humanitarian. This is how the circle is expanded till the circle is so far extended that it just breaks and you lose yourself in the universal being. Most of us, before we have come here, have worked and we know how we used to work. We would work for money, we would work for position, we would work in offices, come back and forget about it. But when we came to the Ashram, and started working for the Divine, few could escape the thrill of joy, feeling the of continuous progress in the being that is common here. The whole atmosphere becomes solemn when one works in the Ashram in the right spirit. Here there is no question of desire because there is no monetary or material return, but still the setting of the work and the fact that the work is looked upon as an offering to the Divine makes a capital difference. And the quality of work has been found to be vastly superior to the work under ordinary motions.

This is what has been achieved in the Ashram and worked for years and years. This should explode the myth that man will work only for economic motives, that only desire can make him work, that society can be based only on economics. Society can be based on love, on harmony and interchange, on a cooperative and not a competitive basis.

It is this idea which Mother has wanted to project in Auroville without the scaffolding that was necessary earlier in the Ashram—scaffolding in the sense of preventing interchange with the lower levels of life outside, with elements who are not wedded to this ideal. Once she was certain that the earth consciousness was ready for this kind of new life, she felt that now was the time to project this work on a larger canvas. The ideas has been taken up in various other places also and encouraging results are being reported. Humanity is ready today.

They may or may not subscribe to the philosophies of Sri Aurobindo and Mother, but the broad principles that the economic base of society, the ego base of the individual are relics of the past and that man is moving towares a different future where he is going to base himself on different values is accepted today by the higher mind of humanity all over the world.

Q.: Mother said that a sannyāsi is more attached to his robes than a householder is to—his wife.

A.: A householder being attached to his wealth, to his home is understandable because he frankly accepts his limitations and he functions in ignorance. You can expect from him only those reactions which a person in ignorance can give. But a sannyasi, a recluse, a person who claims to have left behind this realm of ignorance, to have risen above desire and ego, has new standards applied to him. He can't expect to justify himself in the old way; if he expects a higher recognition, a higher standard is imposed upon him. But what happens is that the old nature continues and by the very fact that he has divested himself of other interests, ego and desire concentrate themselves more pronouncedly upon the little area that is still left to him.

Q.: This fact that we regard things that come to us in a deformed sense must be because the creation is trying to evolve...

A.: This deformation is a part of the process of involution because when the Sat-Chit-Ananda, Existence-Consciousness-Bliss, plunged here for manifestation, Existence turned into Non-Existence, Consciousness turned into Nescience, and Delight turned into Non-Sentience. All the other things, the gunas, peace, etc. also turned into their opposites. So in the course of evolution, from the form that they have taken in the plunge they have slowly to evolve back into their higher terms.

12

THE ELEMENTS OF PERFECTION

We have seen that perfection has two aspects; the
purification of the being, the soul, and its freedom from
involvement in nature. There is also the aspect of the
release of nature from the hold of dualities, from the
play of the three modes, the gunas. Both these movements have to be worked out before it becomes possible
to achieve something of the perfection that is envisaged.
Perfection consists, as we have seen, of two steps: purification and freedom. These are not exactly successive
steps, but more or less simultaneous. Purification has
always to be done limb by limb, part by part, and with
each step of purification firmly taken there is an appropriate release of the part so purified from the elements
that deform its movement.

When both nature and soul have been subjected to
this process of purification to a reasonable extent and
there is a feeling in consciousness of some liberation from
the stranglehold of lower nature, then comes the importance of having the right conception of the divine being,
the divine nature in which we seek to grow. For it is
understood that there can be no perfection as long as we
are confined to the lower being, the lower formulation of
being in which we are imprisoned at present. We have
to conceive of the ideal—divine being and nature—
according to which we have to mould ourselves, our
soul and our nature. And according to our conception
of the Supreme, of the divine being that we want to
attain is the starting point, the process, and the aim of
our sadhana.

There is the traditional view which looks upon the divine being as a sole reality, but excluding the universe. The universe is something that has somehow come to be against the white purity of the divine reality. That reality, exclusive of these lower formations or deformations, is the only reality. It is in an impersonal, aloof, uninvolved reality. If this is accepted, the yoga, the practice and the discipline that is undertaken to achieve this objective is in the traditional line of the yoga of knowledge of the Vedanta.

There is again the conception, popularised by the Buddhist thought, of looking upon the divine as something immensely negative, denying all permanence to the world. The whole world is looked upon as something impermanent without any sustaining being— whether in the universe or in the individual. All is looked upon as a kind of continuation, the stretching out of a thread of thoughts and ideas woven around desire, each desire succeeding another, each desire giving rise to certain movements and so on. The approach is negative and the ideal state is when everything is supposed to be dissolved with the dissolution of desire at its roots.

There are again approaches which conceive of the Divine as the Lord of Love. The devotee practises a nine-fold discipline—to which we have already referred in our studies on the Way of Love—and he builds himself into an image of his beloved. At best he loses himself in the being of the beloved, the Lord. Either he attains a likeness or he approaches a closeness—*sādṛśya* or *sāmīpya*.

In all these approaches the stress is on moving away from the world, on denying the reality of the universe, any objective for life on earth, and emphasising the necessity of withdrawal. This is out of question for a seeker of the integral truth which embraces both the reality in itself and the reality in and as the world. He aims not only at achieving an identity of his individual being with the Divine Being in his consciousness, in his nature, but also at putting out this attainment, this identity in his movement in life. For him there is no inside separate from the outside; he looks upon all life as one. The soul and nature are also seen as two statuses of the same reality. His discipline, his yogic practice is aimed at achieving this unity of life, unity basing the multiple manifestation of the reality.

To achieve this integral objective, the discipline that is described by Sri Aurobindo consists of six elements. The first element is *equality, samatā*. The Gita has already familiarised us with the conception and the necessity of cultivating a poise of equality, whatever our field of life. Life consists of a series of impacts, some of which are welcome, some are not. This interplay of likes and dislikes, of the pleasant and the unpleasant, always evokes in us corresponding reactions. We are at the mercy of every impact and contact that comes upon us, whether we will or do not will for it. So the first indispensable attitude that we have to build is one of equality, and before we build up equality we have to acquire an indifference. Indifference is the first step, which is gradually changed into an attitude of equality. Nobody can have an attitude of equality in the beginning. We always begin with a mental understanding that this is so and this is not so, this is what we have to do. But our nature is accustomed to respond in a particular way. Even if our mind knows, still we cannot help it—the heart, the emotions, even the physical body responds in a way to which it is habituated. The mind has to impose its will and begin by introducing what we may call a stoic indifference, endurance without reacting. When this is fairly well established, the next step is to bring in a positive attitude of equality. Whether it is a welcome contact or an unwelcome one, we simply do not react. We take it that it has to be gone through and accept it as such. We do not shrink, but we do not rejoice either. This attitude of equality is again of two kinds—passive and active. The passive equality is when we do not return any kind of response or reaction, but deal with things in a matter of fact way, do things because they are to be done, without mental reaction. Once this state is attained, passive equality is established in our being, the next inevitable step is to have an active equality. Active equality means to take each contact, establish our strength upon it, treat is as a field of experience and link it to our own progress, utilise it in the best possible spirit, and in the process draw what we may call the *rasa*, sap of the experience. Each experience, in whatever way it impacts upon our surface being, contains elements that promote the progress of our soul. If we are sufficiently objective we can seize the experience and draw the *rasa* from it, and the active equality consists in drawing this *rasa* of experience, benefit of experience, from every contact that we come across. That is what the Gita calls a positive *samatā*—it even goes to the extent of equatting this equality with the whole of yoga. But the yoga that we envisage is something more, with a greater application. This yoga of equality is the first step.

It is a self-evident truth that we do not have or wield the amount of power, force or energy that we would need in every situation. We know what we want to do, we even know what our own desires want us to achieve, but most often we lack the necessary means, the power, because we are content to function within a series of limitations and these psychological limitations entail practical inconveniences, dwindlings of power that we would otherwise exercise. This inability to function at our optimum, this lack of power to achieve what we want, is the next to be remedied. And that can be done only by opening ourselves, our whole being—or at least the concerned part—to *the higher power of* nature, *śakti,* that is active in the universe. Normally we are shut up within the walls of our own ego and the power that can be exercised within those walls. If by some means or discipline we succeed in opening our doors and windows to the inrush of the higher power, the larger powers in the universe, we get hold of a power that derives from a higher source and not from the lower nature. This awakens the inherent capacity of our limbs, of our soul and nature. Each soul, and therefore each nature organised around that soul, has its own temperament, its own shape or form or mould in which it is to function. It is called the *svabhāva,* or self-nature, and each soul as it grows has to find ways and means of expressing itself, of moving into action according to the temperament that has been decided for it, chosen by it earlier. This becomes easier when one is open to the working of the higher Shakti, the higher power. All these three—the awakening of the inherent capacities, the functioning according to its self-nature, and the achieving of things with a power that is not normally available to one—form the second composite step of this discipline.

In so doing we open to the higher or the·divine nature. The individual nature yields to its corresponding part in the multiple divine nature and changes its character. It enlarges itself, it deepens itself, and though the outer form may remain the same, the content gradually changes. To do this more effectively we need to have

the *faith*, *śraddhā*, that we have the power, that we can
link ourselves with a higher power by invoking it, and
we can wield that power to fulfil the demand of our soul
in the pattern that is natural to its mould.

There is, however, a limitation. As long as we function within the range set by our limited, ignorant mind,
all these can be done only up to a certain extent, severely
limited by the limitations of the mind. In our yoga we
do not stay in the mind, however enlarged the mind may
be. We go beyond the mind. There are several gradations
extending beyond the mind, all of which culminate in
what Sri Aurobindo has called the gnostic mind where
the inherent limitations of mind are overcome and their
opposite terms of perfection are founded. After these
preliminary movements have been set afoot we have to
intensify the yoga, to *render mental life into terms of the
gnostic life,* the Vijnana or the Divine Knowledge. This
is the third step. It is only in proportion as the power and
the will of divine, the gnostic consciousness begins to
permeate the mind, inform its movements, uplift its
level that the perfection of equality, making faith a
dynamic, irressistible power, putting on of a divine
nature, become more possible.

Now, there are other elements of the being. There
are the emotions, there is the life-force which is open to
the impulsion of desire, and there is the physical body.
It is possible that on the heights of the mind or consciousness we act and move in the spirit of equality, wielding
the highest power, reacting in terms of the divine nature,
but unless these lower members are also treated to the
light of the gnostic consciousness they continue to react
in the same old way. So the important thing at this stage
is to bring the law of the supramental or the gnostic
purusha to function within the physical body which is

the foundation, the base of the whole edifice. The roots of our ignorance, of the imperfections that drag us down are in the subconscient or the inconscient parts of the physical body. The influence and the working of the gnostic purusha, the *vijñānamaya puruśa*—who on his higher levels reveals himself as the *ānandamaya*, the delight purusha—has to be established in the physical.

And how is that to be done? The physical body that we see is not all; behind the physical body is a subtler existence which is divided into so many sheaths we conceive of this subtle existence behind the physical body as the mental body, the body of the mental purusha, and behind it the spiritual body or the causal body which houses the gnostic soul, the delight soul. It is from this subtle existence that the powers of the divine nature, divine consciousness, begin to percolate in the physical body. The physical body has to be so disciplined, purified that it is set in tune with the subtler bodies, and to do that we must first admit the existence of those bodies, refine the movements of the physical body so that they can express and hold the vibrations of the purer and the subtler bodies. This is purification, and it is in this process of the gradual opening of the *physical body*, physical consciousness to the action of the inner, subtler existence that new faculties unveil themselves, release themselves. These are the eight siddhis in yoga and they can be realised or achieved purely by Hathayoga, by physical means like postures, breathing exercises, exerting pressure on those centres of the body in which these powers are latent. In our yoga this pressure is not exerted, as in the Tantric system or the Hathayogic or Rajayogic from below; the higher pressure, the force of the higher consciousness, as it works, throws open the various centres and these powers, *siddhis*, reveal

8

themselves and function as natural movements. They are no more *siddhis*, wonderful powers, because they arise only when the consciousness to which they are natural is formed. In the traditional yogas they want to excite and activate these latent powers, but they deal with them only from the normal consciousness. That is why to them, who have the ordinary consciousness, it appears that they are miracle powers, but to a person who has got that consciousness of which these are normal powers of functioning, they don't appear miraculous. So where is the question of asking a yogi not to exercise these powers because they are a danger, a snare, a temptation? For the yogi is just not aware that he is doing something wonderful. This is what is likely to happen on the way: these powers revealing themselves as the lower being is taken up and assumed in the higher nature.

When all this is done, we do not shut ourselves up in the attained identity with the Divine or the Brahman. We move into *action with that consciousness*, with the power or powers that are unveiled in us, and as we act with that consciousness we derive a delight, draw an enjoyment. It is certainly not for ourselves because the ego-self which appropriates that joy and enjoyment for itself has long since disappeared. There is only a divine centre and the individual is conscious that he is acting as an instrument, as a channel of the Divine. The enjoyment that he takes, or rather that comes to him in the very act of moving into action, goes to the Divine Enjoyer. This is possible in its perfection only at a gnostic level. Till then the joy, enjoyment, knowledge, sense of power are experienced as reflected in the mind, in a derivative way. But as we change from the mental consciousness into higher grades of consciousness we become aware of a massed and illumined consciousness, what the Upanishad describes as the *caitanyaghana*, which has this capacity to take the enjoyment for the Divine, to act, to put out its forces for the Divine, all the while on the basis not of oneself being separate from the Divine, separate from the world, but of *unity*, *of oneness*. There is one Brahman—that is the basic awareness. All is Brahman, all is the Divine and the Divine is not exhausted, by this creation, he is much more, he is infinite.

So the Divine as One, the Divine as All, the Divine as Infinite—all these are simultaneous verities in the consciousness that we attain, the massed illumined consciousness which reveals itself as but one poise of the gnostic consciousness, even as the same gnostic consciousness, melts upwards into the consciousness of sheer delight.

(From Questions and Answers)

Q.: What would be the distinction between śakti and consciousness force?

A.: They are the same. Consciousness as force is shakti. Consciousness can remain self-aware, static; or consciousness can reveal itself in its dynamic aspect and that force of consciousness is the shakti, puissance.

Q.: And what would be the difference in the working of the śakti and the Light?

A.: In Light the element of awareness, consciousness is more; in shakti or power, the dyanmis is more with the element of illumination held behind.

*   *

Normally the shakti has been deformed, reduced, or you can say, veiled as prakriti. As prakriti is purified of its gross elements and it increases in consciousness and

it realises itself to be a movement of consciousness, changes
into shakti. So what is shakti above is prakriti in our
triple world of ignorance. Prakriti, Sri Aurobindo explains, is the outermost, executive aspect of the shakti.
When you go deeper within, you find that it is nothing
else than shakti; only on the outermost levels it has
acquired the encrustations of ignorance and limitations.
The pure, divine shakti has no limitations. The limitations under which it functions are self-chosen.

*   *

When the body opens to the Divine, the response of
the divine consciousness or the divine force of consciousness may awaken certain chakras in the body. If some
parts are more developed it is possible that when those
parts respond, their chakras also open and you feel the
precise action. But it is not always that the chakras open.
The powers behind that chakra are released into action;
so even without feeling a physical change—as envisaged
by the tantrics—the work may be done. For instance
with the activations of the centre of knowledge, the
centre of love, the centre of expression, the respective
powers may start functioning. A painter or an artist
finds his faculties blossoming—that is because something
in the *ājñācakra* has opened and he sees the vision; or
something in the throat centre has opened and the
faculty for poetry is activised. But we do not put any
pressure upon any centre or any chakra. Whatever happens in this yoga by way of opening of the chakras is
involuntary. In other yogas it is a willed operation.

 Q.: How does the body open to the Divine?
 A.: First the thought or the idea of opening to the
Divine is imposed upon the body by the mind. After all,
mind is the leader of life and body in every human being,
prāṇaśarīranetā. So we start,—whether it is in karmayoga,

bhaktiyoga, jnanayoga or whatever kind of yoga—in the mind. Even when we think of the Divine, first there is imagination. We read books, we conceive—the conception may or may not be correct, the imagination may be wild or regulated—we start in the mind. When we want the body to participate in yoga, to awaken and open to the Divine, we first will it mentally, impose that idea or thought upon the body, communicate consciously that the body must respond to the divine force, learn to awake and aspire for the Divine's possession of it. Each time we take food for instance, or when we take exercise, take a bath, when we do anything with the body, mentally we inject, each time, that this is for God, this is for the Divine, this body must be prepared, it must learn to respond to the divine vibrations, to serve the Divine. At present it is serving desires, serving the ego, it should learn to surrender itself to the Divine Master, to the Divine Mother. When we take food, first we consecrate it to the Divine and then tell the body it is consecrated and made available to it so that it may assimilate it and grow in the spirit of the Divine. When we exercise, we not only go through the muscular movements but are conscious that the element of consciousness in the muscles must be awake so that even when our mind is not attentive, that consciousness functions. That there is such a consciousness in our physical cells, all of us know. We have seen how when there is some danger, without our knowing of it mentally, there is an immediate shrinking, a reaction. So it is there, the question is of tapping it, of articulating it more and more. It has to start with putting a will on the body that it shall be awake. Naturally we respect the body, not treat the body as a slave but as a rich possession given in our hands by the Divine. After all we can do things only as long as the body is there. We treat its minutest intuitions, minutest communications with due respect. If the body intuits something we must not ignore it, we must see what it is, what it wants. We have to spend a certain amount of time in the culture of the body and the body consciousness and orient it towards the Divine, even as we do the same with the mind. We turn the mental thoughts to the Divine, we read what relates to the Divine. In the same way the body also must be engaged in movements and activities that take us to the Divine and not away from the Divine. So the work of the body, the nourishment of the body, the growth of the body—all these are organised around that central objective and the body participates in the sadhana with much more readiness than the life-force, which is always a recalcitrant element until the last stage of perfection has been reached.

13

THE PERFECTION OF EQUALITY

Equality means different things in different contexts, and the first great scripture that laid great emphasis on equality is, as you know, the Gita. The Gita even goes to the extent of saying that equality is yoga, *samatvam yoga ucyate*, and the Gita is right because without acquiring some poise of equality it is impossible to make any headway in yoga of whatever kind. If yoga means to arise out of our lower nature and establish ourselves in the higher nature leading to the Divine, equality is the first step. Whatever the kind of perfection that we envisage, equality is indispensable. In fact, equality is the foundation of perfection. However we conceive of the Divine—as something to be adored, to be loved or to be known—we need have an equality of heart and equality of mind.

It is a popular notion that to love the Divine we must give free vent to the emotions. Some weep uncontrollably, they even undergo certain wild movements of ecstasy. We see so many photographs eulogising them as movements of bliss, but actually one surrenders oneself in these exercises to movements of wild, excited nature, which is far, far away from the peace and the silence of the Self, from the harmony of the soul without which no spiritual life worth the name is possible.

This equality is not of the mind alone. It is common enough to hold that if we are able to bear stoically whatever comes to us—good or bad, pleasant or unpleasant—that is equality. But as we have observed, there is a passive equality and an active equality. Passive equality is when we bear, endure whatever shocks of life, impacts, come to us without giving forth any reaction. Active equality is when we are able not only to receive stoically, but master the impacts, convert them into equal values and make them over to the inner being. Such an equality—passive to begin with, active as we go ahead—is demanded of us. This equality is not merely of the soul, it has to be an equality in nature also.

In the traditional paths, which do not include change of nature in their scheme, nature is left to itself and one concentrates on disciplining the mind, on approaching nearer and nearer the soul level so that there is a spontaneous equality. The first step towards acquiring equality of the soul is to detach oneself with a will from the movements of nature, step back as the Mother says, and get into the poise of the witness self— the self that is not involved but observes, oversees without being influenced either way. It is only as one gets a firm foothold in that witness self that the equality becomes meaningful and not merely a phrase. But even this is the first step.

The next inevitable step is equality of nature. It is through nature that the soul functions. The soul or the self expresses itself, organises its experience through nature and it is in nature that we must cultivate equality—equality of perception, equality of reaction. When we speak of nature it is not just one part of ourselves. As we all know, nature is multiple, nature consists of so many limbs of our being. There is the mind, there is the heart and so many parts of our being. There is the emotional being, there is the vital being, and there is the obvious physical part, the body, all of which are parts of nature in the main. I say in the main because all these have a part which is close to the self,

close to the soul—almost a part of the soul. But the bulk
is constituted of nature. So when we speak of equality
in nature, we have to proceed step by step and induce
this quality of equality part by part, though in practice
things do not go in a logical order. What happens in
yoga is a multi-pronged movement. We proceed simultaneously on many fronts, a victory or a setback in one
sector influencing the movements in others. But for
sake of understanding we can analyse the problem
limb-wise, part-wise and understand how we are to
educate our nature to function from the base of equality.

This equality has to be both of the substance of
our nature and of our dynamism for action. Nature
can very well remain quiet, silent, without acting so to
say. In a sense it is impossible for nature to remain
totally inactive, but beyond a certain surface movement
it is possible for nature to withhold itself from action.
But the equality that we speak of is two-sided—equality
of substance, equality that is built up for affecting a
change in substance and equality that is necessary for a
divine action. When we speak of action we do not speak
only of individual action proceeding from an individual
will. Our action, our life itself, is a part of a general,
universal action that is going on. Each individual is only
a fragment, though a meaningful fragment, and the
action that I do, for instance, is to be seen in the context
of the general action of the universal forces around me.
My actions cannot be interpreted or studied in their
isolation. What makes me do things in the way I do?
Is it entirely my whim, or is it something in the atmosphere, something in the universal forces that impels
me in a particular way? This attention to the laws of
action in the universe, understanding of their processes,

is indispensable before we can assimilate the sense of equality.

If, for instance, someone comes and speaks harsh words to me, is it possible for me to be truly equal in my attitude unless I understand what is behind that action, what makes him speak harshly? It is easy enough to have a rule that whether a man abuses me or praises me I should not be affected. That is a mechanical rule which helps nobody. But if my equality of reaction is based upon an understanding of why people behave as they do, what are the forces or pressures in the atmosphere, that helps me to react in a less involved way, in a more understanding way. This is necessary for self-mastery. An understanding of others, not merely of my own constitution, not merely of my own mental grooves, but of the psychology of others, the behaviour of others, the impulsions that activate them, is necessary for me to acquire self-mastery. And without self-mastery —no all-mastery is possible. They speak of *svarāt*, self-mastery and *samrāt*, all-mastery, but unless one's mastery over one self is complete or adequate one can certainly not acquire any mastery worth the name on others or on all in the environment.

This fulfilled, an understanding and an assent to the laws in the universe, next we have to observe ourselves and see how far our reactions are ego-based and how far based on the soul or the self. Ninety-nine per cent of the reactions of an average person proceed from ego. The first reactions are based on ego, not even on a calculation of what are our true interest. It is the interference of ego that has disturbed the operation of equality, and it is the play of ego that always endangers whatever stability we may have acquired in the way of equality. No equality is possible unless we have achieved an inner conquest of the much that is not visible on the surface of ourselves but is behind the veil, still powerfully active. This inner conquest by the progressive elimination of ego—a negative step—, and the positive cultivation of equality of reception, equality of return, are indispensable.

When we speak of nature, the one part most open to the reactions of ego, of desire, upsetting all the apple carts of equality, is the vital. The vital is under the domination of desire, ego-motive. We think we are separate, we want to dominate, we want to gain control over the environment, we assume an aggressive posture even when we know we don't have the strenth to acquire mastery over the environment. There is what is called a defense mechanism of an inferiority complex. The man who feels inferior reacts aggressively because within himself he is afraid that something is going to harm him, somebody means harm. Actually the other person may not mean anything of the kind, but a person who has that inferiority complex always anticipates trouble and reacts violently even in normal situations. A man who is strong, established in some equality, has no reaction. He can contain, he can digest, he can assimilate, he has the confidence; but not so the weak man. So one of the ways of surmounting weakness in these matters is to cultivate equality. The life-force is indeed meant for enjoyment, but enjoyment in the true sense, not snatching of enjoyment from the cosmos. The Isha Upanishad speaks that true enjoyment, true possession, is possible only when you renounce, *tena tyaktena bhunjithāh*; only when you renounce do you have the capacity to enjoy a thing fully, enjoy it for God. Because ultimately enjoyment is to participate in the enjoyment by the Lord of his universe and this joy of participation in the enjoyment by the Lord cannot be taken away even when things are physically snatched away from us. The movement of what Patanjali calls *parigraha*, covetous grasp, not a physical but a mental and a vital grasp over things that do not belong to us, leads to certain agitations and is an enemy of equality. True equality of the vital can come only when we renounce all claim of the vital on those around us, on the world, on the things of the world, and not the least on God.

They speak of taking the kingdom of heaven by violence, but this is only a phrase which does not answer to the deeper truth of spiritual life. All that we succeed in doing by imposing our will, by knocking at the gates of the Divine with impatience, is to create a disturbance and create a condition in ourselves which interferes with the receptivity to the Grace. We cannot impose our will on the Divine. The Upanishad is very clear on this point: he whom the Self chooses, only to him the Self bares its body. The doctrine of Grace is that the choice is not human, it is the Divine's. So when we speak of compelling the Divine by our intensity, that is again a camouflaged play of the vital. The true attitude here also, even in the spiritual dimension, is one of equality. To surrender and wait upon the will of the Divine, wait without anticipation, without determining in advance that He should open the door today and not tomorrow. The right attitude is: His will be done. Whether it is today or tomorrow it does not matter. All that matters is that He opens the door one day and of that we are certain.

This equality of poise, an ability to wait, is an acme of vital equality. The vital has many fields—it has its own vital field, the vital interferes in the emotions, the vital interferes in the mind, the vital comes in by the backdoor even in the spiritual realm. The seeker can never be overcareful in checkmating the demands of the vital. The one sovereign means for correcting, changing and helping towards the eventual transformation of the vital is the cultivation of equality. Equality must begin in small matters. So often we are asked how to cultivate the will; people say they have no will power. Actually we start with small things, the day-to-day things. We do not wait for a great crisis to take place, putting the choice before us. We have to start cultivating equality in small things. A child's cry, a beggar's wail, somebody criticising us or shouting at us—all these must be utilised as opportunities for progress, to test for ourselves whether our equality is a lip equality or a true equality. And it is only by accustoming our nature in such incidents, in the small day-to-day situations that equality as a habit gets established in us, so that the part of ourselves which is habituated to react in equality responds even in more important situations. The crux lies in the vital.

It is not, Sri Aurobindo is careful to point out, that the vital should be starved of its legitimate part in the cosmic play. It has to change its attitude. Only when it gives up its personal demands, demand for self-aggrandisement and denial to others, when it insists no longer on being what Sri Aurobindo would call the 'top dog', then the vital starts getting educated in the ways of equality.

Then there is the equality of the emotional being. There is not one person, I am sure, who has not been tossed now and then on the waves of reaction, waves of anger, waves of love, attraction, repulsion and so on. But in the true depths of the emotional being, where the doors open to the psychic, the soul, there is no agitation. One can be blissful at a certain level in the emotional part without getting agitated, without getting excited. One can be blissful and fully composed. In fact it is only by the appearance of tranquillity, of a brightness —a sustained and a contained brightness and tranquillity—that one can know there is an ocean of joy, an ocean of bliss. When we find signs of excitement, spilling, agitation—a person needing to dance, needing to shake his limbs to express the joy he cannot contain— we can take it that he is still being tossed on the surface. Equality is nowhere there. The bliss of God, the delight of the Divine, the ecstasy of the soul, can come only when the emotional being has learned to be tranquil, to hold things in an attitude of equality. It receives whatever waves come into it—to use the classic simile— like an ocean receiving the rivers without swelling. Just as the Divine or a Divine-realised person contains the joy and the bliss of existence behind an exterior of immutable peace, it is possible for a trained emotional being, trained in the ways of equality, to strike depths which are never disturbed, where there is no sign of imbalance. Imbalance is a sign of immaturity. Where there is balance, where there is a governing equality, the joy is contained and a joy that is contained always communicates itself in a subtle manner to all who are around. Towards such one, says the Kena Upanishad, all beings yearn and turn. They may not know why they are attracted to the person, they may not understand his philosophy or his teaching, but they all yearn towards him because they receive the sustaining waves of bliss, delight, from him on all sides. But this state is impossible unless we train our heart, train our emotional being to be first detached from the pleasant and the unpleasant, from the good and what we call the bad, to take a neutral attitude in the beginning and thereafter to stand above them and look at them unaffected.

Speaking of the heart, an equal heart is possible only when the desire-soul has been replaced by the true soul, the psychic being. The desire-soul always reacts to outer contacts with a claim, with a fugitive movement, wanting to catch things and that upsets, that does not allow the heart to be equal-spirited. The heart is already inclined this way or that way by the ego or the desire-soul. The desire soul-has been mistaken by many of the psycho-analysts to be the true soul. In their experiments they have stopped at the level of the desire-soul and said that all life is pleasure-motivated. For every action, for every movement, the motive is one of pleasure because pleasure is what the desire-soul seeks. This is a perversion. Both the desire-self and the pleasure that the desire-self seeks are a refraction, a perversion of the true soul inside which seeks delight. Pleasure is a counterfeit coin, the original of which is delight. Delight does not depend upon an external cause; delight is self-caused whereas pleasure is caused from something outside.

'With an equal heart' does not mean that we face every situation externally also in an equal manner. Sri Aurobindo makes a pointed observation that an equal heart gives enough room for the Rudra energy in the seeker or the spiritual man to kill, to remove evil if that is the divine command. The Rudra energy, he points out, even when it kills, exterminates or destroys, has the same love, the same understanding as it has when it saves. Certainly it is possible and easy for one to deceive oneself, but one can't deceive God. If we have such sincerity and transparency in our nature as to give vent to the Rudra energy, anger, heroism, violence as instru-

ments of the divine fury without allowing our soul or
mind or heart to be tainted with the feeling of enmity,
hatred, that is the true equality of the spiritual heart.
We then feel in ourselves something that is identified
with the object that is being destroyed. We feel the
unity but realise that the form has strayed and is becoming an obstruction in the way of divine manifestation
and we are called upon to remove it from the path.
If there is the slightest vibration of hatred, vengence,
that is a taint.

This equality, further, has to be extended towards
the whole dynamic being. All of us have a static part,
calm and the quiet, and an active part which dynamises
things, effectuates things. There also there has to be an
equality. Normally it is the dynamic ego that is mistaken
for the dynamic being. Once desire and ego are spotted
out in each situation and kept under check, the true
dynamic part of the being can be evoked and set into
action.

This done, there is the mind. Man is a mental
being and the equality has to be introduced even in the
mental operations. A mental rule that reacts equally
will not do. We have got our own ideas, our own preferences, choices, likes and dislikes. In a mental way, all
these have to be rigorously subjected to the scrutiny of
truth and we should be able to receive ideas, suggestions
for improvement without feeling that we are forced to
give up our pet theories. This attachment to our own
theories and ideas is a sattvic attachment—'I know the
truth, my truth is the greatest truth, other truths are
inferior; what I know is the final truth, there can't be any
other truth.' Now these are all golden chains with which
the sattvic man binds himself. An equality has to grow by
which we should be prepared to give up our pet notions,

beliefs, faiths; when a greater and more enlightened faith, a larger truth is presented for our acceptance we must not hesitate if it is shown to us that the new truth, the new formulation of faith, is larger, more spiritual and more inevitable in the progress of the soul. With equality one lets go what has to go and accepts what needs to be accepted.

Here too, the ideal is not negation. We are not called upon to denude our mind of all theories, of all mental knowledge. The mind is not to be negated. The mind, Sri Aurobindo points out, is to be transformed from the lower into the higher, from the outer into the inner. At each step, the mental layers have to be exposed to the transforming action of the emerging knowledge, the emerging light. We shall not have any preference as to whether this is consistent with the beliefs and the faith that we have, inherited and given meaning to our life all along. We must not coop ourselves up into small cages of mental formulas. Knowledge is large, truth is limitless and inexhaustible. At every moment in creation new truths are being released for manifestation and the seeker who has achieved equality in the mind welcomes and receives the new truths, the new knowledge without being agitated, without the least hesitation.

When all these types of equality—the vital, the mental and emotional—are established, we grow into a spiritual dimension where also there is a spiritual equality. Spiritual equality is the equality of an integral Sat-Chit-Ananda. The doors do not open only on the peace of the Absolute. We give full play of the diverse formulations of existence, a full dynamism to the force of divine consciousness—the Chit—and allow all formulations of the delight of the Divine to flow through us— not only to flood our being, but flow through us into the

9

environment, all the while standing unaffected on the rock of equality. Equality is the foundation, equality is the crown of perfection.

(From Questions and Answers)

We shall not judge things by their surface moments. The surface moments do not explain anything. We have to go behind the surface, and that is where the science of psychology, para-psychology and the like come in, because there is much behind an act, an expression or a speech. There are forces of harmony, of compassion and love and oneness, as also forces of disunity, disharmony, clash. Now, to which set of forces are we open, how do we react? If you think for a moment of those possibilities, you are surely going to get less angry with the person who misbehaves. The point is, equality shall not be a mechanical equality; it has to be an understanding equality. When it is understanding, it is a living equality and with each exercise of equality you grow. Otherwise it is a mechanical rule, a moral rule, an ethical rule which may or may not further your spiritual growth.

Q.: Which aspect of equality—the passive or the active —should be approached first?

A.: Normally, the passive or the static equality is cultivated first—what the Greeks called the stoic attitude —, not being upset at anything, bearing everything with indifference. That has to be first done because we are all so much involved and lost in the movements of nature. The first step is to bear without moving. The next step is to withdraw, thereafter to rise above.

Q.: Is it ever possible for one to approach first from the active side and then assume the witness side?

A.: Actually what happens in yoga is that we function on all the levels. There is a level on which we live in a sort of passive attitude; simultaneously, there is another level where the will start functions in an active way. These things don't go step by step, though for mental understanding and clarification we study them that way. Man lives simultaneously on so many levels, and the more integral he is, the more evolved he is, he functions on more levels. May be the mind functions on one level, the emotions and the vital function on another level. Usually it is the heart and the vital that are first trained not to give a reaction, to be stoic, to be passive, and the mind decides and directs what is to be done. It is possible to function from a centre in which both these movements are included.

* *

Once desire is given up, equality begins. Mere equality is not enough to lead to the *śūnya*. Equality is only the beginning—thereafter, a good many things have to be worked out. The sense of possession, the sense of want, even need, the sense of reaction, of feeling for others— all these are to be dealt with. There has to be, in the Buddhist sense, a progressive denuding of ourselves of each sheath of nature, step by step, till at last there is nothing left. The Buddhists do not believe in a soul. They say everything is a bundle of *samskāras*, impressions, and as each layer of impression is shed by meditation, concentration, detachment, discrimination, one becomes lighter and lighter till at one fortunate moment when all the karma that has been collected during the past births is exhausted, like a flame that goes out in a wind, what was there is no more there. There are many steps; but the first is the *triṣṇā*, the thirst, the desire has to be removed. The thirst is easily removed from the mind, but to remove it from the vital, from the physical

is extremely difficult because the thirst is embedded
deep within. Mentally we can decide but the vital wants,
the physical craves for it. It is to eliminate them that
more time, more discipline—perhaps lives of discipline
—are required.

*   *

To live in the witness consciousness is one thing,
and to live in the purusha is another because when you
speak of purusha it can be the dynamic purusha, the
purusha who presides over the activities of prakriti or
shakti.

*   *

That is a prescription given in the yoga of Patanjali—*pratipakṣa bhāvanam*. That is to say, when we want
to get rid of habits or movements which have become
natural to us, or when we are born with certain imperfections which goad us into action, even without our
consent, how do we proceed? Some one is habitually
given to anger, another person is habitually given to
meanness, stinginess, another is given to uncouth movements. Well, Patanjali says, set about deliberately
cultivating the opposite qualities, the opposite virtues.
An angry man has to impose upon himself the discipline
of kindness, of benevolence. He must take every opportunity to be kind, to be benevolent. Even when provoca-
tions of anger come, he has to subdue and show kindness
instead. A mean man, a stingy man has to force himself
to be liberal, introduce the opposite movement of giving.
This cultivation of the opposite set of movements or
qualities is an antidote to that with which one is saddled.
This is a great lesson in psychology—particularly in
the Indian psychology.

Q.: *In fact, wouldn't you say that at that moment when
the anger comes, that is the chance to grow?*

A.: Merely to control one's anger is half the step, but to react positively by a movement of kindness, understanding or forgiveness really lifts one out of the movement or habit of anger.

14

THE WAY OF EQUALITY

Continuing our study of equality as a discipline of Integral Yoga, we have noted that there are two sides to it. One is the passive or the negative side and the other the dynamic or the positive side. The first, the passive type of equality, is usually the first step and it consists of three stages, one after the other—endurance, indifference and submission. We learn to endure what we can't help, cultivate indifference to what comes, and we learn to submit. Indeed, we do not submit to events in a mood of resignation, but submit to the higher will, to God, to the universal will. In other words, it is a submission to something larger and higher than our ego-self.

The first step that we take is of endurance. One does not need to be a yogi or a practitioner of yoga to cultivate endurance. Life teaches us to endure. Whether we want it or not, each one is visited by circumstances and events force him to learn in the school of life this lesson of endurance. And as we learn to endure, we find that as a result of this continuous effort our power to endure increases. We never break down. Nature sustains us in our effort and the power to endure with which we start goes on strengthening itself and at some stage we are ourselves amazed to find that the power to endure, to sustain ourselves in the midst of adversity has no limits. We do not break down, there is an elasticity about this endurance which goes on extending itself.

As this endurance gets established, we sail into the

second step. We become aware of two parts in our nature —one is the surface mind, the surface will which complains, which likes to avoid, which suffers, and behind them or above the surface mind and will we become aware of a deeper will, a larger poise of mind which bears patiently. It tolerates without reacting while the surface being frets and fumes. This dichotomy in our nature becomes more and more pronounced as we persist in the discipline till we can at will switch over to our deeper or higher nature and from there impose our will on the normally reacting surface nature to desist from being childish. In course of time the lower nature or the surface nature, habituated to react in an accustomed way, begins to change; it yields. The higher nature assumes the lower one in itself and the customary reactions cease to be prominent. Gradually the higher nature establishes itself, enlarges its range and remoulds the lower nature.

Endurance is largely a matter of exercise of will, whereas the second step of indifference is based upon knowledge. The discipline of indifference to contacts and impacts is based, essentially upon knowledge. The mind knows, the enlightened part of the mind knows that the reactions of our being to life contacts are a matter of habit and they need not be so. As the consciousness grows, as the consciousness gets enlightened, the reactions can be different. It knows also that the right reactions are not what are evident, but different. This knowledge, whether we get it from our own enlightened part, from perception, or from those whose word we take for authority, backs up this indifference.

The first step that we take in this part of the discipline is to decide that these habits of ignorance, habits which have been caused by a state of consciousness or a state of mind where the necessary knowledge is not, have to be cast off. We must not react. Whatever happens, whether the contacts are pleasant or unpleasant, we should be totally indifferent. This determination comes from a knowledge that these reactions are not inevitable, that we can enter into a stage of consciousness where no reactions can be evoked from us and the old habits are dropped.

Here also, as the new habit of indifference starts taking root, we become aware of a division in our being. The surface being, the surface mind, running into the usual moulds, grooves, and reacting while a calmer and a more peaceful and a silent part of the mind refuses to be hustled. It watches, it does not react. Either it concentrates on something else or it is self-rapt, refusing to take notice of what is happening. There is, here also, the ding-dong battle, struggle, the outer trying to upset the inner poise, the inner poise trying to impose itself on the outer surface mentality. But in due course the deeper or the higher mind prevails and the lower one is educated. But it is a gradual and a long process. When this part of the mind that refuses to react, that has decided to be indifferent gains ground, we become aware of an imperturbable tranquility and a peace that cannot be disturbed by contacts, visitations from universal life. They may come through individuals or through a play of forces, but the mind insists on remaining above, overseeing things, not getting involved, not reacting positively or negatively.

After endurance based upon will, and indifference based upon knowledge, comes submission. Submission is essentially based upon the element of devotion— devotion to what is higher than oneself, recognition of a will that is larger than one's own puny individual will,

the universal will. Once we start regarding this will—
God's will, the Divine's will—at work in the universe
and begins to surrender, submit ourselves to its workings,
direct and indirect—through other wills and through
the universal forces—the ego knot gets lossened. Instead
of referring every event, every contact to the ego-point
of reference, we begin to refer to either the standpoint
of the universal will or the will of God, whether it is
universal or transcendent, and we take joy in submitting
to the will of God. In the beginning it may look like a
fatalistic attitude to accept what comes as the will of
God, to go through without complaining, but gradually
as the tendency deepens, there is a joy, an inner happiness in submitting to the Divine's will.

Here also, as in the earlier two steps, there is a
division. The deeper parts or the higher emotions
insist upon keeping to the higher will but the surface
nature goes on reacting in its usual way. It takes
considerable time and effort to educate this outer
nature into accepting the discipline of the inner nature,
to submit itself to the Divine's will.

These are the three steps which form passive
equality. Passive equality is enough as long as one is
engaged in an individual yoga of liberation, for the aim
in such a yoga is to liberate oneself from the lower
nature, from the bonds of ego, and for these ends a
passive equality, an equality by which one arrives
at a state of peace, imperturbable peace, is enough.
But that is hardly enough for a seeker of a yoga like
the integral yoga which insists not only on liberation,
but proceeds with liberation as the first capital step
towards transformation, towards perfection of which
transformation is a part. Here the return of vibrations,
reactions in an equality of spirit is not enough. After

acquiring that capacity of reacting only in knowledge, only in the love of God, only with a will not involved in surface nature, we begin to see that the normal reactions of nature are due to the simple fact that our life is led in ignorance, the consciousness is covered by ignorance, the shadow of nescience, and every contact and movement is to that extent falsified by the surrounding ignorance and even the innate ignorance of the limited, surface mind.

If we are to get beyond the possibility of reacting in ignorance, living in ignorance, we have to take positive steps in active equality and the first positive step in acquiring active equality is to gain knowledge of the Divine in all. The Divine is not merely within us, not merely transcendent of the universe, the Divine is there in all forms and movements in the universe. In all there is God. Once we have this knowledge that God is in all, not only as a mental theory, but as a living knowledge which influences our attitude, our moods, our movements in life, it makes a world of difference. We do not seek to avoid things, do not seek to run away from contacts simply because they are not pleasurable to the senses. We see that everything originates from God, that there is a purpose in every movement, in every contact, and this brings about a revolutionary change in our attitude to the world, to the impacts from the world. All is God—from whom is one to shrink thereafter! asks one of the older Upanishads. For one who has realised that he is one with the Self, that Self is the Self of all and all life is that Self, from what has he to shrink from? If he shrinks it means his knowledge is not complete, his realisation of the Self or the one Divine is incomplete. This is the first step—to acquire this knowledge and to live in it.

Once this knowledge is there as a part of our consciousness, there is the aspect of will, a will for equal acceptance. Since there is the required knowledge, the will has to be trained in the ways of equal acceptance. Once we make a determination and exert our will in accepting things with equality, without getting upset, without getting overjoyed, we feel a growth of strength, a growth of will. It is a slow process, but a steady one. Once the will gets accustomed to greet things with equality, after a time it begins to take joy, take delight in fronting contacts with equality because we know that they are the visits of the cosmic Godhead through so many contacts. We greet the Godhead in every contact and there is an inevitable joy in that step. So there is the knowledge, the will and the delight.

Here also we go through a stage of division in the being. The outer nature is dragged down again and again by its old habits, the inner will insists upon asserting equal acceptance. But ultimately the higher will prevails, as it has to, because always the lower one yields to the higher, the smaller to the larger, That is the law of evolution, the law of life. And as we begin to take this joy, we understand the saying of the Upanishad that there is an underlying delight in all things, nothing could breathe or live without this ether of delight. We begin to understand the science of aesthesis which looks for the *rasa* in things, the sap of delight even in movements, scenes, activities that may appear unpleasant, painful. In each movement in the universe there is, underlying it, a basic delight and it is for that delight that it has been manifested. We fail to tap this current of delight, this source of joy, because of our ignorance, because of our limited consciousness. Once we free ourselves from our involvement in the limited, surface consciousness and

extend our being into a larger ambience, the vibrations
are quite different and our reactions are still more
different. The *rasa* in things comes naturally. We get a
glimpse of this possibility when we witness dramas in
which tragic elements play a part. Some part of the
being enjoys it. Cynics may say you can very well enjoy
it because you know that you are not involved in it,
still a refined mind knows that even in shedding tears of
sympathy, there is a catharasis. They take us nearer the
purer levels of our being. An active equality brings in
this element of feeling the *rasa* in things very naturally.

Active equality means all this in the realm of will, in
the realm of feeling. How does it feel in the realm of
knowledge? Normally our knowledge, our mental life, is
seen to be characterised by ignorance, proceeding
through error, hoping to arrive at true knowledge. In a
person who has acquired this active equality there is
no shrinking from ignorance, he knows ignorance is not
absolute. He does not fly away saying that it is an
illusion, he knows that ignorance is only a deformation
and if the deforming elements are removed the truth
will shine through. So he takes on whatever segment of
ignorance of the universal life is given to him for
participation, studies and sees what are the elements that
deform, knows that the elements that misguide lead to
errors. There is also no finality about these errors.
Errors are, after all, wrong placements of knowledge.
These are corrected, ignorance is tolerated, an attitude
of understanding is cultivated and those who are ignorant, movements that proceed from ignorance, are fronted
with this sense of understanding, toleration, what the
Mother would call, charity. The errors are seen for what
they are and patiently corrected, and he arrives at true
knowledge. Even in this true knowledge there is no

passionate attachment or involvement in what he thinks to be a true knowledge. In an attitude or a poise of dynamic equality he knows that knowledge is endless, that each plane has its own truth. As he develops in consciousness, as he grows in stature, the truth also grows. He does not shut himself into ideas or idea-truths for all time. He allows himself to expand, allows his horizon of knowledge to expand, and this expansion of knowledge goes on till the true and the perfect knowledge is attained at the gnostic level. It is a long way from the mind to the borders of the supermind and it is inevitable that knowledge is always enlarged, extended. The seeker who has that active sense of equality has no regret for his pet theories and notions which are to be left behind, to be replaced by knowledge which he had thought to be wrong. The expansion and the growth of knowledge is made into a joyous movement.

In the realm of will there is a new attitude: this active equality reflects itself as an understanding attention. An enlightened will poised in this active equality identifies itself with things that are happening in order to know, to go to the roots of those movements, understand them and tune itself to the truth behind them. It is here that the active element comes in, a passive equality will just tolerate saying that there must be some truth behind it. But an active and a dynamic equality insists on going behind these movements, knowing their truth and thereafter bearing them with an understanding, helpful equality. In this yoga both the passive and the active equalities are necessary. One leads to the other, not indeed in a logical way of sequence, but as it happens in all movements of yoga, simultaneously. A step gained in passive equality helps to forge ahead in active equality and *vice-versa*. It is enough if we know that there are these two wings of equality and both together take the soaring soul to the heights of the spirit.

(*From Questions & Answers*)

Q.: In the event of an attack by hostile forces, what would be the difference in reaction between a passive and an active equality?

A.: A passive attitude, when it sees a hostile attack coming, will either bear it, endure it, holding to its own truth, or it may pray to the Divine, submit and wait upon the will of the Divine. But an active equality will see what is the strength behind this hostile attack: what is it that gives room to these hostile elements to enter the atmosphere, and precisely what are the forces that are trying to break through. Once you have that knowledge you sound the depths of the consciousness to which you are linked, to deal with the situation, but it is without rancour, without violence. The movement is to correct the situation. If, in the process of correcting the situation, it is found that the hostile elements are to be eliminated, that also is done but without reaction.

Q.: And the effect on the other person?

A.: Naturally, either he has to change or be eliminated, or he will be given a long rope. It depends upon the steps taken against the hostile elements, the nature of the hostile elements—whether they are just forces or elements, or beings. Each case differs.

Q.: I am not clear about the distinction between the inner being, the higher being and the psychic being.

A.: When we say the inner being you can take it that it includes the psychic being. The psychic being is the leader of our inner selves. There are individuals or natures in whom the psychic is not tapped at all. They may ascend in their consciousness through the mental levels and become aware of their higher being. They say that they are not conscious of the psychic, they are not conscious of anything within, they know only what is above. But an integral seeker has to awaken both the ranges—the inner range and the higher range—and the psychic awakening is necessarily the first step for an integral seeker.

Q.: *Can you detail the division between the inner being and the higher being...?*

A.: You can say the surface being and the inner being, but when we speak of the inner it means the higher being also, or the higher means the inner ranges also. The distinction is, really, between what is on the surface and what is behind.

Q.: *Is there any way to know the line of distinction between where one stops functioning with the outer being and the inner being takes over?*

A.: Yes. The inner being, for instance, is not dependent upon outer circumstances. The surface being only goes on reacting. Even in thought, something else thinks for it. The inner being has its own life, irrespective of the outer movements. The inner being lives on its own. It is not perturbed, not overjoyed by any contacts or impacts. But the surface being is always at the mercy, it needs some excitement to feel happy, it needs a pinprick to feel agitated. It has no existence of its own worth the name. This is a simple enough barometer to distinguish the ranges.

In these things you can't have a clear-cut line. Man's being is multiple, each fuses into the other part. Just as you can't have a clear cut-line dividing the mind from the vital, the vital from the physical, similarly between the surface and the subliminal or the inner there is no one line or wall as such. They gently fuse into each other. There is a passage where both appear to be the same—the inner has its outer elements, the outer has its inner elements.

The Upanishads have a very fine phrase. They say *ātmarati*, which means taking delight in the Self alone. One does not look outside for joy or pleasure or happiness, one does not need anything or anybody. His world is all bliss contained in himself. That is a phrase which gives the philosophy of spiritual bliss—that one can live in the soul and be happy without needing the experiences of the senses to lead a happy or a joyous life.

*   *

The Divine will is not the will of others. The Divine will exists independently of others because it has been there before the others have come into existence and it will be there after all have been swept away. It may act through the other wills, but it is not those wills. The way to distinguish is discrimination. For instance there is the Time-Spirit. There may be groups of people who embody that will; you have to recognise it. Somehow they have opened to that Time-Spirit and they manifest it. It is such cases that I had in mind when I spoke of the universal will working through several other wills.

So also, the opposite will, the will of the adversary may embody itself in other groups; that is where the discrimination has to be exercised.

Q.: But in daily life when one has to make a decision...

A.: I think our daily life is too small an affair for the universal will to concern itself with. Each one has only to see what is the Divine will for him, he need not worry about the universal will. The individual Divine will— what is it for me, what is the Indweller's direction for me? That should be enough.

15

THE ACTION OF EQUALITY

We have seen during our previous discussion that equality is both passive and active. According to the needs of the situation the particular type of equality begins to function. Our first experience in the practice of equality is an indifference, a quiescence when there are contacts and impacts from outside. We maintain an attitude of quiet, not reacting. But it is only the first step, that is not enough to give us an entry into the first grounds of the divine life. For that, we need to practise the next step, which is to rise above, to become superior to nature. We not only front things with an attitude of indifference, quiescence, but we rise above the situation of reaction and from there decide which way we are to function. We decide not only the basis of whether a contact is pleasant or unpleasant, welcome or unwelcome, but what is the right thing to do—and that we can do only when we are detached and rise superior to the situation. This ability to rise superior to the situation is the first secret of the soul's mastery.

When I was fresh here, my teacher used to always say, "It is not enough to be equal to a situation, you have to rise above it." I could not fully understand the implications of that statement until I read Sri Aurobindo's explanation of why superiority to a situation is indispensable for the soul's mastery over nature, mastery over existence. Most of us as mental beings use our mind, the mental will, as an instrument for deciding how we are to react, in what manner equality is to be practised. But even after the mind knows

10

and we understand what is the reaction to be given, where exactly we have to confront this contact with the spirit of equality, still after a time as we begin to deal with the situation, the mind is overborne by desire— the desire that is projected by the life or the prana. Once the mind gets mixed up in vibrations of desire, it loses its objectivity, its capacity to react with equality, it tends to take sides. Naturally we start explaining to ourselves why we should do this and not that. It is only a purified mind, a purified intelligence, that can know that already a bias has entered into our mind, the bias created by the inrush of desire. The mind has to be trained in a spiritual discipline, our vision must undergo a revision and must learn to see the one Godhead, the one Divine spread all over the universe. It is only when we not only recognise but accept the presence of a universal Will, a universal Divinity, that we can hope to exercise what Sri Aurobindo calls a "free acceptance of things"; otherwise, we always tend to decide each issue by referring it to our personal self-interest—may be ego, may be desire, preference, prejudice. Whatever it is, there is a reservation and that governs our choice. But if we accept practically —not only theoretically—the presence of a universal Will, and that the Divine is as much in us as in others, in situations that look favourable as also in situations that are unfavourable, when we are convinced of it and by inner discipline ready to face the fact, then our inner being accepts freely any situation that is offered to it, reacts in the spirit of free acceptance to whatever is posed before it.

To come to this level of equality, Sri Aurobindo says that four conditions are to be fulfilled. We have to progressively cultivate and naturalise four qualities, four states of spiritual being. First is equality, a practical equality called *samatā* in the Gita—pleasant or unpleasant, good or bad, cold or hot, whatever the opposites, there must be an initial attitude that whatever comes we accept. We accept what is given to us. Whether we explain it as coming from the will of God or as coming from our destiny, or that it is a process of circumstances in which we are placed—whatever the standpoint, there is a readiness to accept what comes without complaint, without being overjoyed, but with a placid equality. That is *samatā*, the first step.

The second condition is that we must cultivate and acquire a poise in peace that refuses to be disturbed by circumstances. Naturally, this is not acquired in a day but we must find a small corner in our being, may be in the heart, may be at the back of the mind, where we can sense a breath of peace and get a foothold in that corner. Every one of us can experience, at some time or other, some nook, some corner in the being where peace is natural. There we must stick and by rigorous, strenuous, regular discipline extend that area of peace. Naturally we begin in a mental way, There is first the experience, thereafter we mentally visualise that the peace is there even when we don't feel it. We mentally recall that experience, have the faith that there is that peace and we have only to dig at it and we can touch it. Each day we devote some time to the visualisation and the invocation of this peace and naturalise it. Once we do this, experiment with ourselves in recalling that peace, remembering that peace and getting back into that peace when difficult situations present themselves to us, that is a capital gain. The Mother says that each one's way of obtaining peace is different, but if we repeat the word 'peace' or '*śānti*' slowly to yourselves, it unveils itself.

It is not for nothing that the ancients prescribed a
number of peace chants which are prefixed to the
Upanishads, and each peace chant was to inaugurate
the day's session. When they say, "Om, Shanti, Shanti,
Shanti", who can escape that descent of peace! These
words are not letters, these are words which have been
endowed with power by countless seers and practitioners
during thousands of years, and by just repeating those
words it touches a button somewhere and opens the
channel linking us to the Peace. Each language has a
word of peace. The Mother speaks of *paix* in French,
peace in English, and mentions that these are some
of the available techniques to link ourselves with the
Peace that always exists. It is not that peace is brought
on earth by our invocation. Actually the peace is always
there, backing up all the movement that goes on on its
bosom. What we do is to open a door in our being
giving us an entrace into that domain of peace. Each
one of us carries around us an area of peace, only we are
not conscious of it. We are so much extrovert, occupied
with day-to-day things, with what we think to be
important things, that we forget what treasure we carry
within ourselves, above ourselves, behind ourselves.
And the purpose of sadhana is precisely to awaken us
to the potencies that are lying untapped within ourselves. Meditations, relaxation, are intended to focus
our consciousness on peace. Whether we concentrate
upon form or sound or an idea or thought is secondary.
All are intended to silence the mind, to bring the mind
together, silence it for a while—at least in a part of
it—so that we can get the peace. Another important
point is that we cannot seize the peace, we cannot hold
the peace. Whether it is silence or peace, we have to
let it take possession of us. It is larger and vaster than

ourselves. We have only to let ourselves be taken possession of by the surrounding or enveloping silence or peace. Now this peace, this quantum of peace which we succeed in making real to us in yoga, should be always present. After *samatā*, *śānti*, peace which is imperturbable in any circumstances. It must be established at least in some part of us.

The third condition is that there must be an inner felicity; not that bubbling joy or excitement, but a continuous strain of happiness, what is called in Sanskrit *antaḥsukha*, an inner felicity. That spiritual happiness does not depend upon outer reasons, outer circumstances and outer contacts but is there on its own; it must be cultivated and established. And the easiest way to make it natural is to open to the psychic being in us which radiates spontaneously good cheer, quiet joy. We can feel its softness, almost touch it. When the psychic joy, the psychic happiness, exudes we need nothing else. We don't seek for joy, we don't seek for liberation, nothing disturbs, the whole previous perspective seems to be wrong, we do not care what happens to us. It is a natural radiation of the felicity of the psychic part in us. In the measure in which we awake to the presence of the psychic, make it real to us, evoke it, we participate in the natural movement of inner felicity.

The fourth condition is that we not only have the inner happiness, but as a result of its establishment and continuous action in us, we participate in the universal life, the life of the world, in joy and laughter. We participate in the Ananda of manifestation. Of course it can come only after the previous three conditions are fulfilled, but it is a must. It will not do to shut oneself in an inner felicity, closed to outer life, and retreat. We must freely and spontaneously participate in outer life with the joy and laughter of the soul.

These are the four conditions for a spontaneous and a practical equality to function. Till this ideal condition is achieved, it is a hard path. Mentally we know but in practice we have to face situations. The reactions are there, we can't help it. The mind knows, but still it yields. We have to recognise the situation and, as Sri Aurobindo says, take the sting out of these reactions which come from our desires and preferences. Here again, the establishment and the growth of calm is by keeping the mind constantly above the play of desire—mind can watch, mind can sanction, but from a position that is aloof, not only of a witness but of an overseer. The mind has to rise above.

There are reactions, there are elements that are posed by prana, the life-force. It is not difficult, if the mind is sufficiently strong, to put its will on the life-force and suppress it or refuse to participate in its movement of desire. But if that movement of desire or preference comes in the mind itself it is difficult. That can be done only by taking a position even above the active mind. The understanding and will, the buddhi, has to take a poise above the normal movements of mind. As we know, the mind itself has so many layers, but the understanding will must be kept aloof, uninvolved in mental movements. If we know that it is the sense-mind, the desire-mind that wants, then the buddhi can assert itself; but if somehow this preference, this slant, this choice has surreptitiously entered into our understanding and will, how are we going to face the situation? It can only be done, Sri Aurobindo points out, by surrender to the master of our being. There must be constantly an attitude of surrender to the supreme Will.

As this attitude gains ground, each time the buddhi itself is exposed to this temptation, this inner surrender to the master of our being prevails. We allow the higher Will to which we are surrendered to correct our individual buddhi, our individual will.

Even here, as those who practise yoga know, the path is not a smooth path. There are enough backslidings, self-deceptions, too many temptations and each step gained is followed by half a step backwards. But it will not do to get disappointed, discouraged. We have to take it as a process, utilise each setback as an occasion to measure the insincerity in us which opened the doors to the mishap, and know for certain that these setbacks these failures come because room is given to them in our nature, in our being—known or unknown to us. As long as there are defects, as long as there are lacunae, these things are going to arise. They are to be taken as reminders that there is still some leeway to be made up.

With all these preparations we can visualise a condition in which we are calm in all circumstances, and that calm is based upon a sense of unity with all. This sense of unity with all is a result of what Sri Aurobindo calls a universal vision, a vision that sees not only what is relevant to our little selves, but to all. It relates ourselves to everyone else. It is only then that we can be sure that a fundamental equality has started functioning.

In life it is inevitable that with all this calm, with all this knowledge and sense of equality, things evoke a particular reaction in a particular trend. Our nature tends to turn in a particular way. These signs are taken, at that stage, as the direction in which the will of the Lord wants his shakti, his power active in us to respond.

Each has his own way, nature, tendency and direction in which he meets the impacts of life and reacts. This called the *svabhāva*, self-nature, based upon the *svadharma*, self-law. We have to observe which way we naturally tend to react. It is to be observed and, for the time being, allowed to prevail because that is not a permanent stage. An ideal stage would be where we react, the shakti or the power in us reacts, according to the truth of each situation, not according to our own trend. If we are sincere in accepting that one acts and moves according to a higher Will reflected in the individual will, then we function as perfect instruments. As He directs so we function. But that is also a stage. Even this claim to be an instrument, is a subtle ego-claim. A stage must arrive when the personal individuality of even being an instrument, the pride of the instrument, also has to yield. We become identified with the supreme Will, with the Puissance that is acting and we become only channels, not instruments. Then we can say that it is the Master who works and not the instrument.

As such an ideal condition is built up there is the inevitable question of our relations with others. On what basis are we to organise our lives as the sense of equality is established, as a sense of calm becomes permanent and there is the inner awakening to the presence of the supreme Master our being whom we see everywhere? There arises naturally an understanding. We are more charitable towards others, we are no more inclined to find fault with others, but we find explanations why others behave badly, what could have influenced the other person to behave that way. So there is what the Mother calls charity, an understanding of our environment which gradually develops into love. And when we are invaded by this current of divine love which understands everything and helps everything, that is a spiritual status which contributes its own energies to the people around us. We contribute strength, we contribute endurance, we contribute delight—but all in the measure in which we identify ourselves at some level with the divine Presence among those around us and make no distinction between our individual life and the lives of others.

All these states of consciousness, of being, of delight are necessarily imperfect as long as we are confined to the domain of mind. An effort has to go on to transcend the boundaries of our mind in ignorance and open ourselves to the larger and the wider heights of the being. The ultimate perfection can come only when we gain entry into the supramental levels of consciousness, or when the supramental energy enters into us, making it possible for us to participate in an entire plenitude of delight and oneness of being which cannot be described adequately in the human language at our disposal.

(From Questions and Answers)

Q.: *When the three modes of nature are transformed into the supernature, how do they actually work?*

A.: What we call modes—tamas, inertia; immobility; rajas, movement, dynamism, impetuosity; sattva, enlightenment, quietude, balance—they are actually imperfect transcriptions of three higher powers, three higher modes of the spiritual being. They are transcriptions in lower nature. Once you rise above the lower nature you see that these very three lower modes reveal themselves in their original terms. What is tamas, inertia, immobility, reveals itself as peace, *śānti* which is not disturbed by anything. Rajas, the impure self-regarding dynamism of life, reveals itself as the pure

spiritual force of execution. That force may hold itself
or it may throw itself out. Still, it is an effectuating force,
it is the Chit-Shakti. And sattva, the enlightenment,
peace, reveals itself as plenitude of knowledge, radiation of light. All the three were there before they got
deformed by the plunge of the soul into the inconscience
and ignorance. The lower modes convert themselves
into the higher qualities, the divine powers or the divine
values.

*   *

We have seen a practical demonstration of this
capacity of a person who has realised perfect equality.
As Sri Aurobindo says in the last paragraph of this chapter, you are aware, you have the knowledge of why
things are what they are. Even when you fail, even when
you are faced with obstruction there is no upsetting. You
see exactly, step by step, why the failure is coming, why
the difficulties are there, you see the purpose for which
they are there, the reason for which the divine Will has
allowed those things to work, and that very knowledge
gives you the capacity to stand it. I have seen this in the
case of the Mother. She knew very well, in each case,
why things were happening. To know—that itself gives
you the power to correct the situation if necessary or
to bear it, because you know what is going to follow.
Most of us who are in ignorance are blinded by the
immediate situation. As the equality grows and the calm
understanding establishes itself, this capacity to see
behind events—as Sri Aurobindo says, to see behind
your enemy, that he is really an opponent in the game
of life who is contributing to your growth,—grows; that
can be only when you have an established, enlightened,
imperturbable equality and calm. Unless you have the
understanding it is idle to speak of divine love, because

this love can only be a consequence of understanding. If you feel certain waves of divine love with others it only means that the knowledge is within. You may not be awake to that knowledge, but that love is not false. On the surface you have not yet developed enough to see the knowledge behind that love.

16

THE POWER OF THE INSTRUMENTS

We have completed the first limb of the Yoga of Perfection in studying in depth the role of equality. The second limb is the power of the instruments. The question of either the instruments or the power of the instruments does not arise at all in most of the traditional lines of yoga which do not call upon man to uplift or to perfect this world. According to their approach the world, if it is not a total falsehood, is an inferior grade of reality which loses its significance once one attains to a higher level of consciousness. But in this yoga, the integral yoga, where we accept the world to be as real as the Divine towards which we are moving, the call is for action, for a progressive perfection of ourselves and through our perfection the perfection of the society and the perfection of life on earth.

Starting with the individual, it is the instruments that are to be readied for any spiritual action, any spiritual programme to be worked out through us or by us. The instruments through which we function have to be purified and raised to their optimum level of efficiency. If the instruments are flawed, certainly the work is going to be flawed. The aim of this part of the yoga of perfection is not only to purify the instruments, but to raise the power of the instruments to their maximum. And what are these instruments?

The instruments are obviously the intelligence, the mind, the heart, the vital, and the physical body. All of these are in varying states of consciousness. They are to be put in the right condition so that they function at their highest level when we work. And this work, as we will see later on, is not merely external work but also internal.

Let us start with the physical body. Whoever is doing yoga, trying for spiritual consciousness, knows that anything that he receives has a certain effect on the physical body. And the very fact that the body receives the vibrations of the higher consciousness has its results around the individual. The state of the body determines, to a certain extent, not only the state of reception of what he gains from above or from within, but also the spiritual radiation of what is received. The body has its natural limitations. In addition to these limitations, the body has its own habits which tend to pull down the consciousness, which tend to limit the sensitivity of the body or oppose the tendency to go within or go upwards, by a pull always downwards. The pull from the subconscient and the inconscient mostly acts through the physical body. So apart from its natural limitations, the body, at some level is a storehouse of habits, regressive habits, which exert a constant pull downwards on the being which aspires to go beyond. The only way to rectify this situation is to aim at a new body, new in the sense that it begins to function differently, to react in a new way, receive in a new way. The physical body cannot be dissolved and there is no known alchemic process by which we can change the body as it is into a totally new form with new capacities. That is in the womb of the future. But as things stand, to create a new body means, in this context, to train the body to act and react in a new way, not on the basis of past habits but in response to new urges, new pressures from the mind, from the will. We start by dilingently exerting a mental will towards this change. The mind certainly knows how the body has to react. By self-study, byself-observation we know precisely where the body fails to support the yogic action. Knowing it, we exert the will with discrimination, with vigilance, so that it learns new habits, displacing the old ones. And the first step in this direction is to teach the body an entire passivity—not to obstruct, not to oppose, but to hold itself in a passive poise so that what comes from above or what emerges from within is received just as it comes. But this passivity alone is not enough. The body also has to learn to give positive responses. At present what is happening is that instead of responding rightly to the pressures, of the higher consciousness, the body interferes with its habits and dilutes what comes, responds in a half-hearted manner. As Sri Aurobindo puts it graphically, the music of this harp of God is interfered with by the body. The body refuses to respond with the right notes, the new music has to admit into it inferior notes and allow a dilution, a deformation to take place.

We have to reverse this process so that the body responds with a thrill, the right vibrations, to the tune that calls from above. The body must contribute to the fuller orchestration, and by that process the music of God acquires a solid richness.

We said the mental will must exert a control over the body, but that is not enough. We begin with that. We know the limitations of the mental will and once the full capacity of the mental will is used and we find the mental will cannot go further, that will has to yield to a still higher will, the will of the spirit, the will of the soul, ultimately the will of the supramental, but to that we will come later on. As the higher will, the will higher than the mental—starts exerting itself, the body has to acquire the necessary strength to sustain the action of this higher will with its attendant force. The normal body is not able to hold, much less sustain this action. The body needs to be prepared, acclamatised to higher and still higher charges of the spiritual will so that it may not spill what comes, it may not shake and get restless and render the higher action ineffective or less effective. This capacity to hold without shaking must be acquired if we mean to get the body to cooperate in the integral fulfilment.

There is a phrase in the Veda where they speak of how an unbaked jar splits asunder when the divine beverage of ecstasy is poured into it. Unless the clay has been heated, subjected to the proper culturing and made to acquire the right consistency, it cannot hold the inpouring of the divine delight. An unbaked jar is a classic illustration of one who opens himself to the higher forces of yoga without preparing himself at the physical level. That may ensure either an illness or a mental derangement.

Secondly, as the body is being built up, it loses the old habit of getting fatigued. Fatigue is a sign that the body is unable to cope with the situation. Either it has been overworked or it is not accustomed to respond in the manner that is expected of it. When the body stops getting fatigued it is a sign that it is picking up, learning new habits, new ways. Each part of the body must be worked upon not only to make it physically strong but capable of holding, sustaining and enduring the higher action without fatigue. And Sri Aurobindo emphasises, it is not muscular strength, not physical force, after all, that decides things. Whatever it may be when we lead the normal life full of grossness, once we take to spiritual life of this conception, the energy that is required, what the higher consciousness pours into the physical body, is not the outer energy with which we are familiar, the kind of energy that we can get from physical exercise or proper nourishment. There is around us a sea of life-force—*prāṇa śakti*, which really sustains the physical energy. The currents of prana keep the physical energies moving and active. It is one of the aims of yoga to tap this reservoir of life-force in the universe. Normally the body has a certain balance; it receives something and what it cannot hold it does not receive. The outer life-energies try to get in, but when they find that the body is reluctant they do not enter. There is an effort in the early part of sadhana in the traditional yoga to open channels of communication with the surrounding life-force. Those who do not do yoga do it by increasing the physical energies which make their demand on the life-force through exercise and the usual physical means. But in yogas like the Hathayoga and the Rajayoga they have special measures like *āsanas*, disciplines of *prāṇāyāma*, by which a new balance is sought to be established between the physical body and the life-energies. More and more energies from the sea of life are drawn in, so much so that the physical energies form only the last terminal of the life-energies. The more we draw these energies, keep them and arrive at a self-adjusting balance between our own and the outer life energies, we get more control over the body, the body obeys the needs and the demands of the life-force. But this is only a step.

As long as we depend upon physical means like breathing or postures to facilitate the entry of the life-energies, holding them through certain processes of pranayama etc. the gains will be limited. We may live long, may be able to work more, cure ourselves of diseases which originate because of lack of sufficient vital force, but nothing beyond that. Subtler means have to be learned to draw in the life-energies, and that is only when we exceed the mental will and open to the action of the spiritual and the supreme will-power, that the universal prana is spontaneously tapped and brought in. The higher will knows precisely the quantum of life-energy that is required and it draws upon it.

This is what Mother meant when she said that she did not depend upon physical food, that it was the universal prana, that fed her. She drew upon those energies, but she did take the minimum quantity of physical food, just to respect the material law of the physical body. Even a person supremely advanced in consciousness respects the laws of the environment, laws of creation, till those laws are changed. Sri Aurobindo explains in his Letters how even an avatar will not break the rules of the game unless he first changes the rules, establishes new rules.

But that is not the ultimate, to draw the universal life-energy is not everything. That also is a step, though a great step, because even the universal life-energy has its limitations. The universe is in the triple formula of ignorance, so the limitations of this cosmic ignorance apply to the life-force. It is as we near the gnostic levels, the higher will approaches the gnostic, that it draws from still higher levels. There is, Sri Aurobindo points out, what is called the supramental life-force which is not subject to the limitations of the present universal life-force. When the supramental will is made active and functions in us, the supramental prana shakti is set into action.

We must have the faith—faith in the knowledge that is given, faith in the capacity of the body to change,

11

to receive and to sustain the action of the progressively higher and higher forms of the consciousness force. We start with this faith. Man is a mental being and the faith is first mental. But it is always combatted by the opposite faith; the body protests, the vital also shows its incapacity to go beyond a certain level, it throws doubts, the physical mind also has its own doubts. This obstinate habit of doubting the ability of the body to hold and sustain, the ability of the mind and the other instruments to change and reform or recast themselves, is the constant tussle that goes on between the higher will and the will of inconscience. For a long time this struggle continues; there must be the faith, the indomitable and unconquerable faith in the infinite capacity of the life-force to achieve what the will wants. Because after all, what is life-force? Life-force is a projection in the material universe of what is consciousness-force, consciousness as force, on its own higher levels of Sachchidananda. Somewhere there is the core of consciousness, and this consciousness is illimitable. The Vedic mystics attach great importance to this life-force to be summoned, naturalised, and put into operation. They call it the vehicle, the vehicle of the soul. Life-force is symbolically called the horse, the steed; just as cow stands for light, knowledge, the horse in the Veda stands for power, for life-energies. They are the vehicles of the soul, and for the soul to arrive at its goal, the stronger the vehicle, the more ample the vehicle, the better it is.

So far we have spoken of the normal life-energy close to the physical. Then there is another form of prana—the psychic prana, in other words the energies that are yoked to the desire-soul. Here also we must note that all that pertains to the desire-soul is not necessarily evil, not necessarily something to be excised and cast away. This psychic prana is the stuff of which much that we admire in men—character, personality—is constituted. The desire-soul has its own right, it is something in our own being which has a right to possess and to enjoy, but this right is ill-used by the ego and the desire formation organised around the ego. The yogin has to take steps to purify this life-energy by eliminating, as far as possible, the movements of ego and crude desire. The right of the soul to possess and enjoy comes into its own only when this purification has been effected.

It is not enough to be pure. A negative purity is not enough. Once we purify and loosen ourselves from the hold of desire and ego, there comes forward a natural felicity, a gladness and lightness that are from the psychic being. Wherever the psychic is active, lightness, felicity, joy and sweetness are present. But they are veiled by the crudities of our normal desire-soul. Once these are removed, this gladness, felicity and sweetness come to the fore and the yogin is asked to govern his movements with some equality: no undue joy when things are achieved, no depression when things are not. There has to be equanimity; it is only in conditions of equanimity that the psychic prana can function at its optimum and the qualities of the soul begin to emerge.

The physical prana, the psychic prana, and then comes the *citta*. Chitta is the emotional and the pure psychic being. This pure psychic being is free from the least shadow of the vital or the lower vital desire. Here again, this *citta* or the emotional and the pure psychic stuff in us has to be subjected to purification and processed through equality. In the measure in which our knowledge grows, in the measure in which we impose a harmonising will on the different parts of the being through this *citta*, we make a higher working

possible. We have to note that in each person there are
two powers, two aspects. One is the aspect of calm,
equality, silence. The other is one of force and strength.
Both these—the dynamic and the enlightened static
—are to be harmonised, each one has to recognise
what is the hour of the other and what is its own.
They can't struggle among themselves. These two, what
Sri Aurobindo calls the *saumya* and the *raudra*, have to
work in harmony.

If we are so made or allow ourselves to be so made
that we would only be calm and quiet and enjoy the
felicity—not for us is the integral perfection. If we are
only impetuous, dynamic, without knowing something
of the peace, something of equality or equanimity, for us
is not meant the integral perfection. We must recognise
the claims of both, harmonise them, and only then
is the basis laid for the supreme perfection. Thereafter,
Sri Aurobindo speaks of faith not only in our capacities,
not only in our destiny, not only in the existence of the
reality, but faith in the universe, that there is a universal
good. All is moving towards something good; at the
base of all there is a delight, an ananda. God enjoys
his creation and in the measure in which we leave
behind our human perfection and grow into the divine
nature, we also enjoy the play of the manifestation. That
is essentially one of the planks of the Tantric philosophy.

This is a faith in the universal good, that all that
happens is moving towards something good, though we
may not have the vision to see it. But we must not be
disheartened, not allow ourselves to be over-powered
by negative thinking, but seek to know and experience
what is the purpose for which all these, good and
evil as they are called, move. If we have the faith
that the Divine is there in the universe, nothing can

happen ultimately without his will; and if we have the aspiration to reach up to this will and learn how to tune ourselves to the supreme's will in the universe, the universe presents a totally different picture than what it normally does. Once this faith is there in the universal good, our capacity to love increases boundlessly. In everyone there is the bud of love. How far it blossoms depends upon his evolution. In one who believes that there is a universal god, that the divine presence is everywhere, there is a spontaneous movement of love. And as this movement overspreads and ultimately overpowers the individual, he himself becomes ultimately a sea of love.

Lastly, there is the *buddhi*, the intelligent will. That too has to be subjected to the discipline of purity, not insisting upon its own notions, own conclusions, own processes but to convert itself into a clear mirror, a reflector of the higher knowledge. When the mental *buddhi*, the will and intelligence, accepts this role and consents to do no more than reflect the higher knowledge, function flexibly, not hesitating to give up its own likes and dislikes, the *buddhi* too starts participating in this movement of purification and the perfection of the instruments. All these instruments have to be harmonised; it is a full-time discipline in itself. It is here that the awakened mind has to play a great role. The mind has to watch itself, watch the various movements in the system, acquire more and more knowledge of the Self, and what we know we have to practise. And this practice is the *sādhana*, the *abhyāsa*, the yoga.

Thus from the physical body up to the higher will and the highest levels of the mind that we attain, all instruments, tied up with each other, have to be processed through purification, equality, faith, a psychic gladness, capacity for love, passivity when passivity is the need, dynamism when that is the call.

(*From Questions & Answers*)

Q.: *Is the vehicle or the means by which the prana acts on the physical body the subtle-physical?*

A.: Yes, the subtle-physical. We have around our physical body a subtle-physical envelope. That is the channel through which the universal life-energies flow into us. When this subtle-physical envelope is weak for any reason, then those energies can't come in. And how does this envelope get weak? Sri Aurobindo explains how our own movements of depression, defeatism, negative psychological movements, depress the envelope so that not only the healthy currents of life can't come in, but diseases get in. T. B., for instance, is more a psychological disease because its origin—whatever may be the subsequent physical development—is in long periods of depression, mental depression. This acts as an invitation to these deficiency diseases. The subtle envelope gets shrunk, weak. But movement of cheerfulness, of joy, have an effect of strengthening the subtle-physical envelope. From that point of view, positive movements like confidence, faith, dynamism build up a powerful envelope which attracts life-energies, keeps out the inferior energies.

Q.: *What is personality?*

A.: Personality is a formation put forward by the soul through the instrumentality of mind, life and body. The soul comes with some past experience. It wants to gain another kind of experience. So it puts in those instruments in the front—mind, life and body— certain elements from its own stuff which are favourable for the kind of experience that it wants. In the beginning they are undeveloped, but as one grows, these elements start getting into shape; that is called a formation put forward by the soul to gain the experience that it wants. That is the personality. So the mould of the personality, the type, is determined by the will of the soul, though it may happen that this natural personality of the soul may be displaced in the course of life by interference of the ego, interference of the desire-self, and a false personality may displace the true personality. Yoga is intended to dissipate the false personality so that the true personality comes forward. We have seen such a change in many lives—people change their character, change even their facial expression once they take to the inner life. The personality, however, is only an instrument, an instrumental formation put forward by the soul.

Q.: What is the relation of citta in the traditional yogas and citta in Sri Aurobindo's philosophy?

A.: Chitta in Patanjali's yoga, and other systems based upon it, means the stuff of consciousness, the stuff of awareness. It includes the whole system, the mind, the emotions, the life force—all are bundled together as Chitta. But Sri Aurobindo does not go that far. He says Chitta is really the stuff of mental consciousness. He confines it to the mind and the emotional being. The psychic is behind the emotions. To Patanjali and the others even the vital stuff is the Chitta.

17

SOUL-FORCE AND FOURFOLD PERSONALITY

We spoke last time of the perfection of the instruments—the reason, the mind, the heart, the life-force and the physical body. With the perfecting of this instrumentation we arrive at something ready to work as an instrument, but what is it that is to work? That is the question. Indeed, what is to work in the perfected instrument is the divine Power, the Shakti. All preparation has to be done, things have to be readied in order that the instruments may support the action of the divine Force, and as we have seen, a minimum of purity, harmony between the various parts of the being and an upraising of their capacities is essential.

Once the instrument is ready, the divine Shakti also being accepted, on what basis does the Shakti work? It works in relation to the Lord, the Ishwara. Whether in the universe or in the individual, it is the Ishwara, the Purusha for whom his Power, his Shakti works, and the instruments that are readied are used for this purpose, to work out the will of the Purusha. In individuals we call it the purusha, on a cosmic scale we call him Ishwara. And this purusha expresses his will in each individual as the soul-force, the force of the soul. We speak always of force of nature, but there is also a force of the soul. Whatever may be the truth in the case of the average person, in those who make a mark or who do something above average it is the soul-force that makes its impact through nature. Otherwise it is only nature that expresses itself. And those who express or bring out the soul-force characteristically in an impressive measure, in a lasting impression, are called *vibhutis*. Wherever a quality or a divine power is expressed in a pre-eminent manner, that is the vibhuti—a special concentration of the divine Power. A vibhuti is to be distinguished from the avatar which is an incarnation. An incarnation is in a different category—it is the Divine who takes birth in a soul. Here it is a quality or a power of the Divine with which the evolving soul is endowed—may be evolving or not evolving, but the soul is endowed for some particular purpose in creation. By and large this power that expresses itself has some impersonal quality about it. It sweeps not only the instrument but the whole field before it. There is a surge which is certainly not personal. So it is something more than the normal soul-force active in the case of ordinary individuals.

The purusha, the divine being is indeed many-qualitied, infinite in quality—in a certain sense without quality—but in manifestation, with an infinite number of qualities. But he has to work through nature which, as we have seen, has three modes—sattva, rajas and tamas—enlightenment and peace, dynamism and power, inertia and rest. As persons evolve, though the mould of sattva, rajas or tamas is accepted, it is the special power of the soul that is expressed in life. And this special power of the soul which organises itself, builds itself in the course of evolution is fourfold. Put briefly, there is the power of knowledge, intelligence; there is the power of effectuation, strength; there is the power of harmony, mutuality, production, adaptation; and there is the power of work, service, labour. This, in brief, is the description of the fourfold power and Sri Aurobindo points out that in each individual all these four powers are instinct, whether they are developed or not, whether he is overtly conscious or not. Some may be conscious of a particular power which may take the lead over the others and be more prominent. According to the prominence taken by a particular power we call that person an intellectual, a dynamic man, a man of the world, a person who is essentially meant for service, and so on. But as we will see, all these are there in one and it is one of the aims of evolution, to see that all the four develop equally, get coordinated by the will of the soul, and present a fourfold personality in the fullness of time.

The first power or soul force is the aspiration that seeks for knowledge. In each person there is an element that wants to know. The level of the knowledge sought, the nature of the object to be known may differ from person to person. But that longing, that seeking to know, to acquire the knowledge of what one doesn't know, is there in each person. And this seeking is centered in the intelligence, the mind. The mind is alert and probes things in order to know them. There are grades and stages through which this power of knowledge has to develop. In the beginning it may be just a curiosity, later it may be out of necessity of life that some may want to know things, understand them. Some may become sheer dry intellectuals who are satisfied with knowing mentally what is what—they may be armchair philosophers. There are some who go more to the root of things and they acquire wisdom. They are called the sages—not philosophers. If, however, this development proceeds without reference to the other powers, then that knowledge becomes ineffective. It becomes a one-sided development, over-loaded in the direction of the mind, and what the person knows remains just a theory.

Unless what one knows is practised, put into operation, rendered in terms of life, that knowledge remains—as Sri Aurobindo describes elsewhere—something on the top shelf which we rarely touch. It is to be brought down, made use of and only then can knowledge be fruitful. But for whatever we want to do, whatever we want to achieve, knowledge is the first essential, the first requirement.

After acquiring knowledge there is the question of effectuating that knowledge. We want to practise but there are obstructions; we have to break down the obstructions, impose our knowledge-will on our environment, on our own recalcitrant elements, members of our being. And to guard the knowledge that we have got, to express the knowledge with force, to work out the knowledge in life, there is required a certain dynamism, a strength, a power of effectuation. That is the second element, the second limb of the soul-force. If, however, there is an undue stress only on power, only on strength, without a sufficient background of knowledge, then one may turn into something titanic, something asuric. One may go on trying to effectuate one's own unenlightened will. That is why a proper background of knowledge is necessary for the right exercise of will, use of power. Both have to be complementary. Knowledge without power is impotent and power without knowledge is irresponsible.

The third limb is the arranging intelligence. There are those who go on gulping bits of knowledge without coordinating them, without arranging them according to the life situations. This facility, capacity to arrange what one knows, to adapt it to differing situations, not having one rule for all occasions but having what is called a practical intelligence, making the best of the

situation with the available power and knowledge, is
indispensable. And it is with knowledge in whatever
field, with capacity to effectuate it that one produces.
Whether in the individual life or in collective life,
production is essential in life, whatever the kind of out-
put. In society production is always followed by
exchange, by interchange, on a basis of harmony—not
only harmony among the different members of one's own
being but harmony with others with whom one is
associated or thrown together. This capacity of arranging things, producing, exchanging, needs a special type
of skill and only those who are endowed with that skill
succeed in life. Of course here also there are cases where
they have neither the full knowledge nor the requisite
capacities, but they have this practical intelligence. They
manoeuvre, manipulate and manage to get the best
results, but that is not an ideal situation.

And last, one may know, one may have the power,
one may have the skill to operate, but unless one exerts
oneself, one pours one's energies, serves, labours, nothing
can be achieved. This is the fourth power.

In the ancient Indian system these four were symbolised by the four types which constituted originally
the basis of what later came to be called the four castes.
The knowledge type was symbolised by the brahmin.
Who was a brahmin? Not one who was born in a brahmin family but one who sought to know the Brahman,
who communicated the knowledge of Brahman. That
was the original connotation. The power type, the
strength type was the *kṣatriya*, the hero, warrior, who
was called upon to guard the intellectual and the spiritual heritage of the society. Then the producer type,
adapting type, the harmonist was symbolised by the
vaiśya, that is the commercial class, the producer of

common wealth. Exchanging, coordinating between production, distribution—this function was largely attended to by the *vaiśya*. And then came the *śūdra*, the labourer, the person whose dharma it was to serve.

Sri Aurobindo points out that this perception that certain persons are best fitted to work, to serve, to labour has also found an echo in the modern thought of the dignity of labour. Of course some may point out that the labouring classes do not really work because there is a dignity in it; they work out of necessity, economic compulsions. But still, whatever the compulsions of life, service has a great role to play, in a sense a more important role than the others, because it is the foundation. In the Vedic symbology the entire society is conceived as the Cosmic Being—the brahmin from his head, the kshatriya, hero-warrior, from his arms, the vaishya, producer from the thighs, and the shudra, the service man from the feet. The earth is his footing. The footing, the foundation of the whole cosmos is there in service. And in the higher rungs of spiritual fulfilment, Sri Aurobindo underlines, service, self-giving, pouring of one's energies assumes a different complexion. It is one thing when service is separated from one's true self, having to work and earn for one's living only. When the perspective is changed, when the service is meant for God—for God in oneself and for God in the universe, the hue changes. Service is to be coordinated with the other three elements.

We have seen how without power knowledge remains impotent; power without knowledge becomes erratic; the man of production, of exchange, who adapts things, promotes harmony, needs to have a basis of knowledge, the effectuating capacity to translate his abilities into action. Similarly if the service man is

content to remain only serving and labouring, he
tends to become a machine. He also, in his own way,
at his own level, has got that element of knowledge—the
knowledge of his craft, how to do things best, speedily,
perfectly. He has got the power to effectuate what he
knows. Not all can do that service; he has that capacity,
the special type of strength intended for his special
profession. Even if he is a smith there is a power, there is
a strength that expresses itself precisely in the profession
of the smith. And he needs to know how to coordinate
the various parts of his work, how to reach it to others.

In each person all these four elements have to be
coordinated and as man evolves he recognises this necessity. In the olden days each society had this fourfold base.
The names may differ—even in the West they had this
fourfold order. They had the church, symbolising spiritual or religious heritage, the nobles to guard, to support, give strength and then the mercantile classes,
and fourth, the laity. Wherever human society has
been formed, this fourfold classification has had to be
there because it is the cosmic intention. That things have
been travestied in the later development of a caste system in India is another matter, but the true basis is there.
If we miss this basis things get distorted.

Each individual, as he evolves, recognises the necessity of work, the necessity of adapting himself to situations, harmonising with others, then acquiring the
capacity and the power to effectuate what he knows,
and primarily the necessity of knowing the meaning of
life, the necessity of knowledge before he can live. A
recognition of this interconnection of the four different
aspects of the soul-power is a must for an integral, total
perfection.

As early as the Vedas there are hymns which point

out that there is a special class of gods, divine powers, who out of one bowl with which man is endowed at birth, work to fashion four bowls. With the completion of these bowls comes the attainment of immortality. This fourfold perfection is an ancient idea. It has not lost its relevance even today. In the present teaching with which we are concerned, there is a recognition that corresponding to this fourfold aspiration of man, the fourfold perfection that he is called upon to build in himself, the Divine also is described as manifesting in four major Powers. The divine Shakti, the divine Mother in whose hands is given this task of perfecting humanity, emanates four Powers. The first Power, Maheshwari, is concerned with knowledge, largeness of vision, organisation of light; she perfects the limb of knowledge. Mahakali is the divine Mother of Strength, Power—she it is who takes up the human energies, human power and perfects it in terms of her own strength. Then comes Mahalakshmi, the Goddess of beauty and harmony, who teaches man to coordinate things, to harmonise them, to bring beauty in this world of confusion and ugliness. And last comes Mahasaraswati, the Goddess of work, precision, who is not satisfied with anything less than perfection. It is she who perfects the side of work, service, labour. So there is no real deprecation when they speak of the fourth class, the class of workers, because even in the divine manifestation the divine Mother takes an appropriate form, the form of Mahasaraswati to raise this human aspiration for perfection in work to the divine level.

Thus seconding the human aspiration, the human will, the human striving, there is the divine Shakti, that operates, that uplifts and works for perfection. Now what is the divine Shakti, how does it manifest, how does it work, how does it function in individual terms?

(From Questions and Answers)

Q.: *Does the soul-force remain a fixed entity in each person or does it progress, and also how does it work in the Shakti?*

A.: The soul-force is an individual expression of the divine Shakti that wants to manifest through each soul. In each person there is a different stress, in one soul the divine Shakti may want to express primarily its power aspect, in another the knowledge aspect. But all the other parts, the other elements are behind the one which takes the lead. The soul-force, you may say, is only a projection of the divine Shakti and that soul-force works through nature and that nature has three gunas, three modes. So it is a four-fold power working through a three-fold nature.

In the examples of people who have been great successes in life, even though they may not claim to be spiritual, you will observe that they were not one-sided. They had all these powers, though in varying degrees— but all were developed. Take Napoleon, take Shivaji—one thing may have been in the front but all the other three were developed. Napoleon, for instance, was essentially a hero type, a *kṣatriya*, but his knowledge was amazing, not only of literary science, but even of statecraft, psychology. And then he had the power to coordinate a dozen generals around him; he coordinated, he held them in leash and worked. He is said to have slept only on horse-back—he had that capacity for work. If he was only a general, only a military strategist, he could not have been what he was. He was a man of high evolution. When anything outstanding is to be effectuated, all the four elements have to be there.

Q.: Would people in the three lower categories find it difficult to develop in the area of the highest caste?

A.: In their own way they could develop. It need not be knowledge of the shastras, but knowledge of what one is doing. You can go to any man in India—a coolie or a peasant in a village and he will have his own philosophy and a sound philosophy too. He has that element of knowledge, not only of his profession, but a philosophy of life. So you can take man at any level—a civilised man, naturally—and you will find all the four elements. The curse of modern civilisation is specialisation. There has to be a total development. This craze for specialisation tends to narrow our interests, and one of the things which will be swept away as this old civilisation goes is this narrowing of the range of the soul.

Q.: Could you talk a little bit about the different kinds of avatars?

A.: An avatar is a special descent of the Divine and the person who is the Divine descended on earth is always conscious from the beginning that he is the Divine. There are what are called partial avatars. That is, only a part of the divine being takes birth to help humanity in certain situations. There are occasions when great transitions have to be made and there the full avatar, the whole being of the Divine descends. Of course we can't ask what is left there if the whole being has come here; it is said in the Upanishad that if you take out the Full from the Full, the Full remains. So it is not a mathematical total that we speak of. Some come to manifest only a particular aspect of God. They are not the full incarnation. They establish their particular truth.

Q.: Is it so, however, that there is always an evolving soul in that individual body in which the descent takes place?

12

A.: Where we speak of partial incarnation an evolving soul may be chosen and that manifestation may take place through that individual, but where it is a case of a full manifestation, it is not an evolving soul.

18

THE DIVINE SHAKTI

We have seen that the instruments being prepared, perfected, they are to be operated by a power of God. Normally it is a power in ignorance, nature as we call it, that moves. But for a seeker who consecrates himself to the Divine and wants to be possessed by the Divine and made an instrument for the manifestation, it is the power of the Divine, the Divine Shakti that is to function. What we are normally conscious of, what moves us and operates in our instrumental personality is called prakriti. But what a seeker should aim at is the power of the soul, Shakti.

Now the power of the soul and the power in ignorance are not really two different things, there is one power, the divine power, the power of the purusha, the power of the soul, but when the same power has to work in the midst of ignorance with the instrumentation of unpurified faculties or limbs, it becomes prakriti. Prakriti, as Sri Aurobindo has described it elsewhere, is the executive force of the Divine Puissance.

When we look around in the universe we do perceive a power of functioning, a universal energy at different levels throwing out its waves, its currents, but it is more or less a mechanical force, an energy that propels itself and we doubt whether there is any soul at all, whether there is any consciousness, or it is simply a mechanical energy. That appears to be so when we look only on the outside. But should we look into ourselves a little, the subjective experience that we get indicates a different conclusion. We become aware of an energy, of a force, true; but we also become conscious of something that we may call 'I', something that is not totally involved or lost in the working of the force or energy. There is an 'I that observes, that sanctions, that may even get involved, and there is an energy, a force that acts now as physical energy, now as life-force, now as mental energy and so on. This is called the duality of nature and soul.

Different explanations are given of this fact of nature and soul. Those of you who have read the *Essays on the Gita* are familiar with the Sankhya explanation, to which Sri Aurobindo has devoted a chapter in the *Essays*. The Sankhyans speak of a prakriti, nature, comprising three modes, three gunas. That comes into operation the moment it is face to face with the purusha. The purusha himself is inert, he does not move. But in the presence of the prakriti which moves into action in the presence of the purusha, the purusha seems to move. He reflects the activity and the prakriti reflects the consciousness of the purusha. There is a mutual reflection and the game goes on.

There is another approach which speaks of a dual being in us—the higher Self and the lower self. The lower self, ourselves, immersed, involved in the lower nature and the higher being or higher Self which is free from it. We become aware of this double existence when we rise beyond the level of the normal thinking mind.

However, whether in terms of Sankhya or in terms of the dual being, when we go deeper by yogic methods of self-observation, we realise that this duality is only a phenomenal experience. It is not original. It is when we move into phenomena that there is a duality. And this fact of duality being only a result, a part of the phenomenon, becomes patent when we get a higher experience than what the normal mind can yield, when something of the spiritual mind or of the soul is experienced. As this experience of yoga organises itself, repeats itself, becomes natural to us, we realise that the energy, the force that works is nothing else than the power of the soul, the spirit, the Divine Being, the Purushottama, who presides and oversees the whole universal movement. Necessarily this force, this power, shares the character of the soul. It is conscious, self-directing, the appearance of mechanical nature is only its front. It only appears so to the surface vision, but when we go deep we do discover, as even modern science has begun to perceive, that there is some principle that is conscious, is self-aware, directing. If the being is not always conscious that the force that it wields is the divine force, that the life that it leads is a divine life, or potentially divine, it is so because it limits itself to ego-experience. Each one of us shuts himself in the walls erected by the ego, sets himself separate from other beings, and loses sight of the true unity, the true character of the power. If, by any means, we can replace our egoistic will which limits the operation of the power, veils the true consciousness, by a universal will, we become conscious also that the power that acts, whether within ourselves or in the universe, is the universal Shakti, the Power of God.

But this shakti is not outside in the universal alone. It is also there in the individual, because the individual is not separate from the universe. What is there is here and what is here is there. All that can be said is that the universe individuates itself in different forms to give a certain acuteness to the experience of life. And this universal Shakti, which is also in man, is mostly hidden,

Only a part of it operates—or we are conscious of—on our surface being. The bulk of it is stored in us, hidden, involved, and waits to be tapped, evoked by appropriate methods. It can truly go into movement only when the body, the mind and the life vehicles are prepared and become strong enough to sustain and support the unrolling of the universal Shakti embedded in us.

In the Indian tradition this Shakti is called the *Kundalini Shakti* and the same Shakti in the universe is called the *Mahākundalini*. It is the same but here stored in an individual scheme and there spread out in the universal field.

How to become conscious of the stored up energy, the force within ourselves? The first step is to know that the life-energy which normally operates in us, upholding the body, upholding the operations of the mind, is only a fragment of the total life-force kept at our disposal. We utilise only a fragment and we are thus limited in our effectivity. If we can open our doors, free our channels to the inflow of the life-energy from the sea of life-energy around us, then we can become aware of the immense potentialities, on every level of our being, that still wait to be tapped. By opening ourselves to the universal life-force, by linking our individual life-force with that, a means of communication can be established. In the traditional yogas this is done by pranayama and other exercises, as in the Rajayoga or the Hathayoga. Sri Aurobindo points out that it is also possible to do it by the exercise of concentration and application of our higher mental will. It is possible to exert that will, purify the nerve channels and consciously invoke the larger-life-force to flow into us.

And that is not the end. For even then, even if we start receiving the universal life-force, it is not the highest form of force or energy that the divine Shakti takes in the universe. It is only a lower formulation; higher than the life-energy there is the mental energy, the pure mental energy that seeks to impress itself, impose itself on the physical and the life energies, give them a direction, stamp its will. And corresponding to this mental energy is a mental consciousness, a higher mental consciousness, wide, intense, powerful, which can control even the sea of life-force around and make it do what it wills.

Normally our mental energies and life-energies are hopelessly mixed up. The mental will and the will in the life-force, the vital will, are either at war with each other or one subjugates the other and both are mixed. In yoga it is a necessary part of the self-observation and practice to disentangle the mind from the life-force, the activities of life-force—the activities of desire, passion, ambition, all the vital movements through which the life-force throws itself out for domination. The mind has to be trained to detach and disinvolve itself from these entanglements.

Still higher than the mental energy is the pure energy of the spirit, the spiritual energy. When we are in a happy position to feel the working of this higher power of the spirit, we become conscious of both the purusha and the prakriti in their purified aspects. It is here, when the higher power of the spirit starts working, that prakriti is seen to be not something different from the purusha but the power of the purusha or the purusha himself as power, the purusha as prakriti. Once the initial detachment is effected between the purusha and prakriti, the purusha can exercise his will on the movements of prakriti very spontaneously and actively. When this is done, the ascending soul, the aspiring soul can take up a number of positions. One is, in the light of this experience, that all is a working of the power of the spirit; we can elevate the mental life, the mind-governed life that we normally lead to the highest level of the mind, the sattvic level—enlightened, calm, balanced, reflecting the higher light. That is a state which many have attained or can attain.

The second is to normalise the spiritual consciousness, to subject everything to the choice and working of the soul, the spiritual element in us. Whether this spiritual life covers the entire area or only a select area is another matter. We can also choose to acquire and rest in the silence, the static aspect. We let the outer nature carry on but ignore it, concentrating on that silence aiming at an eventual nirvana. But it is also possible, as in this teaching, to base ourselves on the silence and open up the higher levels of the being dynamically to the heights leading to the supramental. But this basis of silence is indispensable and in all these steps the human will alone is not enough. We have to summon the aid of a higher power—call it what you will, see it where you will—maybe through the teacher, maybe through a direct evocation; a power different and higher than the human power is necessary to evoke, establish and normalise the higher states or levels of being nearer to the supramental.

In this process the mind becomes conscious of the higher levels of the purusha or of the prakriti. When it becomes conscious more and more on the side of the purusha, according to its line of evolution, we realise the Divine as the one Self, the Supreme Being, the Purushottama. But if we realise the higher aspect of prakriti in the Divine we become aware of a vast force, a great power, the cosmic Mahashakti.

Though these two realisations are alternately possible, it is also possible, if we lay stress on integration, to have a double oneness. Both the Self and the Mahashakti, both the Purushottama and the Mahashakti can be realised, and actually the individual soul is intended to provide this meeting place, this junction for the Supreme Purusha and the Supreme Shakti to meet and manifest. The individual is the nodus, the soul is the centre through which the Purusha and the Shakti—the enlightened Prakriti—can manifest.

Here again we cannot act on our own. We have to call in the Mahashakti who knows, who has the total wisdom to effect the integration, now to emphasise one aspect, now another and thus to integrate both in a supreme unity.

(From Questions & Answers)

In the question of law, whether the law is only on the material plane and things are fluid on other planes, the truth is not so simple. There is a Law governing the whole universe from the bottom to the top. Each plane has its own law. The material law does not operate in the life-plane; the life-law does not operate on the mental plane. But in our universe all the planes are intermingled. In man, for instance, all the seven planes are embedded. The physical body has life-force in it, has the mind in it. It depends on where we put our weight, where we live more. If we live more in the material consciousness we are bound by the rigidity of material laws. If, by nature, we are more prone to sail with our life-force, to feel light, we are less rigid, more fluidic, more open to changes. But that in itself is not an advantage. Somewhere a ballast is required; it is the divine intention to balance one with the other. Rigidity is less but there is too much fluidity, so the mind comes in to keep a balance. In the process the mind may be absorbed by the tamas of the body or the movement of the life-force. It is as one evolves that one learns the art and the science of harmonising the working of the different laws for the progress of the soul.

Q. : Can the knowledge of the universal laws that you call rigid be gained ?

A. : Yes, it can come as we open to the universal consciousness, it can also come as we begin to grow consciously within ourselves, when we start disciplining ourselves. Instead of being led by our habits, we practise self-observation, self-modification and we come to know to what extent we are still held by the material rigidity, tossed about by the fluid life-force in which vital imagination plays a great part, or governed by the mental operations limiting things, looking at things from narrow points of view.

*   *

Even in the universal mind we are not free from the operation of the lower prakriti. The lower prakriti extends up to the levels where the spiritual mind begins. Till then the rule of ignorance prevails and the universe is within the triple formula of ignorance. We begin to get released as we ascend the spiritual levels.

Q. : At what level does one begin to feel the higher power ?

A. : The power does not wait till you come to that level. Even when you are striving there are flashes of light, there are emanations of that power that come to you and give you an opportunity to acclamatise yourself to them and they in turn help you also to rise above the hold of ignorance. It is precisely these visitations that are called spiritual experiences. When they are organised and built into permanent form they become realisation.

19

THE ACTION OF THE DIVINE SHAKTI

We have now got a conception of what the Divine Shakti is. It is a timeless power of the Divine working in terms of time, spread over all the levels of the universe of which we are a part, working to produce results on the universal scale as also on the individual. We perceive it, from our level of intelligence, as a universal energy, an energy that takes appropriate forms on different levels. We see it working as physical energy, also as a tremendous life-energy, and as an energy flowing in terms of thought at the mental level. Everywhere it is the massive aspect, the unlimited nature of the power, the energy, that we are confronted with.

And yet, individually most of us feel that the energy which is real to us is only a limited energy. We know only that much energy—physical, vital or mental —as is embodied in us, that quantum over which we have control, which follows our will. Actually, Sri Aurobindo points out, what we think to be our individual will or individual energies are not our own. They are only small inlets from the universal ocean of energies, but we feel them limited, we feel a certain constriction around them and we are unable to feel their universal character in their action in our system because our ego comes forward and claims certain areas of the action of energies as its own, blocks off the rest as not its own, as something foreign. This arbitrary division by the ego between oneself and others is what strikes at the root of experiencing the universal character of the energies.

This is so only at the lower levels of the working of the energies. By discipline, by keeping the larger vision before us, and by a sustained effort at extension of ourselves, it is possible, step by step, to arrive at an identity with the universal energies. This is what is called, at the level of energies, universalisation.

Even when our energies are fused with the universal energies as a result of this process of self-enlargement, we should note that the overall stamp on these universal energies continues to be one of the inferior nature, consisting of the three modes, gunas—sattva, rajas and tamas. The perspective is broader, the field is larger, but the character, by and large, continues to be the same. It is possible, however, to break out of this bond of inferior nature by becoming conscious not only of the universal force, the universal prakriti, but also of the fact that this prakriti exists because there is a Person, a purusha behind it. The seeker gradually shifts his gaze from the prakriti to what sustains that prakriti, the purusha, the Divine Being, the One Person who sustains the myriad currents of the universal energy.

As we mentally understand and psychologically and spiritually take our poise in this status of the purusha, gradually there is a detachment, an aloofness, from the action of the gunas, the modes of inferior nature. This detachment, aloofness, gradually develops into a movement which leads towards mastery of the lower nature. As we get progressively released from the compulsive hold of lower nature and develop in the higher nature, we realise that the purusha and prakriti are not really two different things, but are one and the same. The prakriti is the purusha himself in his aspect of power, in his aspect of executive energy and the identification with the purusha extends itself to the truth behind the prakriti. We approach an identity with both Nature and Being, the Lord and his Puissance.

But the process is long, and the first step in this process is for the ego, for the individual acting in terms of the ego, to surrender to this Shakti which is active. And the action of this higher power, in the very nature of things, cannot be continuously at the same level of vibration and intensity. Its force, its action, is felt intermittently. There are ups and downs, days and nights, periods when we feel consciously the action of the shakti, and times when we see only the results but are not conscious of the working. A link has to be established between our mind and the spiritual consciousness, the spiritual heights, as we develop spiritually, which enables this action to become gradually continuous, without a decisive break at any time.

How to surrender? Surrender is a word, the practice leading to the fulfilment of surrender is yoga. The individual has first to give up the sense of the doer, the ego's claim to be the instrument. He should move beyond the position of being an instrument. The doer also—not only the impeller but even the doer—is the shakti. Once he eliminates the ego-appropriation of being the instrument, of the sense of the doer, he gradually opens to the workings of the higher power. Stationed in that working, he cultivates and practises, moment to moment, what Sri Aurobindo calls the Gita ideal of *samatā*, equanimity, equality. If he is not the doer, if he does not have his eye on the fruit or the result, if it is something else that moves him, that works through him, he had better leave the results also to that power. So whatever the result, there is not the longing for a particular result, there is not the straining towards the fruit. It is left to the Shakti, to the power and there is a resultant tranquil sense of equanimity whatever the result.

As this *samatā*, equanimity, deepens, gradually there is an awakening to the presence of the Self—not only at the individual level but also at the universal level. He opens to the Self behind the universal Shakti and to the experience of becoming, for however short a time, one with this Self in a total non-involvement, a total detachment. The interest continues, he continues to witness, to follow what is going on but without any claim, without claim for the action going on or over the results that are to ensue. This realisation of unity with the Self also is not the final step. In certain yogas, indeed, it is, but in the integral path the realisation of the Self is only a door opening to a larger and more consequent realisation, the surrender to the Master of the being. And the Master of the universe and the Master of ourselves is the same divine Person.

Thus there are, as we look around—three powers of the Divine. There is the individual, the Jiva, the evolving soul. Next, God, the reality manifest as a ruling power, not an impersonal state but someone, some Person who can be approached, with whom we can enter into relation. We cannot enter into relation with an impersonal state like silence or nirvana or peace or even Ananda. We can only enter into a relation with a self-formation which lends itself consciously to conscious experience, and that is God. The reality turned towards manifestation, taking a form which can be identified with, which lends itself for conscious relation, is God. The third term is Nature. Nature is the universal power taking myriad forms, coursing through many movements and linking in a way the Jiva and God.

What is the relation of the Jiva, the individual, with

God and Nature? The first relation he realises is that he is a portion of God, what is called in the Gita an eternal portion of Himself; he shares the eternity of the parent Being. He is a portion, a parcel of the divine Being. He has also a relation with Nature—not Nature as we have understood it, the physical nature, but Nature in all its grades, which as we have seen is a self-formulation of the divine Being. The individual realises himself to be a product of the higher nature, the spiritual nature of which the physical nature is only an outer mode. He has been formed by this nature out of the being of God. Sri Aurobindo quotes the two famous formulas: *So'ham*, He am I; and to express the relation with nature, *parā prakṛtir jīvabhūtā* the supreme Nature has become the Jiva.

These are the two spiritual formulas which enshrine the relation that the individual realises with God and with Nature. But our experience in day-to-day life is different. We behave as if we are separate from others, separate from God, and we must guard ourselves from nature. That is, as we said, due to the intervention of the claims of the ego. Ego compartmentalises, ego fragments, ego cuts as under what God has made one. Then why is ego allowed to do it? Because it was a necessity in the process of natural evolution to give a fixity to the flux of the life movement; to centralise the vague movements of mental and life-energies, an ego point was constructed by nature around which all the movements could be organised. But with the arrival of the stage of self-awareness in man, the time has certainly come for this *ad hoc* arrangement to give place to a more natural arrangement. The ego has served its purpose and now it should dissolve itself or should be dissolved by our will so that the true centre, the true point of centralisation, the inner psychic being or the soul, may come forward and occupy its place which today is occupied by the pseudo-self or the pseudo-soul, the desire-soul, the ego. The ego has to be taught to surrender itself, to indentify itself with the true self. Of course in the process of identification the ego tends to evaporate and that is just as well.

There are certain dangers, however, in opening ourselves to the universal workings of the Shakti without the proper knowledge, without having spiritual discrimination. The first danger, and usually a very common danger, is that the ego tends to exploit the Shakti. It wants the Shakti to flow in, it opens all the doors of the being for the inpouring and the action of the universal Shakti. But once things start, the ego begins its subtle claims and exploits the mighty workings of the Shakti for its own purposes—self-aggrandisement, fame, constituting itself as the lord of its limited empire. This claiming to be an instrument of God, but in practice turning God into its instrument, is a danger. The ego always has very specious explanations and it puts suggestions which catch us unawares. We should know that we are but puny creatures. It is only the mighty Force, an impulsion from God which moves us in our best moments that effects the results. It is enough if we don't obstruct it, but it is unpardonable to call in the Force and when the divine Shakti works, to appropriate the workings for the ego. The ego wants the higher force to work in a particular way, according to its dictates, so that it could aggrandise its own interests.

Here comes the role of purification. Unless we arrive at a minimum of purification it is dangerous to invoke the higher power to work in us. The first step in this purification is the withdrawal of the mental purusha from activity. There is an immediate sense of liberation when we so disentangle ourselves from the innumerable rounds of the working force. It is not enough to withdraw, to stand back. Sri Aurobindo says that we have to use our will to raise ourselves into our higher spiritual status. That is, the dynamic part in us must not be left high and dry but should be uplifted into the higher spiritual state, a transition has to be effected from the witness state to the status of mastery. And it is only when we are conscious that we are in the presence of the Master of our being, the Master of works, the Master of sacrifice, that a movement of true surrender forms itself. Once that culminates in an utter surrender, the Master takes charge of our being directly or through his Shakti and the battle is won.

(From Questions & Answers)

There is an identification with the Self, it may or may not move you into action. There is an identification with the Shakti where mostly you are moved into activity. There is an identity on the purusha side of the Divine, there is the identity on the nature side. It is given to the individual to choose which he would have first. If it is to the purusha, the stress is more on the witness, on the transcendental aspect. If it is to the nature side—naturally the higher nature—it is in movement, it is in action. And it is in the scheme of Divine manifestation that both the purusha and the nature recognise each other, fuse into each other, confess themselves to each other in the individual. The individual, the Jiva, is the meeting place, so to say, of the purusha and the shakti.

The first tendency of the mental purusha when he withdraws from action or keeps action on the surface and takes his poise in a silence is for passivity. But it is

13

possible, that instead of living in that passivity one can impart a more kinetic nature to one's life. There is what Sri Aurobindo calls a kinetic yoga, a yoga that proceeds through action from the imperfect to the less imperfect and the beginnings of the perfect and then more and more perfect action. It starts with subordinating myself to the power. I am the doer, no doubt—I do not have, at the outset, the consciousness that I am not the doer. Mentally I may know, but the whole being feels that it is the doer, very well. I can at least start with the recognition that I am a subordinate doer. The Shakti, the higher power works through me. It is easy for an enlightened or a seeking mind to accept this position. As this sense of subordination deepens and I grow in the divine quality of humility, humbleness, I come to recognise in time that I am only a servant. From the doer the sense changes into being a servant of the Shakti. That too is a step, though not the final step. The next step is that all is done by the Shakti. It does not need me, even as a servant. I am just a point through which the universal Shakti individualises itself and goes on to effect what it wants. So all is done by the Shakti. That too is a stage. If I am content to stay at this level accepting the Shakti as supreme and the final truth—as certain traditions in India do—that is a way, but it is a half-way.

I have to become conscious of what is behind the Shakti, that is the Self. Behind the Shakti there is the Shākta, and in each individual behind the motive-force, behind the energy, there is someone who wields that power through the will and that is the Ishwara, the Lord. It is his will that is effectuated by his power. The Shakti as such does not have an independent reality apart from the divine Master. And just as I realise myself first as a servant and then as a point through which the Shakti flows, I also realise myself to be a small portion, an infinitesimal part—though a significant and a meaningful part—of the Divine Being, the Divine Ruler, the Ishwara.

The next step—Sri Aurobindo just indicates the possibility—is after one realises oneself to be a part, small or big, of the Divine, the next realisation that opens its vistas is that of embodying the Divine. That is, one is so much completely identified and merged in the Divine Being that one becomes the Divine itself. There is no difference left. The Divine Being, the Divine Consciousness is wholly there—nothing separate of myself is left anywhere. I am one with it and I am it.

Q.: *What is the difference between avatar and vibhuti?*

A.: A vibhuti is a phenomenon when a divine quality or a divine power acts through an individual; it is something super-human, pre-eminently a divine power beyond the normal range of human faculties. For purposes of evolution the Divine puts out such emanations of its power, its knowledge, its various verities and either these emanations take human birth, do their work and withdraw or they manifest in some extraordinarily developed evolving beings. There need not be a divine consciousness accompanying it. One may feel that it is his own power. Napoleon always felt that it was his own power, Shivaji did not go to that extent. There are other vibhutis, Shakespeare for instance, who are not conscious of the origin of the divine power they wield, but an avatar is not that.

An avatar is a descent of the Divine Consciousness, along with all the powers implicit in that Consciousness, on earth in a form—usually a human form, as Mother points out—and that form is conscious always, whether he expresses it or not, that he is divine. The divine nature of the consciousness is always there. The avatar comes once in a while at crucial junctures in the progress of human evolution, but vibhutis come comparatively frequently. They take birth and effectuate the divine will in different spheres of activity—maybe in statecraft, maybe in literature, maybe in science, maybe in the military field and so on. All fields are proper fields for the divine work and these radiations of the divine powers are called vibhutis.

Sri Aurobindo points out in his elaborate discussion on the subject in *The Essays on the Gita* that an avatar can be a vibhuti, an avatar need not have only a divine consciousness but he may also have certain powers in a striking manner. So that extent he has the vibhuti aspect also. But a vibhuti is never an avatar. The vibhuti is a secondary delegation, a limited formation for a limited purpose. A number of vibhutis prepare the field, prepare for the advent of an avatar.

Q.: If an avatar does not come in human form then what other form would it take?

A.: You must have heard the parable of ten avatars in the Indian tradition. It is not just a story. If evolution is a fact and it has passed through so many stages, at each level of transition the Divine has to embody itself in that form to effect, at a physical level, the transition.

Q.: But now there cannot be any more animals, it must be a human form?

A.: Yes, because that stage is over. There is a stage when a new form has to appear so the avatar usually takes that form, either ready or in the making. And the work of the avatar during his life period is to prepare for the establishment of that form, the corresponding consciousness and power in that form.

*   *

The Mother says on this question that there is a universal healing power in the cosmos. Its function is to heal, make whole. Obviously it derives from the plane of ananda, delight, but each one expresses it according to his level. There are those who give it a totally physical form by the laying of hands etc., there are those who can direct that healing force through the mind, through simple vibrations. Naturally the level at which you receive and put out that healing power of God makes a difference.

You can say that the healing power is a part of the functioning of the universal Shakti. The universal Shakti has its aspect of knowledge, its aspect of power, its aspect of delight. And delight can't come where there is fragmentation, where there is a limitation, lacunae. So the role of delight, or what flows from the delight, is to make whole.

*   *

If we are content to shut ourselves in one realisation we are allowed to do that. The soul is always given a freedom by the Divine to choose its direction of evolution, to choose its goal also.

Q.: Can one choose whether one will realise the purusha or the nature or can one realise both and if so, can both realisations come simultaneously?

A.: Why not? One can choose first this and next that. They can go on simultaneously, but one of them has to happen first. It depends upon your line of evolution whether you are more purusha oriented or nature oriented, whether you are more active and dynamic in nature or tending to be more passive and silent. One can prepare the field for the other.

*   *

It is not simply a succession. In spiritual or mystical

matters when they speak of lineage it does not mean that one man goes and another comes in to occupy the chair. It does not. When a tradition or a path or a yoga or a teaching starts, there is a divine impulsion, a divine consciousness fathering that movement. First it works through the person chosen. And the next person who occupies the seat is not merely one who has a spiritual realisation on his own account, but one who continues this charge of divine consciousness which the first person carried. That is why we see that even when the person occupying that throne or seat is ordinary, what he does has a different effect. Among the other disciples there may be more gifted people, more developed people, but they can't deliver the goods in the manner in which the person in the seat of authority can do. That is because of that charge of consciousness which is transmitted from person to person. Of course, in course of time things fall into disuse and the consciousness dissipates; afterwards they remain just figureheads. That is the truth behind the *paramparā* or the lineage.

Q.: You mentioned about purity and how purification takes place. Can you aspire towards purity by aspiring towards vastness?

A.: Yes. In the Upanishads there are passages which call for vastness to acquire purity. But there are also other passages in other Upanishads which speak of purity in terms of heights of consciousness or depths of consciousness. The point is there are certain movements which release you from the hold of impure nature. Now nature being practically ubiquitous, you have to tackle the problem from different points. To extend yourself is one way of getting release from the hold of ego. But there is still the hold of nescience; you must exceed the lower nature.

Then there is also the purity of the consciousness, the divinity that can be evoked from within. You go not downwards, but within and from there bring out the psychic or the soul-light or the soul-power which dissipates the impurities. So for a seeker all the three are necessary—to go deep, to go wide, to go high, Each has its time and role.

20

FAITH AND SHAKTI

We have so far spoken of perfection in its three limbs—
the perfection of the instrumental being, the mind, the
mental intelligence, the heart and its emotions, the vital
energies and the physical body; perfection of the soul
powers, four of them; and perfection of surrender to
the Divine Power, to the Divine Shakti. Now all these
movements, necessary movements, towards perfection
are not possible without a supporting faith, and what is
faith?

Faith is an assent of the being to a truth, to an ideal,
to an idea, to something which it wants to reach, to
realise, to embody. Elsewhere Sri Aurobindo describes
faith as the soul's witness to a truth that is yet to gain
acceptance by the external being. The soul has perceived,
the inner being has perceived and that knowledge of the
inner being communicates itself to the surface being as
faith. Faith is a natural, spontaneous conviction that
this is so and this is not. Now this assent of the whole
being is indispensable in the path of perfection. Faith in
what? First, faith in the Divine. There is a divine
Intelligence, a divine Reality that exists and that is
expressing itself. Faith in the Shakti, the power of the
Divine to effectuate its will, to work out the manifestation. If we do not have faith in the Divine or in the
divine Power which are the supreme powers of perfection, we cannot tread the path.

But that is not enough. To have faith in the divine
Reality or the divine Lord and the divine Mother, the
Shakti, is not enough. We must have faith in our own

capacity to tread the path, to stick to the path. It is easy enough to be attracted to a path, but to stick it out we cannot do unless we have the faith that it is worthwhile exerting ourselves because the goal is sure to be reached one day.

And the enemy of faith is doubt. Wherever we have faith, confidence, the mind also poses a doubt: supposing it is not so, supposing it is otherwise, we are unnerved, the whole nervous being sinks. At any rate the first experience of doubt, attack on faith, is that however strong the faith, for a moment we tend to falter because a possibility is shown with such vividness that it could be that the faith is moonshine, is misplaced. Somebody has said so and we blindly believe or it could be a wrong perception. Is it wise to tie up ourselves with this project? This doubt can be an honest doubt, it can also be a mischief of the hostiles; the anti-divine forces which want to create division and delay, if not prevent us from advancing on the path:

This said, it does not mean that all doubts are wrong, and this is the danger. If we take it that all doubts are wrong there is no problem, but the trouble is that some doubts are legitimate. Not doubts regarding the fundamentals of faith like faith in the Divine, faith in the rightness of the path, even faith in our capacity— because once we choose a path it means we are chosen for it. Doubt has a certain legitimacy where half-truths, half-way measures and half-way stations are concerned. The path is long and perfection is not achieved in a day. The whole course of spiritual evolution proceeds from ignorance to less ignorance, from half-light to light, from light to greater light. In the process many things change. Ideas, opinions and convictions which are valid today become out-of-date tomorrow because we have travelled, grown into a newer consciousness and the old thoughts and ideas which suited once do not suit any-more. A person lives wordly life, he has a family and he has duties, responsibilities to his children, wife, parents. But if he receives a call and takes to the spiritual path he may be obsessed, troubled by those loyalties. Then a doubt can very well arise that those loyalties do not apply any more because he is no more a member of the family. He is an aspirant, a seeker to whom the whole truth is the Divine and not truths of the family. That way doubt plays a useful role in the growth, in discarding values that are no more relevant, that have become out-of-date. This applies not only in intellectual and mental ideas but even in spiritual matters.

There are experiences and experiences. No one experience can be treated as a whole, shutting out all other possible experiences. Then there is the load of superstition, wrong formulations that have encrusted the past traditions; there also no liberation from that ignorance and wrong belief would be possible unless rational doubts were permitted and allowed to play their role. This is the use of doubt. You can take it that everything in God's creation has a purpose, a use. Things become misfit, dangerous only when they outlive their utility and seek to poach in domains which are not their legitimate concern.

In this faith in the possibility of perfection, it is inevitable that a number of minor faiths crumble down. Faith in colleagues, faith in mental reconciliations and compromises, acceptance of certain standards as neces-sary for the norms etc. are possibilities. But the divine Shakti that works strikes down many such faiths in order to create place for new faiths. Left to himself, man would be a prisoner of his smaller, more convenient

faith. He would not care to grow. But when the hour
arrives the old faiths become jailors in a prison house,
and the divine Shakti, strikes. One feels as in a wilder-
ness, having lost the old moorings, old supports, till new
ones take their place. One is at sea. This happens in the
life of almost every seeker and these are the periods of
confusion, what the old masters called the periods of test.
But as long as we have a basic faith in perfection, basic
faith in the Shakti we stand it. We know it is an inevitable
process. These smaller, incomplete, imperfect faiths have
to go so that more perfect, more whole faiths take their
place.

Then we must have faith that the influence from
the Spirit, the impartial Spirit, is active for the liberation and the perfection of man. There is a grace, there
is a compassion, there is a helping consciousness—we
have that faith. And this influence goes on acting as a
leavening agent in the strife and stress of life. One may
succumb to temptation, one may take wrong path even
under honest beliefs, one may fall, but one can always
be sure of standing up again as long as one has deep
faith in the reality of the path and in the certainty of
reaching the goal. To analyse; first is the faith in the
principle of liberation, the principle of perfection, the
principle of spiritual evolution. We must have that faith.
Once we have it we accept all the consequences. If we
have a doubt that this world may after all be an illusion
and all this talk of perfection is just speculation, then we
may succumb at any moment. That cardial faith in the
basic objective and the possibility of realising these objec-
tives in this life must be there firmly embedded—faith
in the principle. Then next, faith in our power to achieve,
not only at the end but even now—what Sri Aurobindo
calls a working faith. We may be imperfect, our know-

ledge may be incomplete, we may be weaklings, but
still we have certain circumstances helping us, we have
the guidance assured to us, we have the teacher, we
have the field—well, we exert ourselves and to the extent
that we do so, even if we commit mistakes, we will be
seen through. A working, practical faith is enough to
start and go a long way. And in the growth of this
faith it is necessary, Sri Aurobindo warns us, that we
do not erect any premature certitudes. As we grow,
as we evolve, we see that truths which apply in one
sphere do not necessarily apply in other spheres and the
Shakti strikes them down without mercy. We must
always have a plasticity. When a faith is proved wrong,
we have only to discard it. When the framework changes,
our faith, our beliefs also have to enlarge themselves,
modify themselves. So Sri Aurobindo cautions: do not
have any premature certitudes, and even if you have,
have the faith in the Shakti that what is premature will
be removed and what is permanent will take its place.
Recognise also that there is always a possibility of error.
Till the last threads of ignorance are removed, the last
shade of ignorance is dispelled, no one can be sure that
he is always right. There is always the possibility of error.
We must never be cocksure that we are right and others
are wrong, never feel that we can do no wrong. We never
know because we are not of one part. The enlightenment that the mind has, the enlightenment that the
heart has, may not be active in the vital or in the physical mind, for instance. So it is just possible that under
our very nose things may be going wrong. This possibility of error must be recognised. It is usually the ego
which asserts, 'I can do no wrong.' That can never be
so till we are completely transformed down to the last
cell and the supramental consciousness suffuses our

being. We cannot say that all our movements are only movements of truth; there is always the possibility of mixture, possibility of error and these possibilities of error are well recognised in spiritual life. They can take place on any level. To start with the level of mind, our beliefs, our philosophies, our placings of things in life are true at a certain level of understanding, but as the understanding grows, widens, we may have to modify them.

These are what are called the steps of Shakti. As the Yoga Shakti develops in us, as the workings of the higher Shakti expand and take root in us, these possibilities are thrown before us again and again emphasising the necessity to change our rigid stance, to have certain plasticities in our mental make up. Similarly, the assent of the heart and life to these steps of the Shakti, to these incidental and necessary changes of poise, changes of perspectives, is indispensable. Not only the mind, but the heart and life also are so much involved in certain workings, in some experiences, that they cling to them as the very guarantee of truth. May be, but it is a lesser truth as we will realise one day. Greater truths take their place and it is time that the heart and the life let them go without pain, without regret. There are truths and truths, formations and formations, which are best described as steps of the growing spirit, and the steps have to be free.

Then there has to be the ascent of the soul. Because even in matters pertaining to the soul, which are necessarily purer, there is always an intrusion of occult experience. In the West they call it psychic experience, we call it occult experience. They need not have anything to do with the soul but they interfere with spiritual experiences and a time does come when the seeker has to choose the spiritual and relegate the occult to the background. Even in the spiritual experiences there are various types of experiences. It will not do to accept any one experience as total or final. Each experience, however great, prepares for a still greater experience.

Many of the traditionalists made the mistake of accepting one capital experience as the final one and were in a hurry to formulate it in mental terms, erect philosophies, taking it as the sole truth of the spiritual life or the destiny of man. Today, however, we cannot afford to take those limited views. Each spiritual experience is to be taken as valid in its place, but it cannot shut out other possible spiritual experiences. If my spiritual experience is great for me, I should have the spiritual humility to recognise that your experience is equally great for you, and who knows, one day I may find it to be greater than my own! This gradation of spiritual experience is very important and the soul's faith shall not be shaken when this truth is revealed to the soul. Faith has to be enlarging, comprehensive, accommodating to new experiences, new realisations.

Apart from these individual assents of faith, there has to be the assent of the whole being to the presence and the guidance of God and his Shakti.

It is impermissible to have a lack of faith in one's own discrimination and capacity. To have constant self-distrust, to be constantly defeatist, is a tamasic movement. The opposite is a rajasic pride: "I have the truth, I have experience, anything else is inferior." An ideal seeker has to be free from either of them—constant self-distrust on one side and an offensive spiritual pride on the other. We must know, we must realise, that the Power that effects is the Divine's. It is not possible for the puny human power with which we are endowed to negotiate all these corners, to tread the path all alone. It is His power that guides, His power that shows, His power that lifts us up and puts us across when there are difficult channels.

Finally we must have the faith and the vision to see that whatever the field of life nothing is impossible to the Shakti, the Divine Power which Sri Aurobindo again describes here as the four-fold manifestation of the Divine Puissance—the Shakti effectuating the divine will in the realm of knowledge, light, enlightenment; in the realm of power, strength; in the realm of beauty, wealth; in the realm of work and continuous perfection. This is possible for the Shakti because behind the Shakti is the one who wields the Shakti, the Ishwara. As Sri Aurobindo describes in *The Life Divine*, the Shakti is the Lord himself in the poise of action, dynamic action. There is one Will at work in the universe and it is the Will of the Supreme Lord. This is the climax of faith, when we see in every movement and every moment the working of the Supreme Will through so many instruments. The prime one is the Divine Shakti. That is the last word in faith.

(From Questions & Answers)

Q. : *If the integral yoga consists of having all the different realisations one after the other including nirvana, how does one re-emerge from extinction?*

A.: Extinction comes only when you pursue the path of nirvana exclusively to the end. But in this yoga you take that experience, that realisation of silence and immobility, and aspire for the dynamic element of the Divine from that foundation. You don't move towards the extreme of nirvana, even as you do not always engage yourself in the extreme of the path of works;

you always take care to maintain touch with the immutable Self, with the Silence. So throughout there is an integrated approach, not a one-sided, exclusive thrust. The ancients, those who spoke of extinction, found it very tempting to leave the problem to others. They even convinced themselves that there was really no problem. It is only as long as we are in that flux that we feel a problem. But here one does not pursue that way. One takes the experience or realisation of nirvana for what it is worth and what it is intended to give in the perfection of life and makes it an element of perfection.

21

THE NATURE OF THE SUPERMIND

We have now arrived at a stage where the discussion approaches the concept and the constitution of the supermind. Naturally, these portions are somewhat stiff because they deal with areas which are not familiar to the human thought as it has developed so far. Still we shall try our best to understand and assimilate—at least in substance—what is described here. Perhaps those of you who have read the *Life Divine* would detect some difference in his description of the supermind and its workings in the *Synthesis* and what he wrote later on in the second volume of the *Life Divine*. That was inevitable and Sri Aurobindo himself wanted to revise and recast what he had written, particularly in the later chapters, but that was not to be. However, what has been written gives us an idea of the labour ahead and the present chapter deals with the nature of supermind.

The supermind is the goal of the integral yoga, and the supermind, as you know, is not something that is higher than mind, some kind of magnified mind; it is a consciousness or a Truth-Will which is clearly above the highest domains of the mind. The highest levels of the mind are the overmind, the overmental levels; even beyond those levels are those of the supermind. The supermind also has its gradations, a number of them, and the seeker has to ascend them step by step. The integral yoga which aims to realise the truth of the supermind means a radical change of consciousness— consciousness in the mind, in the heart, in the life-regions, and even in the physical down to the sub-

14

conscient. And such a radical change of consciousness as this cannot be achieved by the traditional paths of yoga. That is why out of decades of experience and realisation Sri Aurobindo has chalked out what we today call the integral yoga. In other words it is called the yoga of self-perfection and this yoga which we have traced so long goes step by step, beginning with purification—purification of the instrumental being, the mind, the emotions, the life-energies, the physical energies. Purification is followed by liberation of the self from the knots of nature; and once this liberation is achieved in a certain measure, an attainment of equality, a spirit of equality which receives the impacts of life with detachment and equanimity. All these prepare the being for the direct action of the Divine Shakti. Even as it is, the action goes on, but indirectly through several inferior formulations of that Shakti in ignorance. But the direct action of that Shakti can take place after the preliminary steps of this path of perfection have been taken.

With the action of the higher Shakti proceeding apace, the perfection of the instrumental nature becomes possible. Till then however much we may purify, however much we may discipline them, there is always an element of ignorance; an element of inconscience pulling them down and diluting the working of the higher Shakti. But as the direct action proceeds, the instruments shed their past legacy and they are given a new turn and set to working in new dimensions. Perfection of the instruments becomes possible.

But through what medium is this Divine Shakti to operate? As things stand, it is through our mind that it has to act. Mind is the highest faculty so far evolved by nature and naturally it has to act through the mind, but mind as it is is not equal to the situation. What is

required to function as an unsullied and an uninterfering
instrument of the Divine Shakti is, let us say, a kind of
mind which is receptive to the Truth, expresses the
Truth, embodies in a certain measure the Truth and also
wields the will to translate this Truth into action or to
express it, manifest it. Our normal human mind is far,
far from being able to discharge these functions. It is
only what Sri Aurobindo calls the Gnostic Mind, the
Mind that is based on Truth-Knowledge, established in
Truth-Power that can function as the effective instrument of the Divine Shakti. And this Gnostic Mind is
what is termed *vijnāna* in the ancient Indian system,
what Sri Aurobindo calls the supermind.

What is the fundamental nature of the supermind
if it has to replace our evolving human mind and function as the leader of evolution? We should understand
in what way it differs both in nature and function from
our mind. In the first place the knowledge that is natural
to the gnostic mind is a knowledge by identity and oneness. The knowledge that our mind commands is, after
all, a separative knowledge. The mind holds itself separate from the object of knowledge, studies it as something
other than itself, and arrives at a formulation of perception, constructs a structure of what it calls knowledge; the
approach being from outside, we can be pretty sure that
the knowledge is not the full or the complete knowledge
of the object. We know only as much as our mind can
skim on the surface of what it holds to be separate. But
the gnostic mind does not have to seek for this kind of
knowledge with the aid of reasoning, based upon sense-
data as our mind does. It has a special faculty of embra-
cing, becoming one with, comprehending the object of
knowledge. In fact at that level there is not this distinc-

tion between the knower, the known and the link of knowledge. There is a oneness of consciousness.

Some idea, though not the full idea, can be had from the analogy of ourselves knowing what goes on within us. We become angry, we become happy—we know we are happy. We do not separate the happiness from ourselves. There is a certain identity at a deeper level and by oneness the knowledge is natural. I know I am happy, I know I am angry — I do not need to convince myself with logical aids. I do not need to study it, I have only to look at it and I know what I am. Similarly, though in a different way, the knowledge of identity and of oneness that the gnostic mind commands at all times is its natural and most important possession. It does not have to concentrate upon an object, assess it, go round and round, but has only to direct its gaze and immediately the knowledge arises. At a deeper level my consciousness and the consciousness in the object become one. The moment I want to know, my consciousness covers, comprehends the consciousness that is in that object and that yields its knowledge-content to my comprehending consciousness. The whole action takes place in a split second because the operation does not work according to our mechanical rules. It is a direct possession, a direct seizure of this knowledge, of the truth.

The poise of the gnostic mind being this, it is natural that the awareness that all is one, that the spirit is one everywhere—the oneness of creation, the oneness of forms, oneness at every level—is a self-evident truth to the gnostic mind. We have to convince our present mind, for instance, that all matter is one. My body is constituted of matter, the bodies of all are constituted of matter, so at that level all of us are made of the same matter and we are one. So too at the level of life, we all breathe the same life-force, are filled with the same life-force; it is the same life-energy, the universal ocean of life-energy that flows into all of us. There also we are one. So too on the mental plane. There is one universal mind of which our minds are so many self-postings. So also spiritually. The mind has to be convinced again and again till it gains a conviction that all is one. The world is one, behind all the various multiplicity of forms there is oneness of spirit which expresses itself at every level. This knowledge is natural to the supermind or the gnostic mind.

Sri Aurobindo adds a note of caution in pursuing the analogy of subjective knowledge too far, as far as the supermind is concerned. We spoke of being aware of becoming angry, of becoming happy, and so on. But even that gulf, that distinction between my mind and my body, the part in me that knows and the part that is known, does not obtain at the supramental level.

The second characteristic is that this knowledge is a total knowledge. The mind can only collect bits of knowledge, fragments of knowledge—it can know only one thing at a time. What it knows it may know thoroughly to that extent. But of things other than what it knows, it is not aware of. That is why the mind is a seeker of knowledge and the knowledge that is acquired is only in fragments. The supermind, the gnostic mind, has a total knowledge. And what is this totality? Certainly not the whole world only. The totality of which the gnostic mind is in possession in knowledge is the reality of the individual, the reality of the universe, the reality of the transcendent. It knows the totality of the scheme. It knows not only vertically but it also knows horizontally. This integral nature of knowledge is, again, a special character of the gnostic mind. Our mind is not capable of it.

We can conceive of the individual being, at its core, as a
formation of the Reality. The mind can also conceive
that the individual can merge in the universal. But at
the same time to think of the Transcendent and relate
itself to the Transcendent, is a thing which is not natural
to the mind, though the mind may have that faith. It is
not natural for the fragmenting mind to have a total
knowledge.

Thirdly, the gnostic mind is directly truth-conscious.
It does not have to proceed through grades of knowledge, through various stages of understanding to arrive
at the truth. The gnostic mind, being constituted directly
from the operation of the supramental consciousness, is
conscious of the truth directly. Our mind can conceive
of truth, but it is not directly conscious of the truth.
It has to pass through many grades, break through many
walls of ignorance. The background of mind is error;
the mental consciousness not being fully evolved, there is
always the element of error, limitation, restriction.

The supermind, Sri Aurobindo points out, is not
only the knower but also the creator. It knows, but what
it knows it wields the power to create, to manifest that
knowledge in form, in movement. The mind knows,
but what it knows it is not in a position to fully render
in terms of manifestation. But here, both the truth that
the supermind knows and the will that is the power of
that truth are in perfect balance; unlike the mind where
there may be knowledge but power may be lacking,
and to that extent the knowledge remains ineffective,
impotent. It may happen that the mind may have the
power, the dynamism, but it may lack the knowledge
to back up the power, which leads to an anarchic use of
that power. This defect is not there in the supermind
where truth and will are evenly balanced. And in the

higher grades, Sri Aurobindo points out, it is wrong
even to speak of truth and will as two separate things.
Truth and will fuse into one, truth is an aspect and will
is another aspect. Or to put it more simply, it is truth as
will. It is not truth *and* will, but truth *as* will. There is
absolutely no possibility of conflict between knowledge
and power in the supermind.

Wherever the supermind works, this combination
of knowledge and will being effective, things are always
kept in line with the vision behind. A thing is intended
to take a particular line of operation and the knowledge-
will behind it sees to it that it is followed. And it is a
reflection of this truth that has led to what we call the
perception of karma, necessity, fate; what we understand, at our level, as fate, necessity and karma, has
a truth behind it and that truth is that every manifestation being divine, the divine truth-power basing and
conducting every movement in creation sees to it that
it follows the Idea behind. And this imperious compulsion of truth gives the element of determination to
movements in manifestation. We call it karma, we call it
necessity which we can't escape, we call it fate which
governs us. Naturally the significance of fate, necessity
and karma changes once we understand the truth behind
these concepts. They are not mechanical determinants,
but original, luminous and conscious determinates of all
that goes on in the creation.

This knowledge-will has before it, mapped out, as
it were, in one vision the past, the present and the future.
Our mind can know only what is before it, it can recall
by memory—a secondary operation—what has gone
before; it can perhaps imagine what is going to be the
future but it can be sure of nothing. But the gnostic
mind has the entire expanse of time—past, present and

future—mapped out before it; and it may take its own time to effectuate what has been conceived, what has been embodied in the real Idea. There is not the human compulsion of time as far as the gnostic mind is concerned.

(From Questions & Answers)

Q.: *Is the gnostic mind capable of distinguishing between past, present and future?*

A.: Yes, the gnostic mind, as you will see later, has two operations—the comprehending action and the apprehending action. We are now speaking of the comprehending action. When it chooses to know point-wise, section-wise, part-wise, it changes its mode, it undergoes an apprehending movement of knowledge.

This Truth-Will on the cosmic scale is experienced as the active Light and Tapas, the light and force of Ishwara, the Lord. What they call the Ruler in religions and mythologies with different names is really this Truth-Will, this Light and Tapas governing the universe. At its level the Truth-Will is supreme. As it descends in creation it goes through several stages of self-modifications. After the gnostic level comes the intuition, the self-evident truth takes the form of intuition. And that intuition is there at every level—there is an intuition of the intellect, an intuition of the lower vital, an intuition of the sub-mental. Intuition, the flashing of truth, the certainty of truth, is only a projection of the gnostic truth, the gnostic knowledge. The gnostic knowledge cannot function directly at our level, it radiates itself in the form of intuition. When it is said that the supermind is involved in matter it is not a figure because supermind really means the Truth-Will, and if Truth-Will bases the whole creation, necessarily it must base every form in creation. In everything there must be the supermind involved. And what we call intelligence, a ray of consciousness or a spark of consciousness regulating things, controlling and guiding them, is nothing but this working of the involved supermind. When we begin to be aware of it at our level we call it instinct because an instinct, like intuition, like the supramental working, does not proceed according to reason. It does not collect data and then arrive at conclusions. There is a spontaneous feeling, a spontaneous perception in the mind that this is so and that is so. This is as a result of the action of the involved supermind veiled behind the mind, vital and physical. At· the purely material level we know that the energy at work in matter is self-directing, it leads to certain results. It may have a mechanical appearance, but all evidence points to the fact that it is self-guiding. It has an object and it reaches that object even without the intervention of the mind. We begin to get a greater evidence of the working of this gnostic consciousness when the vital creation starts. In the animal, for instance, there is the right instinct to take to things that are favourable, to avoid things that are unfavourable. This intuition that is active at the level of the animal reaches its height in the higher species of animals. But as the human mind develops, the instinct —which is a veiled operation of the intuition,—withdraws; that is the direction of evolution. It is the intention of nature that the consciousness has to evolve through the mental grades and not simply be directed by a blind instinct. As long as nature was following a certain course up to the level of man this veiled intuition called instinct was a governing force. But once man has appeared it is the mind that has to be developed, he has to work out his own guidance, in other words become

self-aware. That is why at the human level the instinct
has receded into the background and man is working
out the mental consciousness and is now reaching out
to the heights of intuition proper.

Finally, there is a difference—Sri Aurobindo notes
pointedly—between the supreme supermind as it is
there and the supermind that is attained by the *jiva*,
that is the human being. That is so because whatever
truth, whatever consciousness is attained has to be embodied and has to manifest in the mould of the attaining
jiva. Each *jiva* has its own mould, its own nature, temperament, way of manifesting the consciousness; the
supramental consciousness shapes itself accordingly and
manifests itself differently to different individuals according to their soul-type, according to their nature-type.
This is the difference between the supermind as Being
and the supermind in becoming.

Q.: Nature-type depends on what?

A.: Nature type is usually ordained by the soul-type.
The soul-type chooses its appropriate nature-mould.
That is the idea, and usually universal Nature sees to it
that each soul is provided with the mechanism that is
best suited for its evolution.

*Q.: What was the original argument in favour of the
so-called passive retirement of the spiritually realised person?*

A.: When they retired they felt the world had no
more relevance to them; it was an interference between
themselves and their spiritual realisation. So they chose
to withdraw and they never thought of this universe or
of perfecting their life. Such of those, the Rishis, for
instance, who did think of the world and who exerted
themselves spiritually by emanating thoughts, feelings,
impulsions that would lead to the progress of humanity
can't be said to have retired or to have gone into retreat.

They may have taken up residence in forests for their own reasons, but they did continue to take part in the universal movement.

*　　　*

It will come later when we discuss the operation of the supermind—where the divine mind comes into existence when this Truth-Consciousness poises itself as if separate—not separate but as if separate—and observes itself there. It is fully conscious all the time, but it is itself that is being observed, just as I observe my hand. It is itself that is observing and it is gaining its own knowledge at a particular point. That is called the operation of the apprehending consciousness as distinct from a comprehending movement, an enveloping movement; it absorbs the knowledge. This action, this apprehending movement is characteristic of the divine mind, and the divine mind is truly the progenitor of the movement that ultimately turns into the separative mind in ignorance. The last step on the borders of truth, the domain of truth before it comes out and into the over-mind is the divine mind. And that is the term into which our mind has to convert itself before it can enter into the poise of the comprehending supermind.

Q.: In most places where Sri Aurobindo deals systematically with the Truth-Consciousness, he always speaks of Knowledge and Will, but very rarely discusses Love. But in one letter he says that supramental love is not cold, so you know it is there but why...?

A.: I think the love aspect of it comes on the levels where there is the Ananda, the Delight principle of the supermind; love comes in on ranges where the Delight principle is active, on the heights of the supermind, because love is an expression of Delight.

Q.: What would be the effect of the supermind on the karma of one who has attained the supramental consciousness?

A.: Most of it would stand modified and cancelled, but there is a certain element in karma—what is called the ineluctable karma—which has to be gone through even by an avatar, unless it is absolutely necessary for the divine purpose to cancel it. It is a part of the rules of the game. If that ineluctable karma is not worked out it disturbs the whole karmic machinery of the cosmos, so the realised ones have usually chosen to go through and work out that karma; even if is in their power to dissolve that karma—they do not do it.

Q.: An avatar has karma?

A.: Yes, an avatar has karma in two respects. Whatever he does in the human body registers a karma. Then, to the extent he identifies himself with the earth-being he shares the universal karma also. Mother was saying during the later periods how falsehood from the universe was torturing her. She said her physical pain was nothing compared to the torture to which she was subjected when the universal falsehood was striking at her. What is this if not the universal karma? She could very well have withdrawn herself, kept herself in a different poise, but she did not. She underwent, she suffered it so that that karma could be worked out. Sri Aurobindo explains somewhere that unless it is necessary for the divine work, that karma is not cancelled though the Grace is capable of completely wiping it out.

Q.: This is far ahead, but will the supramental beings have karma, will they have a chain of karma?

A.: Supramental beings or the gnostic beings will not have karma in our sense of the term. Whatever they do will produce only positive karma giving positive results to the rest of humanity.

Karma comes when we do things with a selfish motive. But when we are identified with the divine consciousness and it is the divine consciousness that works through us, we don't build up any binding individual karma. From that point of view the gnostic beings in a gnostic community will not be building up that karma. They will be only manifesting. If, in the course of manifestation, in the course of their contact with lesser beings like us, some karma is produced, it will be a superficial phenomenon.

*   *

They are expected to pour out energy which will help humanity to get rid of their detaining karma and build up a strength for a positive karma. Even a liberated man—not to speak of one who has the supramental consciousness—a Jivanumukta like Buddha, the Maharshi,—when they live, individually they have no such karma in their life. But to the extent that they interfere with the karma of others, even by way of help, they take on something of that karma themselves. That is why in the death of most of these great people there is pain.

Q.: Then as long as they are doing work in relation to the creation they are subject to karma even if they have the supermind?

A.: Yes. Only there will always be a certain mitigating process, but the universal karma is bound to fall upon them.

22

THE INTUITIVE MIND (I)

We have now come to a stage where it is necessary to have clear-cut conceptions of the terms we are using and are likely to use more frequently than before. As we have seen, this creation of which we are a part starts at the summits with Satchidananda. There is first in Existence, Sat. The nature of this Existence is Consciousness, it is Chit. And this Chit, again, has two aspects—the aspect of consciousness, awareness, and the aspect of force. And the nature of this Conscious Existent is Delight, Ananda. Sat-Chit-Ananda are not three different things, but a triune truth at the head of manifestation. This Satchidananda is the highest conception that has been given to us of the Reality in so far as it lends itself to our understanding. The Reality itself, which is beyond human conception, is called the Absolute, the Parabrahman. We can say nothing of it—we cannot say that it is or it is not. Any kind of an attempt to define it would amount to an offence to the purity and unknowability of the Absolute.

We can know something of the Absolute only as far as it is turned to manifestation. In itself we cannot know it. We can know it as turned to manifestation, but not in the way of the mind. We can know of its nature through our consciousness, but not through our intellect. That is why they say in the Upanishads, "Speech and mind fall back when they approach the Reality". The Reality escapes the grasp of the mind, the intellect, but what cannot be known by the mind can be known in other ways. Our consciousness can identify itself with this Truth and know it in its own way. That is how we know of Satchidananda, the triune truth or reality that heads the manifestation.

When the Satchidananda moves into manifestation, it determines itself bringing together the knowledge of what it wants to manifest and the will or the power to effectuate what it wants to do. And this self-determination of Satchidananda in the creative poise is known as the supermind. The supermind, again, has three broad grades. At the highest it is characterised by utter unity, there is oneness. When it needs to manifest, naturally there is the many, but the many are held in the close grasp and embrace of the one. At no stage are the many separate from the one. It is the one as the many, with the emphasis on the oneness. The second stage comes when the emphasis is shifted to a kind of equality—the one and, supported by it, the many. Both are equal truths. The utter dependence of the many on the one is not so much emphasised here. The many are also true, they depend upon the one, they derive from it, but both are true. The third stage comes when the emphasis goes more on the side of the many. The one is at the background but the many are preponderant. This is the third stage. This play between the one and the many bases the triple gradation of the supermind. When this emphasis upon the many, upon the individual unit goes a little further, so much so that the sense of oneness is left behind and each pursues its career, aware indeed at its centre that it is part of the one, but in practice looks ahead and pursues its career as if it were separate, we come into the region of the overmind. And when this movement reaches its culmination in an effective sense of independence, of separativity, we are on the level of the mind. In between the overmind and the mind there are different gradations in which the consciousness, the manifesting consciousness limits itself, narrows its range till in the mind it reaches a definitive stage of self-forgetfulness and ultimately it leads to the levels of life and matter, to an utter nescience, complete forgetfulness not only of the unity but of everything. That is the nadir, the lowest point of the plunge of the Reality.

On the reverse path—the path of ascent following the path of descent—once we reach the level of the mind and further evolution is to take place, the mind itself can be analysed into three grades. The lowest layer of the human mind is the sensational mind, the sense mind. Our senses—hearing, seeing, speech, all these—go as errand boys, get the report and that part of the mind which is presiding over these movements of the senses collects the data and formulates its reaction. This part of the mind which depends upon the senses for its data and moves in the realm of the senses is the sense mind. In the Indian tradition it is called the manas. Above the sense mind is the dynamic mind, the mind that effectuates, the mind that has power, the mind that wills to do things—whether it has knowledge or not is another matter, but what little it knows it wants to effectuate, it wants to work. That is the dynamic mind. Above the dynamic mind is the reasoning mind. As the mind develops the faculty of discrimination, reasoning whether this is right or that is right, whether this is correct or incorrect; as this faculty develops we have the reasoning mind. But that is not the end. Reason today has recognised its severe limitations, it has been forced to recognise areas in consciousness which it cannot grasp, which it cannot decipher.

Above the mind there are levels which we call the higher mind, the higher levels of which are called the spiritual mind. Above the higher mind and the spiritual mind is the illumined mind. That is, whatever mind knows, that knowledge is lighted up by a spiritual light. One knows in the normal way but that knowledge is lighted, one has no doubt about it. Above the illumined mind is the intuitive mind where truth and knowledge play in the form of flashes, and each flash is an edge of truth, a direct reaching of true knowledge to the mind. This is the intuitive mind. Above the intuitive mind is the overmind and above the overmind is the supermind.

Now, with this background you will appreciate what is the role of the intuitive mind in our ascent to the supermind. The transition from the highest level of the mind to the supermind cannot be direct. Supermind, as we have noted, is not just a superior mind. It is differently made, its texture is different, its process is different, its vision is different. The mind is a labourer in search of knowledge; supermind holds knowledge in its sovereign grip. It doesn't have to seek for knowledge, it has only to turn its gaze and it has the knowledge that is needed; that which is pertinent, that which is relevant comes before the supramental vision. The chief characteristic of the supramental knowledge is that it is self-aware and all-aware. There is a knowledge of itself, what it contains, the truth that it carries; it is also accompanied by a knowledge of the all, of what is manifest. So this just combination of self-knowledge and all-knowledge is a characteristic of the supermind in every poise. In itself it is supreme; but when this supermind is being manifested or organised on our earth plane by a divine being—call it a god—that god has to take account of the conditions—mental and other—in which he has

to express or organise this double knowledge, self-knowledge and all-knowledge. He has it with him, the difficulty is in creating conditions in which alone this dyna-
mis of knowledge can work naturally. The difficulty is
much more in the case of the individual who is rising
from the mental plane, evolving from our levels towards
the supermind. The individual, the sadhaka, the seeker,
has first to grow into the nature of the supermind.
Theoretically, philosophically, he may know what is the
nature of the supramental knowledge, but that remains
a conception. For it to become true—a part and parcel
of his being—the individual has not only to perfect his
mind, but to take it up, level by level, into the supramental domain.

Secondly, even if the supramental knowledge were,
by a miracle, to manifest in the human mind, there are
no organs, no faculties to express that knowledge. We
have evolved the necessary faculties, the necessary organs for our mental knowledge. But for the supramental
knowledge, the gnostic knowledge, the organs are yet
to be shaped. The present organisation of the mental
apparatus has to be completely changed.

Sri Aurobindo cites the analogy of the great change
that the animal mind had to go through, how the working of the animal mind had to be overturned and completely recast by nature before the working of the faculties
of the human mind, the reasoning mind, the discriminat-
ing mind became possible. The gulf between the animal
mind and the human reasoning mind, Sri Aurobindo
says, is nothing compared to the gulf that exists between
our present mind and the supermind. A greater change
has to be effected than was effected by nature when the
transition was made from the animal level of the
mind to the human. And for this change to be possible a

spiritual development is indispensable. Our highest
developed reasoning mind has to undergo modifications
that are inevitable when it is being spiritualised. Spiritualised means the mind giving up its sense of separativity, its sense of confining its idea of truth and reality
to material forms, of separating the abstract from the
concrete, of placing itself separately in a subjective poise
and observing the object of knowledge in an objective
way. This kind of self-separation and observation of
things as other, characteristic of the human mind, has to
undergo a spiritual change and modification. The mind
has to learn in the way of the spiritual mind, the spiritual
consciousness, to identify itself with the object of knowledge and learn to grasp the contents of that object.
This is just one illustration of the change that is expected
of the mind when we ask it to undergo spiritualisation.

Then comes the stage of perceiving the unity of
life, unity of mind in the universe, and this, too, can
come only to the extent to which the mind opens itself
to the spiritual sense of oneness. In a word the mind has
to abandon its nether basis and take a leap into the spiritual heights so that it becomes familiar with the operations of the higher echelons of the mind, particularly
the spiritual mind which is an open field for the play of
still higher faculties like illumination, intuition. If faculties like these were to operate at our level, they are
bound to be diluted, mixed with the inferior workings
of our sense mind and the interested vital mind, and
even the rigid reasoning mind. All these interfere with
the play of the higher faculties like intuition or illumination, but if the mind has been spiritualised, converted
into a spiritual mind, that possibility is much less. The
spiritual mind provides a more natural field for the play
of those higher faculties than the reasoning or the sense

mind. The spiritual mind certainly is not the highest that we can attain, but it is a necessary stage before we can hope to enter into the still higher realms of consciousness.

So between the spiritual mind and the supermind there is still a gulf and it is here, in bridging this gulf that comes the role of the intuition. We have seen that at our level whenever intuition acts our mind interferes, it wants verification. Even if there is a self-evident certainty about a suggestion or a perception that is clearly intuitive, our mind insists on its credentials and it is thus that action of intuition is diluted and delayed. However, we have moments when we have experienced the action of this intuitive faculty. We go on labouring, organising our thoughts, seeking solutions to problems and we despair. Suddenly, when we are perhaps not thinking about it, there is a flash and we know that it is the solution. Those who lead the spiritual life know that it is intuition, but others deceive themselves by saying that it is just a rapid action of the mind. In some cases it may indeed be so, but we can know by the freshness of the revelation that it is an act of intuition.

Now this occasional play of intuition has to be naturalised, maximized before we can claim to have a direct working of the intuitive mind in us. We have to extend the action of intuition. We are aware in our best moments of how the intuition acts not only in the mind, but in the heart, even in our physical body. They call it instinct. There is the play of self-evident truth at all levels. Sri Aurobindo says that we must make it a practice to open up all the levels of our being to the play of intuition. Intuition should be made an active acquisition. That is easy enough because intuition, as a faculty of the revelation of truth, is already there embedded right from matter upwards. The working of a concealed intuition is there. At the lower level of the animals we say it is instinct—they instinctively know what to eat and what not to eat, how to avoid danger. That instinct is nothing but the play of intuition disguised at that level in the form of an instantaneous perception and reaction. But with the arrival of the mind at the human stage, the play of intuition gets subdued. We are so much full of our own thought activity, sense promptings, that even when intuition acts we dismiss it or treat it on par with the hundred and one suggestions that play in our mind. We have to learn to discriminate between our own imagination, our own conclusions of laboured thinkings, and this sudden prompting of the intuition—whether it is in the heart or in the mind or at the vital level.

Indeed it is not possible for us to have direct experience of the play of intuition. The mind, unless it is developed, can't receive, can't provide the field for intuition. The play or the working of intuition is bound to be erratic unless we provide for it a sound mental base. So a combination of both, development of the mind from below and an evocation of the intuitive faculty from above, are recommended. We have to purify our mind, enlarge the range of our thought, emphasise on movements which expand the horizons of the mind—in a word, to culture the mind wider, higher. And at the same time, by aspiration, by call, by will, invoke the play of intuition. Both the processes should go together and it is only after we have got well under way that intuition starts becoming part of our mind so that it is no more an occasional play but a normal action of intuition.

In what manner these processes are to be combined —the lower ascent and the higher descent—is not left to our puny mind, but to the Divine Shakti to which we open ourselves in yoga. It is the Shakti that decides at which time to emphasise the downward movement, at which moment to tone up the upward process. It is the supreme, omniscient Shakti that alone knows and the seeker has to have the aspiration, collaboration and surrender.

Then Sri Aurobindo goes on to describe the various limbs of this process of the development of the mind upwards so that it can be open to the play of the higher faculties. The first and the more usual step in all spiritual yoga is to silence the mind. The mind is so much lost in its own noise that even if truth perceptions were to sail in, it is very unlikely that the mind will notice them. That is why the mind has got to be quieted, silenced. As to how to silence the mind, we have already discussed in our study of the yoga of knowledge and I presume that mentally we all know what are the processes of silencing the mind. Slowing the tempo of mental activity, narrowing its range, bifurcating the mind leaving the surface to deal with the thoughts and centering the consciousness more towards the immutable self, or keeping out our thoughts by an exercise of will and making the mind blank, vacant—whichever the way we pursue, the mind is to fall silent for it is only then that the Self discloses itself. Whether it is the intuitive part of the Self or the illuminative or the sheer Self within, Atman, that reveals itself depends upon the individual, his readiness. But at this stage where the mind is silenced and the inner Self starts disclosing itself, there is a likely interference. The mind questions what could this be, what could that be. It tries to interpret, drawing upon what it has heard or read. This is what Sri Aurobindo calls the intrusion of the inferior mentality. It is for this purpose that the mind has to be cultured, the consciousness has to be vigilant. These intrusions, interpretations, doubts are to be kept out and eventually eliminated.

For those who choose not to go by the path of the mind, who do not live that much in the mind but who live more in the heart, for whom devotion, love, understanding and sympathy are more natural than mental understandings, theirs is the way of devotion, bhakti. Their way is to indraw the attention. The gaze, which is normally outwards, is withdrawn and steadily pulled within. The whole consciousness is gathered up and directed within in search of the Lord, the divine Master who is stationed within the lotus of the heart. And it is from there that the direct, intuitive intimations start coming. The feelings are correct—whatever thoughts come are touched by this warmth of heart intuition. One doesn't think, one doesn't reason, one doesn't argue but one knows. The mind just reflects the knowledge that is unrolling itself from the heart. That is another way. Even here there is bound to be interference from the vital, from the inquisitive mental. Some of the movements of this awakened and enlightened heart centre open to the action of intuition are apt to have the colour of miracles, because they are not reasoned out. In spite of it, the opening of the heart centre to intuition can only be a stage. It cannot take us, by itself, to the supermind. Though it can normalise the action of intuition in us, it cannot take us beyond because the heart centre is not our highest centre. And what is that centre?

(From Questions & Answers)

Q. If the supramental consciousness is increasing its content in the earth consciousness, is there not some sign that things are happening that way, some things characteristic of the supramental consciousness that are more in evidence on earth?

A.: I do think there are. For instance, the convergence of the various movements of human activity towards oneness. Whatever the political quarrellings and bickerings, at the level of culture, at the level of industry, science, trade, commerce, the movement towards oneness, wholeness is increasing. There is no going back on this trend. The trend is towards unity. There is already a recognition that the world is one. The point is how to translate this knowledge into effective practice. There is a resistence from the 'haves' to provide for the 'have-nots', but by and large there is a recognition that they both have common interests. This was unheard of about 25 years ago. Today those who used to fight on the battlefields meet in councils. This trend towards unity and oneness is a special result of the pressure of the supermind.

Secondly, the impossibility of a world war today is a clear sign that the force of harmony has taken root. There may be local battles and skirmishes, but a war of the type the first two world wars were is ruled out. That is because the force of harmony, the force of oneness has come to stay. The mental barriers self-imposed by modern empirical philosophers and thinkers are breaking down and new sciences are emerging—that is another sign that the mental barriers have yielded. Knowledge is expanding, the life span is increasing, ways and means are being found of conquering the forces of disintegration and death. All these are a direct result of a pressure of a new knowledge and a new consciousness upon the earth mind.

Q.: Will the vegetable and the animal kingdom receive the benefit through the agency of man, since he is the peak of evolution at this point?

A.: All orders of creation will receive the benefits directly in their terms. Things that were suppressed, submerged, will come up. For instance with the plants, the higher type of consciousness for which they are struggling will form in them without much effort. The animals also want to know, they want to get beyond their limits. They will get nearer the human stage. And in spite of appearances of man moving towards the animal stage once again, the soul is moving towards the godhead.

At each level there will be an uplifting action in the evolutionary scale. Gold will be more gold, a horse will more horse. And man will be a real man—he will express his manhood which is to express the truth.

Q.: I just heard this morning that a doctor who is the head of one of these world organisations, said in a speech that by the end of the century there won't be any more bad souls, that there has been a decision by the higher forces. It sounds a bit funny, but then the leader of another world unity organisation said, independently of him, that by the year 2000, it would be very difficult for bad people to continue to sustain themselves in the world because the forces of goodwill be so strong.

A.: It is true. It is a mental formulation of a higher truth that is manifesting. The lower tendencies will lose their hold.

23

THE INTUITIVE MIND (II)

To recapitulate what we were discussing: the super-mind, we noted, is plenary self-knowledge and all-knowledge. It is supremely self-aware and at the same time aware of all. Along with its knowledge it wields also appropriate power; in other words it is omniscient and omnipotent. If this is the poise of the supermind consciousness on its own plane, when the supermind is being organised in the earth consciousness by a divine being, the same characteristics will surely be there essentially; but in the course of its working, account will have to be taken of the terrestrial conditions and the establishment of this consciousness has necessarily to be progressive. Much more limited will be the working of this consciousness in an individual who is growing from the mental levels to the altitudes of the supramental. The individual has his roots in the ignorance that casts a long shadow on the workings of the mind. However hard he may try, the effects of this basic disability prolong themselves in a hundred ways. So the growth from the mental to the supramental is slow, often obstructed, often diluted and it takes considerable time if it is worked out by the individual alone. Luckily we have admitted a new factor into the situation, the factor of the Divine Shakti, which takes charge of the situation and conducts operations in its own high wisdom.

Another difficulty is that we have at present no instrumental faculties appropriate to the supramental consciousness. The mind has forged its own but the supramental consciousness has still to have its own instruments for direct functioning. At the moment it functions indirectly through our highest developed faculties like spiritualised mind, intuition, flashes of illumination and so on. And the process of establishing new organs, modifying the workings of the mind and uplifting them into the higher workings of the gnosis, entails larger change than what was imperative when the animal mind had to change and transform itself into the reasoning mind of man. The change is infinitely more, the gulf is greater, and it needs a long spiritual development before the present mental organisation can be assumed, lifted up into the next higher dimension. And in this process of transition, intuition has a mediatory role.

At present the functioning of intuition is not organised. Even in those few cases where intuition can be said to be active, it is more or less an intrusion into the mental workings. We can never be sure that it is always intuition that we experience. All that we can say is that we have periods when intuition works more than during other periods, that certain conclusions that we arrive at are based more upon intuition than on mental reasoning. This action of intuition, however intermittent, is to be extended and put more or less on a permanent basis. The extension of the action of intuition, the purification of the mental processes so that they may not interfere with the action of the intuition are two parts of the same process. The wise seeker leaves it to the Divine Shakti to determine which part to emphasise and when. There are three or four movements in the process of this change.

One is to silence the mind. The mind is withdrawn from its restless, surface activity, thought activity, quieted and turned towards the Self. And the mind waits for the Self to disclose itself, it waits for the intimation from the Self. The mind does not think, it does not

reason. It refers to the Self, the intuitive Self that is
within and waits for the response. When the mind is
silent and quiet, the illumination of the Self reflects itself
in the calm waters of the mind. Even then interference
by the old processes of the mind is possible. When the
knowledge gained in the silent poise is sought to be
translated into mental terms, the inferior mentality
intervenes. It gives its own coating, its own interpretation. Now this element of the inferior mentality has
got to be pitilessly eliminated.

The other method, which is more natural to some
temperaments is the way of bhakti, devotion. One is
conscious that there is a divine Indweller. One is drawn
to the presence of the Lord, the divine Lord within.
All emotions, all mental movements spontaneously flow
towards the Divine within. This Indweller, we must note,
is not situate in one physical position. There is this divine
element in all parts of our being—behind the mind,
behind the emotions, behind the life-energy, behind
the physical—though the heart centre, connected as it
is with all these different locations of consciousness, can
be described as the capital of the Lord. The seeker
enters into communion with the Lord within for intuitive
guidance. The inner purusha gives that guidance—may
be in the form of words, may be in the form of feelings,
may be in the form of silent direction. Still, as long as
the outer nature is not sufficiently purified, interference
is to be guarded against. Whenever the purusha guides
there is a certain quality of a miracle because that
guidance has to gain ascendency over a number of other
voices and noises that are current in the being and it is
with a miraculous impact that the guidance makes itself
felt. This impact while it is spectacular in the earlier
stages needs to be normalised later on. If it is always

kept in its miraculous character it may be sabotaged at
any time by the upsurge of the lower workings. And it
cannot be normalised in the existing state of things. The
inner guidance has an element of supernormality because,
Sri Aurobindo points out, the heart centre is not the
highest centre that we have got. The highest centre of
consciousness that we have organised in our being is at
the crown of our head, on the higher levels of the mind,
embodied mind, and that is called the lotus of a thousand
petals. Now when we speak of a thousand petals, it is not
to be taken literally that the lotus or the configuration
has exactly a thousand petals. In the ancient systems,
spiritual and occult, there are certain figures which indi-
cate an amplitude, a fullness, a plenitude—ten, hundred,
thousand, hundred thousand and so on. So when they
say a thousand petals it means a plenary manifestation
of the consciousness, the highest, fullest manifestation of
consciousness in the human system. Now this *sahasradala*
at the crown of our head is not to be confused with what
is called the brain centre. The brain is only a physical
organ, but this highest centre, the centre of the thousand-petalled lotus, is above the physical brain. In fact
it is not at all situated in the physical body. If we are to
be in direct contact with it, if we are to receive guidance
from the knowledge enshrined there, we have to make a
habit of lifting our centre of thought, centre of action
above the head. Above the physical head is the subtle
physical realm which opens above it to communication
from the still higher centres of spiritual mind, intuitive
mind, illumined mind and so on.

That is one way, to lift our centre of action and
thought to the highest centre of the thousand-petalled
lotus above the brain. Sri Aurobindo describes how his
brain never functioned when he wrote the *Arya*. He

always wrote from a centre above the brain, above the physical head. Most of you would have read that passage in *Sri Aurobindo On Himself*.

The silencing of the mind, communing with the inner centre, lifting our centre of thought and action above the head—these are three difficult processes. But there is a fourth process open to the seeker which is not that difficult and that is to develop the intellect, to develop the mind as it is, upwards: not to accept its present working as the only possible way, but to recognise that the mind can be developed, the processes which are familiar can be toned up, changed in their character, extended in their range, uplifted, subjected to a transforming change. The transformation of the intelligent will so that it does not depend only upon the sense data or the data given by the reasoning mind, but recognises a different range of phenomena which also demand acceptance. And it is here, in this process of developing the mind with all its different faculties into something superior to itself, something above it of which there is daily evidence—the mind itself doesn't need any proof of it—that the intervention of the supermind becomes imperative. Where the upward effort of the mind is to be done and in what area the descending action of the supermind is to be encouraged, promoted—this is beyond the human intelligence; it is left trustfully to the discretion of the Divine Shakti. The Divine Shakti, when it is left to operate in its full freedom without interference by our arrogant mind and its egoistic claims, takes up all the four methods depending upon cases, depending on which part is strong in the individual. It is indispensable, whatever the path, whether the path is that of devotion or work or knowledge, to silence the mind in a spiritual consciousness, quiet it so that it may be suffused with a spiritual vibration, calm it so that it may reflect the image of the superconscient truths. There is also the awakening to the intuitive being within at all levels. Intuition does not operate only in the head. There is an intuition in the heart, an intuition in the body; everywhere there is the divine consciousness as intuition. We may or may not be aware of it, we may or may not perceive its action directly, but whether in the form of instinct—what we call hunch—or a sort of a premonitory feeling, it makes itself active, awakening us to the action of the intuitive being within us. All this threefold upward action evokes the descent of the supramental energies which descent alone can give completion and permanence to spiritual silence, intuitive guidance and the elevation of mental workings to the higher spiritual workings.

With all these methods the first result that we see is what Sri Aurobindo calls an intuitive change. The working of the mind undergoes a change. Though the mind may imitate some of the intuitive workings by the rapidity with which it comes to certain conclusions, still we can know the precise nature of the intuitive knowledge by the certainty with which it speaks. Intuition, as Sri Aurobindo says, is an edge of truth, a ray of truth coming and striking directly on our being. Fitful at present, the working of intuition can be normalised, established as part of our system, but that is not the end though there is a temptation to stop at the intuitive level as the direct working of knowledge. As Sri Aurobindo points out, it is still the mind, maybe the intuitive mind, and wherever there is mind there is always the possibility of the basic and fundamental limitations of the mental apparatus exerting themselves, coming into their own at some time and undermining the reliability of intuition.

It is wise to recognise intuition as a link between the human mind as it is and the divine mind as it is waiting to be formulated in humanity. A necessary link, a luminous link, but only a link. The perfect perfection to which the integral yoga aspires can only be attained at a still higher level, at the level of the divine gnosis, the supramental consciousness, beyond the possibility of being diluted, of being coated with mental operations.

That brings us to the next theme, the gradations of the supermind, because the supermind is not of one piece as we have observed earlier. There are gradations and after the intuitive levels are crossed we go to the lowest levels of the supermind.

(From Questions & Answers)

Q.: *Does mathematics operate in the subtle physical?*

A.: What is mathematics, after all? Mathematics, as I have understood it, is a science to arrive at a direct understanding of the processes of nature: how things happen, by what processes, at what speed etc. Now if the same results that mathematics can give, as the result of long processes, are given by intuitive flashes, mathematics as we know it today won't have that function. It will continue its role to subtilise the mind, to accustom the mind to move into dimensions other than the purely physical, into the domain of the symbol. After all, numbers are symbolic. they symbolise certain truths. So, mathematics is a science which helps to subtilise the mind, to lift it up from being always engrossed in physical details and processes, but it too, in its present form, has a range beyond which it cannot go. Grammar, linguistics, these are all included in what are called the lower sciences. They don't give you direct knowledge of the reality, though they prepare and fashion the mental apparatus to receive the higher knowledge later on.

*   *

When P.B. was the chief engineer of an important river project and afterwards an adviser to many engineering projects, there were times when, with their best skill, the engineers, both foreign and Indian, could not come to definite conclusions. So he brought the maps and showed to the Mother. When the Mother was told what the problem was, she placed her finger on a spot. And it was found that that was precisely the spot which other engineers later on arrived at after long, long calculations. It was the right spot. Now what do you say to that? A spiritual comprehension of the truth, the higher knowledge, the supramental or nearing it, lands exactly on the solution to arrive at which you have to have months of mathematical calculations.

Q.: Mother stresses that even after a certain stage of development one still continues development of the mind and the physical body.

A.: For expression. It is not that difficult to acquire a state of high consciousness on the summits of one's being or in the depths. But to express it, to organise it in one's being, training is necessary. The mere fact that one has that consciousness is not enough. There can be interference when one starts functioning on that basis. That is why even after you get the knowledge the instrumental being needs to be educated.

Q.: Beyond the mental knowledge is the occult knowledge and beyond that is where is the intuitive plane...

A.: Occult knowledge is not beyond, it is behind. At any level, there is an occult knowledge—an occult physical knowledge, an occult mental knowledge, an occult spiritual knowledge. What is occult? Occult is what we

16

don't see with the naked eye. It is always behind the veil. What we know is only a surface formulation of what we can know. So even without being spiritual, even without arriving at the heights of mental knowledge of which man is capable, he can have some occult knowledge. He can do tricks, that famous rope trick, or whatever it is. For spiritual knowledge one has to go beyond mind. For occult knowledge, one just withdraws behind the surface and the occult ranges open.

Q.: *Does intuition always make itself known through a voice?*

A.: Not always. There is in many of us what we call conscience. Conscience is a formation in our consciousness created by the environmental beliefs, ethical standards and our acceptance of those standards as our rule of life. Certain beliefs that we have or have come down to us from the elders and which are honoured in the present society become our governing principles. Now when we have strong faith in them, they constitute our conscience. And when that conscience is alive, when we do anything right or wrong according to that conscience, it makes itself felt either as a strong feeling or in words; Socrates called this the Daemon. It was not really his soul. It may happen in spiritual life that the soul or the psychic being may also guide directly, either in the form of a voice or as a feeling. But we need not go to the psychic level to hear a voice, because the ego is very clever in projecting voices, imitating the voice of conscience, the voice of the soul, the voice of the teacher, the voice of God. Our own desires and preferences are very clever in taking the form of these inner voices. Apart from that, hostile forces are more clever than we are in injecting themselves. They will even imitate the voice of the teacher. These voices are a very dangerous proposition. For myself I have made it a principle and I always advise everybody not to be guided by voices and visions. Sri Aurobindo asks us to leave voices and visions to themselves and look for experience.

24

THE GRADATIONS OF THE SUPERMIND

The subject today is the gradations of the Supermind.
Very often when these chapters are taken up for discussion I have a gnawing doubt as to the utility of discussing or expounding things which are still of academic value to us. Because those states of consciousness, states of being, are so much beyond our present attainments that even conceptually it is difficult to relate ourselves to them. But then I remember Sri Aurobindo writing somewhere that while it is true that this kind of knowledge remains mental, an intellectual acquisition, without any necessary impact on the practical life, as things stand, still such knowledge is necessary because our minds must be accustomed to that climate, they must know the course that is charted out, the way that we have to journey upon, and mentally we must be prepared for corresponding experiences when they come upon us in our inner quest. When we have an experience, it is better received and assimilated, if we have a mental background helping us to appreciate its bearings. If we were in a total blank, then the experience is not likely to yield its full benefit. From that point of view it is something like a guide giving advance information of what we are going to meet, the situations that are likely to arise and how they are to be met, where we have to change trains—the vital for the mental, the mental for the intuitive reason and so on. So it is necessary and I convinced myself before proceeding with this section of *The Synthesis of Yoga*, that we should go through all these chapters and

discuss, in our own way, what he describes as the ascent of the mind though the intuitive levels of consciousness to the various grades of the supramental knowledge, will and ananda—in other words the supramental gnosis.

We have seen that above our normal reasoning mind are the levels of the spiritual mind which lead us to the intuitive levels. But the intuitive mind is still a mind. At best it can be a link between the reasoning mind and the gnostic mind. But it is a necessary link. Intuition is a direct presentation of knowledge. It may not come in masses, in comprehensive ways, but still there are flashes of intuition building up a milieu of right knowledge, right feeling and possibilities of right action by their constant action. This working of the intuitive faculty, to which we open more and more in the course of yogic development, translates itself into an ever-present feeling of the presence of a higher spirit or a greater Purusha on the altitudes of our being with a different degree and kind of knowledge, consciousness and delight. But there is a radical difference between that state which we feel on the heights of our being—or by reflection in our depths—and the state of our normal mental faculties. There has to go on a double action—the descent of the higher consciousness with a higher charge into the lower mental formations and the ascent of the lower mind. From that point of view the highest that we are is still the lower mind. There has to be an ascent into the higher degrees of consciousness where the intuitive light is playing. As this double action proceeds the action of the divine spirit on the intuitive level of our being becomes more organized, more natural.

But clearly that is not the end. It is only the middle. The intuitive working reveals itself as only a middle element, even as the reasoning mind has revealed itself to us as middle between the outer world and the higher spiritual knowledge. And once we recognize that the intuitive level is not the terminus, the final resting place, we proceed in our evolution upwards. Intuitive openings occur, giving us revelations of still higher states of knowledge—what we may call the divine reason. Not the human reason but the divine reason. Still it is a reason, in this sense that the activity of the consciousness is idealized thought-wise, form by form. May be the mental reason thinks that each form is all, and the divine reason does not—it is aware of the unity behind—still reason proceeds by a de-piecing, in effect. So even the divine reason functions on the pattern of the mental reason, though with a different background and with a different result. It is what Sri Aurobindo calls the luminous supramental—not the original supramental but the luminous action of the supramental. It is a delegated action of the gnosis.

On the heights of the intuitive being, leading to the supermind proper, we first meet the action of the divine reason, which is a delegated activity. When we stand at this level, we perceive that there are four faculties, four powers through which the supramentalized intuition acts. From our human point of view intuition is a flash or truth, but on its own plane, when the intuitive faculties function in their full force and rhythm, we find that there are four powers or four faculties through which the intuitive knowledge gathers and becomes effective.

First, there is what may be called the suggestive intuition. We get ideas, the ideas don't form as a result of our reasoning, but they just sail into our minds with the suggestion that they are the right ideas. This is what is called the suggestive intuition. Ideas are thrown and we know they are the right ones. But that alone is not enough. If we were to immediately act on these ideas, it may land us anywhere because there are always imitative ideas. So there comes in the second faculty of intuition called the discriminative intuition, intuitive discrimination, which immediately relates these ideas to the circumstances around, to other mental formations, to other possible intuitive ideas which may or may not have relevance at the moment. This kind of sifting of the values of the suggested idea helps us to assess the significance and the role of the ideas that are given to us.

Third, there is the intuitive inspiration, which helps us to find the right word, the right rhythm, the right process of expression, manifesting the idea. That too is not enough. There is the fourth faculty, the intuitive revelation, which brings before our mind the full body or the form in which the truth or the idea clothes itself. All these four powers are necessary before there can be an organized action of the intuition. Suggestive intuition, discriminative intuition, inspirational intuition, illuminative intuition—these are the four powers. They are naturally different from the mental operations of these very same powers because in the mind they are subject to the shadow of ignorance, but at the intuitive level they are not, though they are not in their plenary action, which they can be only when they reach the supramental heights. In the suggestive intuition there is not the labour of acquisition of knowledge. Normally, we read books, we take data, we argue and discuss in order to arrive at some knowledge, get a content of knowledge; we have to acquire at the mental level, but where there is the suggestive intuition there is no acquisition but only a disclosing, by intuition, of the truth that we can have.

In all this action that goes on through the four-fold

powers, there is a continuous pulling upwards. If the pull upwards were not there, the pull downwards would prevail. There can be no stationary functioning on the higher heights of consciousness. Either you continuously go upwards, gathering the whole of the being in the process, or you are subject to the downward gravitational pull of the lower mind.

Sri Aurobindo distinguishes between two belts of the gnosis. One is the lower intuitive gnosis and the second is the higher intuitive gnosis. The lower intuitive belt, or the gnostic mind, is where the faculties of perception and discrimination prevail. The active suggestion and the discrimination are nearer the mental process. In the higher intuitive gnosis, the powers of inspirational intuition and illuminative intuition are more active. And both these together constitute what we may call the intuitive gnosis. After this operation of the intuitive gnosis is complete, after all the lower mental levels have been assumed in the intuitivized consciousness, the next step of going direct into the supramental consciousness becomes possible. And the first character of this transition is a complete reversal in our way of functioning. Till the supermind is reached, even on the heights of the intuition—as we have seen—there is some kind of projection of the mental process, mental way of thinking and doing things. But here the whole process is reversed. We do not proceed, in the pure gnosis, from outward to inward as we do here. At our mental level, we first see things, the senses gather the data, the sense mind presents, the intelligent mind interprets, the reasoning mind argues and ultimately the *buddhi*, the understanding will, sanctions. So knowledge proceeds from the grosser to the subtler, but here in the gnosis the process is the very reverse of what is natural to us.

One does not exert the consciousness to form a knowledge, to get an idea of what is what, but the consciousness directly receives the knowledge and transmits it to the lower members. The thought and will are not built up, not slowly given shape as at our level. The thought, the will are already there—they sail into our consciousness. We have to receive them, transmit them, as they are, to the other levels for their formulation in terms of the other members. In the spiritual mind the purusha, if he is not involved in the mental operation, is behind, a witness. But here in the gnosis of the supramental reason he rises above, he stands above the process of knowledge.

So the first character is a complete reversal of the process. The second is the luminous will and knowledge from above which are transferred by the intuitive faculties to the other members. But in this transmission there is a good deal of dilution, dispersion, and even a certain amount of deformation. It is for that purpose that Sri Aurobindo calls for a yogic preparation for subtilizing our members like the body, the life, the mind, the emotions. They have to be purified, lifted out of their limited movements so that when higher things are transmitted, they are allowed to work in the system as integrally and with as pure an impact as possible. Till the supramental reason starts functioning, it is the spiritual reason that reigns. After we have gone beyond the borders of the logical mind, touched the spiritual, it is by and large the spiritual reason that rules the movements of our consciousness. And Sri Aurobindo points out that even the spiritual reason is not the last. The supramental reason is a stage still ahead. Even the supramental reason has the same four powers—suggestion, discrimination, inspiration and intuition. The way of its functioning is that the spiritual reason, on the height of the intuitive gnosis, possesses the truth, discloses the truth, harmonizes all of them and the data presented by the senses—including the sixth sense, the inner mental sense. It does not mean that the circumstances, forms and movements of the world in which we live are excluded. They are taken up, only they are given the right interpretation and put to the right use. They are not abolished simply because they come from a lower plane of consciousness. They are lifted up and the plane from which they come is helped to receive more and more of the light of the higher plane.

But the spiritual reason alone is not enough. Sri Aurobindo points out that even the spiritual reason acts by a kind of representative idea and will in the spirit. It does not have the truth directly. Using a simile, he says it is a power of the sun, the light, but not a power of the soul, the Self, *sūrya śakti* and not *ātma śakti*. The sun is after all secondary; the Self is the primary fact. Spiritual reason can only emanate the power of the sun, the light of sun's radiation. In the supramental zone one moves into action in union with the universal and the transcendent spirit. The difference between the spiritual consciousness, spiritual reason and the supramental consciousness and the supramental reason is simply this: in the spiritual one is in touch with the universal and the transcendent spirit either in the depths or at the centre or on the heights of the being and remains there. But in the supramental or the gnostic that unity, that identity spontaneously translates itself into action whether one wants it or not. Just as we breathe, that consciousness of the universal and the transcendent spirit pours itself in action. There there is no practical distinction between status and dynamism. Both are two wings

—not one behind the other. They are almost involved in each other, each supporting the other, each presuming the other and this action becomes very natural at the gnostic level.

In the spiritual consciousness, in the spiritual reason, we have the idea that all exists in One. The idea is there, the mental knowledge is there but we don't function upon it. In the supramental reason, this knowledge that the Self is in all, that all are in the Self and the all are the Self, the Self is the all—is dynamic at every moment. It governs our slightest thought, slightest feeling, slightest action. It doesn't remain a background knowledge which we know but may or may not be able to act up to. All is seen and experienced as the luminous body of the truth.

Having pointed out this difference between the spiritual reason and the supramental reason, Sri Aurobindo goes on to discuss how the spiritual reason insists on being lifted up into the supramental status. And there also is this four-fold action, though the fourfold action distributes itself into a threefold action in this sense, that the discriminative action does not need to take place separately. Along with the dawning of the idea, along with the representative action of the thought, the right relation is struck. The discriminative work is not a separate function. Thus it is a threefold action in the process of the conversion of the spiritual reason into the supramental reason. First is the representative action, which concerns the actualities of life, the actualities of facts. For instance all forms are One, the many and the multitude are the One. The actualities of the many being one, that knowledge is firmly organized and expressed in the representative action. Second is the interpretative action, which concerns the potentialities. If these are the actualities, what do they lead to, where do they point? Manifestation, yes, but in what way? What are the right manifestations? So this awakening of the sense of potentialities and working them out belongs to the interpretative action of the supramental reason.

And then, there is the knowledge by identity. This action of the knowledge by identity governs one's life and experience. It's not a matter of knowledge, not a matter of comprehension, but a matter of intimate day-to-day life. The knowledge of identity with the consciousness, the being, and the delight of truth spontaneously renders itself into life and experience. Sri Aurobindo adds at the end that though he has discussed these in a kind of a mental order, step by step, in order to let us understand how things are to be done, in actual practice things don't follow this precise mathematical order. Some higher elements may come up earlier, stir up things, then the lower things may come to the front. So there is a mixed and intermittent action of the various principles and forces, but the higher yoga force or the supramental shakti knows. He makes a very profound observation when he says that from the lower end we may not be able to know how the higher works, the lower elements may not be able to put themselves in tune with the higher or understand, but the higher very well knows what is the position of the lower. It can stoop, it can identify itself with the lower and help it grow into itself. It is not only possible, it is natural. The higher can always contain the lower, lift it up and impart its character to that. So the lower has no reason whatever to shy away from the higher.

25

THE SUPRAMENTAL THOUGHT
AND KNOWLEDGE

To continue our discussion, it is clear that there has to be a complete conversion of our consciousness before its further ascent. The activities carried out by our mind have to undergo a radical change in their process before the mind can be said to have been converted into the workings of the supramental consciousness. We see that normally the mind proceeds with the data assembled by the senses, interprets and comes to its own conclusions. The feelings, the will, all these depend upon the processes or the decisions taken by the mind in which the intellect, the reason takes a leading part. This has to change.

In the working of supramental reason, the movement proceeds from within outside, not from outside to within. And the first step for bringing about this change is: there are periodical descents from the higher consciousness, eruptions of the higher movements, sudden invasions from on high taking up the mental activity. But there is always not only the possibility but the actuality of the mind interfering, imitating and putting forward its own rapid workings as the action of the higher supramental reason. It is for this purpose that yoga insists upon a certain purification before the conversion can be attempted. The mind has to be purified so that it takes on the character of a luminous mind which can be a direct instrument of the intuitive faculty. The intuitive experience can be undiluted only if the mind has undergone a purificatory discipline, and it is only the intuitive mentality that can be drawn into the supramental. The supramental reason cannot draw mind as it is into its own province because mind has many disabilities which don't permit the intellect, the thought, as they are, to be assumed in the supramental reason.

Purification of the thought mind is not enough. There is also the question of will, the question of feelings, the question of the body. They also contribute their thickening elements, their grossnesses, and for the supramental action to be complete and adequate, the vital and the physical body also have to be taken up and exposed to the purificatory discipline. With all this the mind can go beyond itself, the mental activity can be assumed into the supramental, because, Sri Aurobindo points out, the mind always draws from the secret supermind. The supermind is not overtly active, but it is always there secretly behind veil, exerting itself and reaching its influence, the last find point of which is the mental reason. And it is because of this its basic source in the supramental that the mind can hope to arrive at full knowledge one day. Till then, the mind can only command a partial knowledge, and in this partial knowledge the mind assembles details after details, fragments after fragments, and puts them together and calls them one. The supermind also presents the details, but differently. Different forms exist even in the supermind. But the difference in the seeing and the handling consciousness is this, that at no time, at no stage, does the supermind feel or look upon these details as self-sufficient, living by themselves. It is always aware that they are self-formulations of one unity, the one. The Self posits itself into so many places and each one has an individuality, each one is true, but all derive from the one and all exist because the one indwells them. So the one not only creates, but holds them in its consciousness and the one lives in them also. This deep possession of the governing unity and harmony among the various forms, movements, is natural to the supermind, whereas to our mind it is an acquired knowledge; it is a knowledge that has to be taken on trust.

The mind, for instance, has a typical action of the thought mind. It consists in what we may call the representative action; the thoughts organized, created by the mind, mentated by the mind and built up into knowledge, are representations of certain realities. Ideas are there; those ideas represent things which, however, are not real to us when we think. We know that these thoughts, these ideas stand for something, they represent things which are not in them. That is what is called the action of representation of the mind. If we want the thing itself we make that thought perhaps a spring board, a starting point and then work to get at the thing. But as the mind is treated to the supramental light, as the mind is taken up, the ideas, the thoughts become full of a substance of light. So they are not just fluffy ideas or mental conceptions; thoughts acquire a solidity, thoughts radiate a light and the substance of that light belongs to the thing which the idea or the thought represents.

Now this representative action of the mind, which acquires a different significance as the supramental influence starts working, is truly a projection of what Sri Aurobindo calls the representative supermind. The representative supermind has, again, two actions—the higher and the lower. What is the representative supermind? It is that action of the supermind which presents the various actualities that are present on that plane. The higher action shows things in their full light, in their full substance. The lower action is what is called the supramental reason—each one presented as it is. In the higher action all are presented as they are, without making a distinction of each.

We spoke last time of two or three grades or elevations of the supermind. The representative supermind presents the actualities as they are. Higher than that is the interpretative supermind, which is not satisfied with presenting the actualities as they are, but takes up the potentials, the possibilities as they exist—which are necessarily larger in number. So the interpretative supermind has a larger range, it presents possibilities which have not yet matured into actualities. And the third stage, you will remember, is the knowledge by identity where each thought, each vision, each movement is pregnant with identity in being, identity in consciousness, identity in delight. There this identity with the object of knowledge is always present and there is no distinction really between the knower, the knowledge and the known. These three elevations or grades of supermind were discussed last time, and all these grades are to be allowed to be organized in the mind that is ready for transmutation.

Then, in the mind there is always a conflict, as you know, between thought and thought. I get a thought, and after five minutes I get another thought which is opposed to that thought, puts a doubt on the past thought. There is always a running conflict or a rubbing between thought and will. The will may not be prepared to exert itself to translate the thought because it may not be convinced. Again, I have a certain will at this moment, and after fifteen minutes I change my will. There is a changing, a clanging of wills; the same with feelings. So within the little mind there is always a bundle of contradictions—between thought and thought, between feeling and feeling, between will and will, and among wills, thoughts and feelings.

Now this perennial conflict between thought, will and feeling becomes a thing of the past as we cross over into the higher ranges leading to the supramental. The keynote there is harmony—harmony between thoughts and feelings and will—and unity. All this is because this triple movement of thought, will and feeling is really based upon the knowledge of truth, and in the expression of truth, in the manifestation of truth there can't be conflict because a truth consciousness governs the thought movement, the will movement and the feeling movement: harmony and unity.

When this harmony and order of the supermind starts exerting itself, pressing its order upon the mind, there is a reaction. However ready we may think our mind to be, there is a resistance when the mind is forced to abandon its natural and characteristic activities. The mind may protest, the mind may appear to get deranged because there is no immediate coordination between the higher movement and the lower impulses of the mind. So till some sort of harmonization is achieved between the higher and the lower, there is some reaction. And to avoid this reaction in its extreme or articulate form, a purification is necessary. The mind must learn to surrender itself to the higher action of the supermind. The inequalities that are characteristic of the mental movement are gradually replaced as the mind opens to the working of the intuitive mind. And the intuitive mind, in so far as it introduces the element of intuition, right feeling, right action, right thought in the being, promotes an integral development towards the supermind. We do not have to wait for this harmony till we reach the supramental level. As the mind recognizes its

17

limitations, as the mind accepts the necessity of outgrowing its tutelage to ignorance and allows the intuitive workings on its summits, the integral development begins. The culmination comes after we cross over into the domain of the supermind. And as we rise from the intuitivised levels of the mind to the supermind, there is harmony between thought, will and feeling. And this pronounced harmony between them, as it gets established, promotes unity between them so that these three no longer function as three separate faculties, but as three movements of one being. Another point to be noted is that the supramental knowledge is not thought knowledge. We make the mistake at our level of thinking that all knowledge is necessarily thought knowledge. Knowledge is not true to us unless it presents itself in thoughts, in an organized thought pattern built into a system with a beginning, middle and an end. It is a sort of a weaving of a thought mass. But those who have experience of higher consciousness know that thought knowledge is not all. Thought is only one of the many movements of knowledge. There is, for instance, the knowledge of self-awareness. It is not that the knowledge has to filter through the mind and through the form of an idea or a thought; before the mind knows, there is an instinctual self-awareness. Something which exists by itself in the heart, you may say. One has not undergone the processes of thought but still the knowledge is there. So even at our human level we know that thought is not indispensable for the formation of knowledge, though knowledge may use and does use thought activity at the level of the reasoning mind. But not so above.

What is the supramental knowledge if it is not thought knowledge? The supramental knowledge is knowledge by identity. Identity is a word, but what does it mean? It means that one is aware of a thing, of what a thing is, of the truth of a thing because one is in touch, one is in rapport, one is identified with the soul or the Self of that thing. And how do I get into the Self of this thing? I get it through my Self. I don't get at the Self of this object through my mind. My soul, my Self is awake and from that level I contact the Self of the object. And the linking, the bridge between my Self and this Self is also the Self. So the Self in the Self, by the Self, *ātmani ātmānām ātmanā*. So the whole process is woven within the Self. It is because I am awake at the Self level that the knowledge of the Self of another rises in me spontaneously. And this making contact between Self and Self is a direct operation of the Self, you can call it a Self movement. Now this character of the supramental knowledge by identity has to be gradually imparted to our members. That is supramental knowledge by identity.

There is also what is called the supramental vision. Thought is completely dispensed with, there is only vision. We see things and the very seeing leads to identity. If we see, based upon our physical sight, we have to build up a relation. We have to think, build up thoughts, build up ideas of what it could be; it was blue so it must have been painted blue, there were dark spots on a blue cloth—all these the mind observes and upon that the mind works. But here in the supramental vision thought has no role. We see a thing and the truth of the thing reveals itself to us. That is, the supramental vision brings the spiritual identity straight, without having to mentate upon it. There is also not only the supramental seeing, but there is also the supramental hearing, the supramental touch. Each one of these operations puts in contact with the thing concerned. They become gates to awaken the knowledge by identity. At the mental level, we see a thing, then the idea comes into the picture and it translates the vision into knowledge and will. But in the supramental, knowledge comes first. Thought may or may not arise. Or, to justify, to relate that supramental vision to the mind in our body, the thought may come in later.

Another point to be noted is that intellectual thought takes an objective reality, goes on thinking about it, and then leads to some abstraction. It is not satisfied till it analyses, dissects things and arrives at a certain abstractness, abstract principles. Then only is it satisfied that it has arrived at true knowledge. But the supramental thought does not lead to abstractness. It leads to what Sri Aurobindo calls spiritual concreteness—not a gross concreteness. In each supramental thought, there is that light, substance of light, and the spiritual concreteness.

And the supramental thought, as we said, has got three elevations—the direct thought vision, the interpretative thought vision, the representative thought vision. Direct thought vision is what we described as knowledge by identity.

We spoke of the supramental hearing. Now, the supramental word may or may not have the outer form of the word we speak, but there is its own kind of word. As the supramental truth, the vision, reveals itself or the supramental word impinges upon the consciousness, it renders itself into an inward speech. We have spoken of the four grades of speech, of which the last is the human speech. This is an inward speech. The knowledge formulates itself in a kind of word, a kind of speech, of which the outer form is the most gross form. And even when the supramental hearing or word tries to express itself, uses the human language, the significance it gives to the human words is quite different. That is the difficulty which we have experienced in the human language used by Sri Aurobindo and the Mother. The dictionary meaning of certain terms which Mother and Sri Aurobindo have used is quite different from the meaning which they intend. When they say transcendent, they mean quite different things than what systematized philosophy means, whether in the East or the West. But they are not prepared to change because that is what it means. Simply because we have accustomed ourselves to give a narrow meaning to a particular word, it does not exhaust the full content of that word. The real content of that word is what we see. That is the case with the word psychic, so also the word transformation. It has meant different things in different ages.

However, there is another difference between the supramental consciousness, the supramental thought and the mental thought. The mind relates everything to the individual. It is confined as far as the individualized human mind can go. Everything that the mind sees and records is conditioned, related to the development of the individual consciousness. But for the supermind, the supramental thought, the range is as wide as the cosmos. The individual is not even a center there, the individual is a point where the cosmic and the universal movements converge. And even this universe is not the limit. The supramental vision and thought go beyond the universe, beyond this physical universe. They go and touch the various planes of existence which are occult to us. The supramental man so developed sees not from within this world, not involved in the world-movements, but standing above in his consciousness. He commands a view from the high spaces of the infinite. He sees truth in essence, but not that only. He sees the truth in potentiality, he sees the truth in actuality. He sees into the heart of things, he is aware of the essence of each thing and in that sense he draws nearer and nearer the omniscience of God. He stands above the highest heights of the will attained by man, conditioned by so many factors. He stands at a height which commands a free power of will, and in that sense he approaches the omnipotence of God. The human mind is shut in the present. It may be aware of the long past, it may try to speculate and peep into the future, but it is most sure—to the extent that it can be—only of the present. But in the supramental consciousness the past, the present and the future lie unrolled, like a map, making possible what is called the *trikāladṛṣṭi* of the knowledge of the three tenses, three periods, three movements of time—the movement that is gone, the movement that is on, and the movement that is building. The supermind or the supramental consciousness exceeds the present formulation time.

Then, the supramental knowledge is realized best with what we may call pure thought. Sri Aurobindo discusses what areas or what ranges of the mind are touched by the supramental knowledge. Necessarily, the highest achievement of the human mind, the realms of pure thought are first taken up by the supramental knowledge. But it doesn't stop there. The supramental knowledge percolates and gradually takes over even what is called the applied thought. No range of the human mind is excluded from being taken up, possessed and changed by the direct action of the supramental knowledge. It makes itself felt in pure thought, in applied thought, and it spreads itself in the past, the present and the future.

26

THE SUPRAMENTAL INSTRUMENTS—
THOUGHT-PROCESS (I)

In speaking of the supramental instruments, we must know that the faculties that we are using at present are, in their essence, projections of the faculties of the supermind. It is not as if these faculties are going to be rejected and new ones come in their place. Actually, at their source, all the faculties that we use in life are connected with the supramental consciousness. They may be something else in their functioning, but in their origin they are projections of the supramental faculties. And that is why it is possible for the supermind, once it starts getting organised in the human consciousness, to take up these lower faculties, change their character and impart its own nature and make them function as direct instruments of the supermind. These faculties and powers are not merely those with which we are familiar as functionings of the mind. We have other faculties, the subliminal ones, the subtler ones, which are not normally active in our life; they are faculties which are to come into operation with the progressive expansion of our being. The supermind takes up even these less known, but nevertheless true, powers and faculties of the subtle being, of the subliminal.

In the first place the action of the supermind starts on the highest level of our mind. That is the plane of ideative knowledge where the mind pursues knowledge, where the mind organises its ideas and studies things from various approaches in order to come to a definite understanding of the principles of things. And in this

ideative action, the normal thought activity, the mind
has a triple motion. First, from our end, is what may be
called the habitual thought mind. We are used to think
in certain grooves not only because of our own habits,
but because of the environmental habits, the habits of
collective mind. We take for granted particular ideas,
thoughts, forms of thinkings and coming to conclusions
and the mind habitually flows into these moulds. These
activities are more or less mechanical, habitual. We give
the same responses to the same or similar data. One
thought leads automatically to another thought, we
don't reason. It has become a habit. This is the action of
the habitual mind—what Sri Aurobindo calls the physical mind, mechanical mind—, it goes on and on. It is a
great hindrance when we start attending to the mind
and want to correct its action, open it to the higher working. It is this habitual and mechanical mind which
presents the most obstinate difficulty. We get a doubt,
we reason it out and reject the doubt and when we think
it is over, that doubt comes once again. Again we go
through the whole process a second time, a third time
and so on. It is a mechanical movement. Unless we make
up our mind, exert our will and say we will have none
of it, the turnings of the mechanical mind cannot be
stopped. It goes on like a clock whatever we may be doing. This is the lowest level of the working of the thought
mind.

Above is what we may call the pragmatic idea mind.
That is, we get ideas, we assess them, decide whether
they are right and wrong, whether they are to be enter-
tained or rejected—not from the point of view of the
truth contained in them, but from the standard of their
utility to life, whether they can be translated into action,
how far they would help to enhance our life. We relate

ideas to their utility, not to their own intrinsic value. This is called the pragmatic idea mind.

Higher is the pure ideative mind, where ideas are received, related, organised and tabulated to build up knowledge. We are not concerned whether they are practical, whether they have a background, whether somebody else has tried them. We weigh those thoughts, those ideas purely from the point of view of how far they serve the knowledge pattern which we have before us. The habitual mind, the pragmatic idea mind and the pure ideative mind—these are the normal three movements of the thought mind. And as it happens, all of these don't work in harmony. At times the habitual mind pulls strongly, at times the pragmatic idea mind tries to march over the ideative mind, at times the pragmatic and habitual mind defeat the ideative mind, and so on. Thus even within the thought mind there is a lack of harmony, a conflict between its three movements. When the supermind comes into action, when it starts reforming the mind, taking over the functions of the mind and changing them, the first result is that there is a coordinated movement between these three elements and movements of the mind. A harmony is introduced, each one helps and buttresses the other urged by the supermind. No obstructions are allowed to stand in the coordination of the three minds. Each level, each layer of the thought mind has its value, its function. The knowledge, the light of the supermind helps us to decide precisely which part of the mind has to be operative at what stage and for what purpose. The supermind is able to do that because it is in possession of the essential truth of things. It proceeds from that basis, it does not have to build up knowledge entirely from the data gathered and presented to it by the external senses, or even by the subtle senses.

The supermind does not lose itself in the multiplicity of data and experiences like the mind. It is always in possession of the Self that constitutes the essence of things. What it studies, what it organises is the expression of that Self, it is the varied manifestation of that truth, the truth which is in its possession. And because it is in full possession of the basic knowledge of the truth, it is easier for the supermind to get at the truth of the varied forms that are, we may say, the self-placings of the truth, of the self.

The pragmatic mind, for instance, is not abolished. Only it is not allowed to decide the value of an idea or a thought. The pragmatic mind is made an instrument. The knowledge is there, but through the pragmatic mind the knowledge is linked with life. So the pragmatic mind functions as a link between life and the truth in the supermind which is to be manifested or organised in life. The pragmatic mind does not bind the supramental consciousness.

And even the habitual and mechanical movement is used in its transformed action as something that orders the thoughts. The habitual mind is used to streamline the running thought activities, to build up a kind of an underlying order. Sri Aurobindo speaks of an order of thought, a cycle of will and stability in motion. These are the three things which are built up on the basis of the habitual and mechanical movement of the ordinary human mind. Each activity of the human mind is rendered into its higher, diviner term and the habitual and mechanical movement is rendered in terms of order of thought, a cycle of will. The will is to be exerted, but in what direction? It is to be exerted repeatedly in similar junctures. And stability in motion, otherwise everything is in a flux. The only difference is that the thought mind draws its support from outside, from below it. The senses bring the data, the human reason or logic organises those data. They draw from below, but the supermind draws from above. The foundation of things is above, the truth of things is above, and the supermind, instead of drawing things from below like the ordinary unenlightened human mind, draws from above. Whatever difficulty there is in doing so is only due to the habits of the mind, which still form a sort of an undercurrent to the whole operation till the mind is completely transformed. The mind's characteristic action on the lower plane dilutes the functioning of the supermind and lessens its effectivity.

Then there is the reason. Reason plays an important part in the normal functioning of the human mind. Of course reason is not alone. We know what are normally the functions of reason, but looming over the reason, enveloping the reason—whether we are aware of it or not—there is the intuition. The intuition is the link between the supermind and the mind. Whenever it gets an opportunity intuition percolates and gives us glimpses of truth, even when we are reasoning, theorising. Certain flashes come because the intuition is pressing from above. Pressing from below also is what we call the life-mind, the desires, the impulses of the life-mind or the vital mind. They tend to colour, to pull the reason in their own direction. Whether we are fully aware of it or not, much of the slant of our reason is due to this pull of the life-mind from below. So the reason does not function, ultimately, on its own. Always it is a triple action —from above the intuition, from below the life-mind, and reason-proper.

In the action of the supermind replacing the mental functioning, all these three undergo a change. Reason continues, but it does not confine itself to the data supplied by the senses. The working of the intuition is not sporadic, it is more regular, more organised and constantly corrects the tendency of logical reason to limit things, to fragment things.

Similarly, the supramental light falling on the human mind, the intuitive discrimination prevents the mixture of impulses of the life-mind from diluting and vitiating the action of the reason. Reason is allowed to continue its role as the link between the intuition above and the sense mind below.

When reason is exposed to the continuing action of the supermind its field enlarges. Note that reason is not displaced, reason is taken up, uplifted, enlarged, stretched out till it ceases to be the reason that we know. Behind the human reason is the supramental reason. Reason persists because of this supramental reason at its back. And reason, in the process of transformation, is not only active in the outer field, but also in the inner. Even at our level, while our reason looks at what we call the objective field. It is also aware of the truth within ourselves, the inner field. It judges them, assesses them from its own angle. Then it tries to understand what happens to other beings through their gestures, their words, through so many indirect channels. It tries to get knowledge of what is going on in others. And then there are planes of existence which are beyond and behind the physical—you may call them the occult—reason tries to analyse those phenomena also, study them and come to its own conclusions. And then there is the Self of things. Here also reason tries to understand the principle of things, principles not only of nature, but also of living beings, principles of creation. The reason is active in so many fields. The same processes continue, the same fields continue, though in an enlarged way when the supermind takes over the functioning of the mental reason. The data are enlarged upon, the judgements are more sure. The necessity for full and precise action is felt more and more when the range is extended, when more faculties come into operation and the supramental reason can deal with all more securely because it is in possession of the fundamental unity of things. Our human reason has to arrive at unity in a conceptual manner, but the supramental reason is naturally in possession of the fundamental unity and the variations are seen and studied by it in the context with the background of this unity.

After reason comes memory. In the functioning of the mind, we are all aware of the role that memory plays. Things have been stored up in our consciousness and there is a particular faculty called memory through which we recall, at any rate we attempt to recall what has passed. This individual memory, helped by what is called the race memory—not the recorded memory in the form of books and things, but the instinctual race memory where things come naturally to us. Each race has its own memory, the western races have their memory, the eastern races have theirs and these different kinds of memory—individual memory, the environmental memory and the race memory—all add to our fund of knowledge, our means of knowledge. These are deepened and much more is tapped through these memories by the supramental action than by the mental action.

Then there is the question of judgment. The human mind assembles the data, compares things, compares what is happening with what has happened in the past,

elsewhere, and then comes to a certain judgment which
may or may not be correct. Now proceeding from a base
of truth and guided by intuitive discrimination, the
supramental reason naturally comes to a correct judgment of things, never a wrong one. One judgment may
have to be revised in terms of a larger judgment, but
there is never a wrong judgment.

Imagination plays a wasting role in our life, our
mental life, though there have been cases where imagination has been helpful but by and large, imagination
leads to day-dreaming. When the supermind starts
functioning, imagination becomes a power, it becomes
what it originally was. That is, it assembles the various
possibilities that are still waiting to be actualised. When
we speak of human imagination we don't think of possibilities; our desires, our wishes are what take a mental
shape. In the supramental reason imagination becomes
a power of evoking a number of possibilities that are
behind the actualities of the present. And in the very
act of projecting these potentialities and dwelling upon
them, it gives them a power to realise themselves. So
imagination is made a link between what is manifest
and what is yet to manifest; whether all of it to be
manifested or not is decided by the supramental will,
but before the will can come into operation the will needs
to have before it all the possibilities still lying untapped.
Imagination plays that helpful role in the supramental
reason.

The mind can give us only knowledge of phenomena, the reality itself is not grasped. But when the
supramental reason starts, first comes the reality and
then come the phenomena, first comes the unity, then
the multiplicity. Everything proceeds from the base

of oneness, unity, reality; all else is a consequence. So
the whole process is reversed in the supramental reason.
Our reason comes into operation after the senses
contact. What does the supramental reason do? The
supramental reason also utilises the contact, but it is not
bound by the contact. The supramental reason may
make a physical sense contact or a subtle sense contact
a starting point, but it does not build its knowledge
upon that alone. It may use it as an occasion for a direct
contact of the consciousness with the object of knowledge.
You see a thing; that sight itself may be enough to form
a bridge, to form a link between the supramental reason
and the object of knowledge. But it is not bound. Even
without that sense contact, if there is a wish or a will in
me to know a thing, the consciousness contacts it directly.
If that object—it may be a human being, it may be anything—wants to yield its contents to me, my consciousness immediately responds and takes cognisance of it.
There is no indispensable need of the physical sense
contact. There can be a subtle sense contact, there can
be a thought contact. You may think of me or I may
think of you and a contact may be established. But these
kinds of contacts, subtle or gross, are not indispensable.

The supramental reason acts even as it takes cognisance of an objective field. It is, as Sri Aurobindo says,
subjectively objective. That is, it envelopes the object
with its own consciousness. I know intimately what is
happening in me—I am getting angry. I am feeling
happy, I have a warm feeling, there is a certain movement in my stomach; I don't need any other logical
proof, I know it. Similarly, the supramental reason,
when it takes knowledge of an objective reality, an
objective field, does it with the same facility, directness
and intimacy as I do today only with my subjective self.

Again the supramental reason, the supramental consciousness is cosmic or universal in its range. There is nothing really other or outside to it. At one level it is one with the universe. So when it wants to know a thing there is a spontaneous envelopment of that object. I can know things in the same way as I can know today what is happening within myself. There is a natural and a spontaneous oneness with the known. It is not that the knower is here and the known there with knowledge linking the two. The knower becomes one with the known. Knowledge becomes self-evident, there is a knowledge by identity.

If in the supramental reason we speak of observation, observation becomes a movement to bring out a latent knowledge. The knowledge of all things is there latent. An observation, a contact, a hearing—all these become occasions for the canalisation of consciousness, —the supramental reason in this case—to bring out the knowledge relevant to it. Otherwise there is an all-knowledge and a self-knowledge, but when I want to know a particular thing I observe it and that observation becomes an occasion for a flow in the particular direction, to bring out the knowledge that is there regarding that object. And this observation becomes a bridge of connection. What we discussed as *samyama*, concentration on an object to know its contents, in the yoga of Patanjali, is no more necessary, it is spontaneous. We do not need to concentrate, it is enough to direct our gaze, enough to have a thought of a thing in order to be filled with the knowledge of it.

*　　　　*

27

THE SUPRAMENTAL INSTRUMENTS— THOUGHT-PROCESS (II)

Among the questions raised at a recent seminar, one would be of interest to you because this question has been asked again and again, and has occurred to practically everyone who has thought about the subject. It is this: if and when the supermind is fully organised, will the whole creation be supramentalised and what will happen to the various levels of creation that we see to-day. Will all of them be perfected and all be supramental? Obviously, the answer is that it not going to be so. A new gradation, a new dimension will be added to the existing gradations of the creation. There are various levels of consciousness, of the forms of consciousness and the functionings of consciousness, and when the supramental is properly organised one more level will be added. That cannot mean that all will be supramentalised. Just as the fact that there is a mental level, a mental humanity, has not eliminated sub-human or sub-mental types, sub-mental orders of creation. Evolution will continue to be there doing its grades, and since creation is a continuous process, all the levels of life will be there. For those who want to be supramentalised the possibility will be open. But one important difference will be that the very fact that the supramental grade is fixed on earth will have its indirect effect upon all the grades in a more pronounced manner than the establishment and working of the mental grade has had. This plenary force of truth and knowledge and oneness which goes with the supramental consciousness will definitely weaken the hold of ignorance, limitation and division. The forces of disharmony will be contained and there will be a general uplifting of life, a more definite establishment of the movement towards oneness and harmony, a more pronounced movement of love and unity. But this does not preclude the continuation of the lower orders of creation, though their evolution will be expedited. Their course will be more speedy, but they will not be eliminated.

Q.: Supposing several persons advance along with path of transformation and then they die. How does it affect the next generation?

A.: Every advance registered in a human body becomes a permanent possession of humanity. Those persons may die, but what has been achieved in their bodies becomes a permanent possibility to others. So that is gain for humanity; that much has been achieved and established. It means nature has yielded to that extent and anyone who makes an effort thereafter can achieve what has been achieved already. It is just like an invention or a discovery. The person who does it may die, but what he has discovered, what he has achieved will be there open to all for all time. So any progressive movement done in creation is never lost. It becomes a permanent gain so that the next person really proceeds from that point onwards. The evolutionary spirit takes up from the point where it has been left before. And naturally, when those who have arrived at that particular state of evolution take birth again, they won't have to start with ABC. They will continue from the point they have left.

*   *

We were speaking last time of the supramental instruments. To recapitulate what we discussed, we said that all of our faculties, our mental and life-powers are truly distant projections of the workings of the supermind. Behind every moment of our mind, body and life there is the impulsion of the secret supermind. And when we speak of supramentalisation or the supermind taking over and changing our life, it means that all the faculties that we exercise today will be uplifted and changed into their supramental terms. Not only all the normally active faculties of the mind and external nature, but even the subliminal powers of which we are not conscious. The supramental consciousness will bring out these latent and occult powers from the subliminal, normalise them in our nature and add its own touch, give its own character of truth and will to them. So all the powers that are imbedded in man stand a chance of being uplifted and rendered into terms of the supramental faculties.

The highest faculty that man has developed so far is that of ideative knowledge in the mind. Pure knowledge, not knowledge loaded with considerations of practical life, but knowledge for its own sake—what is called *jnāna* in Sanskrit or ideative knowledge in English. Even though the thoughts, the ideas that move in that belt of ideative knowledge are true in a way, still they are not totally true. There are some limitations which are inescapable as long as we function through the mind. Now, the normal thought action of the mind, we noted, has a triple motion. There is what is called the habitual thought mind; the habitual thought mind is what is accustomed to receive the data collected by the senses, pass judgments and build some thought knowledge upon that basis. Thoughts revolve around these conclusions, these sense experiences—not only our own, but of those in the environment. Then there is a part of the habitual mind which is open to new knowledge, new ideas, but always they are made to flow into the mould of the previous knowledge. This is more or less mechanical; we accept certain ideas, thoughts, repeat them and whatever new knowledge or experience we gain, we give them that habitual, old coating. This is called the habitual mind. Then there is the pragmatic idea mind. We get ideas, we never evaluate them or assess them in their own light. We immediately relate them to our needs of life, what they mean for life, how far they can be translated into practical utility. This is what is called the pragmatic idea mind. Higher than that is the pure ideative mind where ideas and thoughts are received and considered in their own values, irrespective of whether they can serve life or not. They are pursued for their own knowledge content.

These are the three grades of mind—habitual mind, the pragmatic idea mind and the pure ideative mind. All these three are there in developed individuals but they conflict with each other. They function simultaneously, trying to seize a situation, they may conflict with each other and ultimately what we have may be a mixed action or a mixed judgment. In the supermind all the three will exist but in a coordinated movement. There will be no obstruction in their functioning because the supermind is in possession of the truth of things and the mind will not be obliged to lose itself, as it does today, in the ideative regions. When the mind is pulled up from our present state, above a certain height of the ideative mind, and exposed to the vastness of consciousness—to thoughtless peace, for instance—the mind tends to lose itself, lose its identity, but this will not happen in the supermind because the essential truth of things is always present. Secondly, the pragmatic element also will be there but it will never be the deciding factor. It can be an instrument, it can be a link between the higher consciousness and the life-mind. Even the mechanical movement, habitual mechanical movement, will change its character but the movement will be there. There will be, instead of the pure ideative mind, pragmatic mind and habitual mind, what Sri Aurobindo calls an order of thought, a cycle of will and stability in motion. This habitual mind movement is really an expression of what nature strives for in order to bring about stability in a flux. By constant repetition, by constant habitual movement, a kind of stability is introduced in a situation full of flux. This habitual mind renders itself as an instrument leading to stability in motion in the supermind. What is pragmatic mind becomes cycle of will. It is the will that decides. And the ideative mind becomes an order of thought. All these will not be based or derived from lower nature but from higher nature whose foundations are above and not below.

Again, in our mind there is a play of three elements —the life-mind or what we call the mind embedded in life, the intuition and the reason. Reason is the bridge between life-mind and intuition. All the three are interconnected. Intuition has to be organised by the reason and then communicated to the life-mind. Similarly the impulses of the life-mind have to be assimilated by the reason and then submitted to the light of intuition. All these three will also continue in the supermind, but in a coordinated action based upon unity. The reason, however, cannot be the absolute power that it claims to be at our level. It can only act as a link.

Further, we noted that the human reason, in the normal mental functioning, has an outer field, nature, and an inner field within ourselves. It takes note of other beings, what is happening to them, how they react to us; and then within ourselves or within nature there is the occult which starts with the Self. All these will continue, the process also will be the same—namely gathering the data, arrangement by the reason and the arriving at a judgment. The necessity for more precise action leads to the development of reason and to the faculties like intuition which are above it.

Helping the mental reason is memory. Memory, as we noted, is not only what each individual remembers, but it also means the race memory. Memory, not only artificially recorded in history and literature, but something that has sunk in the consciousness of the race and which comes to the forefront when we will to know it; or nature pushes it up when the situation demands. So this memory which is playing a part in the mind plays a greater part in the supermind because the range of memory is enlarged. Similarly not only of the past but there is a memory of the pre-known, what is going to happen. Somewhere it has been decided and that is projected as the memory of the future.

And there is the power of imagination, which does play a constructive part even at our level. It plays a greater, an interpretative part and the role of summoning many possibilities into the field of actuality. So judgment, imagination, memory—all these which help the human reason have a larger and a greater role to play in the supermind. The supermind lifts up the reason, converts it into the supramental reason, but the procedure it adopts is not that of the normal human reason—mainly collecting the data, arrangement of it and then coming to a judgment. The supermind may use this process but it is not bound to it. It has got its own means. It can use the contact of the senses, the thought contact, without the necessity of the outer senses. The subtler sense can contact the object, a thought can contact the object without even seeing it. But more than that, the supermind being in possession of the truth of things, it has only to will to know and the knowledge is self-evident. It does not have to move through our procedures. It may do it but when it wants, it can know directly because it is in possession of the knowledge by identity. The supramental reason also acts. Its way of action is described by Sri Aurobindo as subjectively objective. That is, even when we are subjective there is a certain objectivity about it. It is not coloured by our subjectivity. Within ourselves the knower can observe objectively.

Then there is the universal consciousness without which the supramental consciousness cannot come. And that consciousness being always there, there is an undercurrent of oneness with the known. Observation is a movement to bring out the latent knowledge, but even observation is not indispensable. It can provide a bridge of connection if we need it. There is a state of the supramental consciousness where no such bridge is required.

There are three movements of the supramental reason. I project myself and know the object or the object emanates its knowledge to me and I know or I know simply by supramental cognition. A will to know a thing or a will to be known is enough. A will to know in me or a will to be known in another is enough to make the knowledge present in my mind, rather the supermind. Again, the supermind is not analytical in the mental way. There is a direct seizing. It does not need to assemble the various multiple forms and say this is the one. There is a simultaneous presence of the truth of unity and the truth of multiplicity. Both are present, the mind does not need to remind itself that this multiplicity is a many-sided projection of the unity. There is a simultaneous awareness, cognition of unity and multiplicity.

Similarly, the supramental consciousness knows the *gunas* or the qualities or the modes of each form, in what proportion they are active, what is the nature or grade of consciousness that is active in each form. And this it can know by identity or by wanting to know it. The knowledge of the supermind is not confined to the physical plane, but extends to what happens on other planes also. The human mind, the human reason is confined to the domain of the physical, but the supermind is simultaneously aware of all the planes of existence. The supermind does not need to get evidence or data for judgment, it is its own evidence. The judgment is spontaneous, natural. And even what is called logic at the human level has a place in the supramental consciousness. Logic in its transformed role links knowledge with knowledge, organises the different placements of knowledge. Because though essentially all knowledge is one, for purposes of manifestation the knowledge may organise itself into different stresses—now a stress on one aspect, now a stress on another. There are still higher ranges of knowledge above the supramental reason, and they are the ranges of knowledge essentially based upon identity.

Sri Aurobindo adds that as long as there is still an undercurrent of mental working, all that has been described will not be absolute. It is only when the supramental consciousness or the supermind functions entirely unpolluted, undiluted by the mental elements that things are in this strain. But till the mind is completely transformed, the lower we come the more diluted the action is likely to be; the higher we go, the nearer the action is likely to correspond with this description.

(From Questions & Answers)

Mind has various grades. There is a part which is always restless, agitated, running about. There is a part which is practically occult or subliminal, which is quiet, receptive to larger vistas of knowledge. Now what he means is that the frontal part of the mind which is normally agitated, in movement, has to be silent so that the deeper part of the mind is free and can develop. After all the main part of the mind which develops is not on the surface. The surface mind has to be quieted and silenced so that we can become aware of the deeper mental consciousness evolving—and not only become aware, but open ourselves to its action and participate in its growth. It is a simultaneous process.

28

THE SUPRAMENTAL SENSE (I)

During the course of our discussion of the various means of knowledge we have had occasion to speak of the highest mode of knowledge as being knowledge by indentity. Knowledge by identity is when our consciousness is in full touch with the object of knowledge and has a spontaneous knowledge of the contents of that object. One does not have to make an effort—mental or otherwise—to know it. The consciousness identifies itself with the object and there is a self-aware knowledge that emerges from the contact. This is called knowledge by identity.

There is another way and that is when the consciousness embraces the object, envelopes the object and comes to know by a kind of comprehending action. That is called *vijnāna*. The third is when the identity is pushed into the background and there is an operation by which the knower separates the known from himself and studies it, keeping the object in front. That is what we would called the apprehending movement or the *prajnāna*. And there is the fourth, which is the contact of the senses. It is not like the contact of the physical senses which provide only the data. These are subtler senses—the vital sense, the spiritual sense or the mental sense. The moment we want to know a thing, it immediately contacts it and seizes the knowledge. That is called *samjnāna*. These three or four modes have been discussed at length by Sri Aurobindo in his commentary on the Kena Upanishad though he refers to them in passing in the present chapter on the Supramental Sense. The point is, there is a knowledge that can be got sheerly through the senses. Only they have to be subtle senses, they do not need the instrumentation of reason, of discrimination and other mental apparatus. There is a spontaneous contact of the sense with the object.

In day-to-day life, as things are organised at present, though we speak of the five senses, we know that those five senses have to report to the mind and it is the mind that builds the knowledge based upon the data of the senses—hearing, seeing etc. That is why the mind is called the sixth sense. In fact it is the only real sense. There is a mental sense and in the supramental consciousness also there is a sense of its own. On each grade of our being there is a corresponding sense and as we rise higher, each sense is more free, less limited. As the spiritual sense rises in its consciousness, in purity, it becomes the power of the spirit. There sense does not mean something that we have to inhibit, to negate, as is true in the life of ignorance. When the Upanishad speaks of being aware of everything as Brahman—we see Brahman, we hear Brahman—it is not a metaphor, it is not a poetic figure. It is an actual experience of the spiritual sense.

Sri Aurobindo was asked once what he meant by "seeing Brahman everywhere". He said, "When I look at this table, it is not a table for me. I actually see Brahman in that form". This is the knowledge yielded by the spiritual sense.

Now the supramental sense is something more because it is based entirely upon the total truth. The spiritual sense may be based upon a partial truth, but a supramental sense is based upon the total truth. When it starts functioning we see all as God and all in God. The sense action that takes place is a manifestation of this knowledge. This knowledge pours itself in a dynamic form and that is its sense action. On our mental plane, when we go into trance or a tranced condition, we are superbly self-aware. When we come out into a waking condition that awareness changes. We become aware of things as a manifestation of that consciousness—the consciousness is not self-gathered but self-rolling. Both are true, but in the supramental state there is a simultaneous knowledge. There is not a separate know-ledge of self-awareness and other-awareness. There is a simultaneous state of knowledge in which the self-aware, gathered condition is present even where there is the varied knowledge. And when the supramental sense starts functioning it has a totality, a sense of truth, a largeness of range that extends even to things which are not yet in physical existence. Because the senses are subtler, they take cognisance of things which are in manifestation on a subtler plane but not yet organised or seen by the physical eye in the physical existence.

When the supramentalisation starts, Sri Aurobindo describes, there is a complete transformation of all the parts of the being—gradually but steadily. As the supra-mental consciousness flows, there is a constant downflow and at a certain stage it turns into an outflow—outflow from the senses, outflow from the being and the faculties —into the universe around. So there is first the downpour of that consciousness, then the outflow, and then the supramentalisation. And this supramentalisation extends to the physical—not only to the mind, not only to the heart, but even to the physical faculties. When the supramental sense sees or comes near a physical object, there is an automatic report, not only of the thing as it strikes the physical eye but even what is behind, what is above, what is within. That is, by one stroke of action it shows the supraphysical truth of a physical thing, not only the physical. It removes and eliminates the deforming element and looks into the soul of things and makes the knowledge of the indwelling soul, the indwelling truth—undeformed—a part of our knowledge. And this is not a laboured knowledge. The supramental sense, yielding the supramental knowledge, uncovers the physical form in no time but it does not ignore the physical form. It reports the physical element, the physical form in its highest value, and also what is behind the form, the truth that activates that form.

And here, Sri Aurobindo mentions, the supramental sense adds a fourth dimension. We normally speak of three dimensions, but the supramental sense adds a fourth dimension concretely, and that is the dimension of a certain internality which we normally ignore. Each object is seen not as a separate unity by itself but always as a part of the whole. When you see a thing it is immediately revealed to you what is the part it plays in the total scheme. Even with things that are unpleasant, things that are ugly when their ugliness strikes you, you know why it is ugly, in what way it is serving the cosmic scheme by being ugly. The intention behind it is immediately revealed so that your reaction is one of understanding, not one of disgust, not one of condemnation.

If this is an outline—for an outline is all that we can understand—of the supramental sight, the supramental sense vision, there is a supramental hearing also. Whatever sounds you hear, whatever words you hear— it is always a part of the cosmic harmony. Always the things behind the words or sounds make an impact and it is the voice of the Divine that you hear behind every sound, behind every word. In that state it is the Infinite that is heard, the Infinite as it expresses itself to the hearing but also the Infinite in its silence. When you hear the word you also hear the silence supporting that word. This is the supramental hearing.

There is an opening of new ranges of power, both in sight and in hearing, without making any effort. The subtler ranges open themselves in their full intensity. So when a supramental person is seeing he apparently sees all that we see, but at the same time he sees much that is behind, much that is above. So his assessment of things, his evaluation of things is bound to be different from ours —we being mentally governed human beings who see only the surface of things, who hear only the outermost speech. And this is where even the discordant elements reveal their *rasa*, their part of the delight of existence. Immense ranges open up before the embodied mind, the physical senses find their fields enlarged. The supramental sense also takes note of the enlargement of the life-range, the life energies and their origins, their field, their action—all of them are opened to the cognisance of the supramental sense, even as the physical energies and the physical workings are. But that is not the end. Even the vital sense is spiritualised. So what Sri Aurobindo calls the supramentalisation of the vital, adds an undeformed truth dimension to the life ranges. The supramental awakes in us the consciousness that supports the vital sheath, the *prāna kośa*. Our physical body is able to move, function because of the vital body that supports it. Now when the supramental sense starts functioning we become aware of the vital sheath, the vital body as concretely as we are conscious of the physical. Practically no gulf is experienced between the physical and the vital energies so that there is a constant streaming of the life-energies in the body, streaming not only from our own vital self but from the universal.

We become conscious of the interchange that goes on between the universal life energies and the individual life energy. We can stop them outside before they enter and act, we can control them. With the enlargement of the range there is also the enlargement of the control, of the power. With the growth of the supramental sense all these take place, one after another. Each has its own action on every level of the being. The limitations of individual life are broken down and man feels himself standing in the midst of an ocean—ocean of mental energies, life-energies, physical energies—as a fixed point of solidity, an individual frame. And as the supramentalisation proceeds, the vital energies reveal themselves as currents of the universal Shakti, a universal Power. And that universal Power also, as the supramentalisation proceeds and our sensitivity increases, reveals itself as the Chit-Shakti, that is the consciousness-force of the transcendent who is also the universal and of which the individual is an instrument.

So there is a continuous linkage between the transcendental, the universal and the individual. That is vertical, you can say. Horizontally also, there is a live interchange with the ocean of energies around. There is nothing hidden from the supramental sight, there is no word, no speech, that cannot be heard by the supramental hearing.

Sri Aurobindo wrote these chapters somewhere before 1920. Now in the Sonnets, on the same subject, written about 16 or 17 years later, the same idea is there
. in a more expressive form. For instance, he speaks in
The Divine Hearing:

> All sounds, all voices have become thy voice
> Music and thunder and the cry of birds,
> Life's babble of her sorrows and joys,

Cadence of human speech and murmured words,
The laughter of the sea's enormous mirth,
The winged plane purring through the conquered
    air,
The auto's trumpet-song of speed to earth,
The machine's reluctant drone, the siren's blare
Blowing upon the windy horn of Space
A call of distance and of mystery,
Memories of sun-bright lands and ocean-ways,—
All now are wonder tones and themes of Thee.
A secret harmony steals through the blind heart
And all grows beautiful because Thou art.
All is the voice of God.

Similarly, there is the *Divine Sight*:
Each sight is now immortal with thy bliss:
My soul through the rapt eyes has come to see;
A veil is rent and they no more can miss
The miracle of Thy world-epiphany.
Into an ecstasy of vision caught
Each natural object is of Thee a part,
A rapture-symbol from Thy substance wrought,
A poem shaped in Beauty's living heart,
A master-work of colour and design,
A mighty sweetness borne on grandeur's wings;
A burdened wonder of significant line
Reveals itself in even commonest things.
All forms are Thy dream-dialect of delight,
O Absolute, O vivid Infinite.

Then last is *The Divine Sense*:
Surely I take no more an earthly food
But eat the fruits and plants of Paradise!
For thou hast changed my sense's habitude
From mortal pleasure to divine surprise.

Hearing and sight are now an ecstasy,
And all the fragrances of earth disclose
A sweetness matching in intensity
Odour of the crimson marvel of the rose.
In every contact's deep invading thrill,
That lasts as if its source were infinite,
I feel Thy touch: Thy bliss imperishable
Is crowded into that moment of delight.
The body burns with Thy rapture's sacred fire,
Pure, passionate, holy, virgin of desire.

Significantly, someone met me yesterday and gave me a sentence or two which the Mother had spoken somewhere about 1970, when there was some discussion about a Tamil saint who is said to have conquered death, but all the same died. When the Mother was asked for an explanation, she said there is something in the atmosphere which brings about death as long as things are what they are. Then she proceeded to say, "What is important for those who are here now is to develop their consciousness of the physical world so that they are conscious of it without the physical organs—eyes, ears, fingers, etc. And this is perfectly possible,". That is, one must develop the faculty of being conscious on the physical plane without making use of the physical senses. It should not be that we see only when the eyes are open, hear only through the physical ears, feel the touch only through our fingers. She says it is possible and we must develop our consciousness—the Supramental Sense, ultimately—so that we are conscious of things even when the senses do not function physically. And then she added, when the body goes, the body goes. That is, the consciousness remains. The physical body is not necessary to get into contact with things. The senses are

19

no longer necessary. You can be conscious of things, you can act upon things without using the physical senses. When the body goes, the being remains, the consciousness remains.

There is one more section of the chapter which we shall take up next time. All that we are discussing is only to give us an idea of how things can be. This is not an exact description or transcription of the functioning of the supramental sense, but compared to what we are, compared to how the mental senses function, this gives an idea.

*   *

The supramental sense will be more in correspondence with the delight principle; supramental thinking will be more in correspondence with the truth; supramental action will be in correspondence with the force aspect, with the *cit-tapas*. The basic reality of the supramental person, his existence corresponds to the *sat* principle, his thinking and knowledge to *cit*, his dynamic action to *cit-tapas*, his sense to the delight or the *ānanda* aspect.

29

THE SUPRAMENTAL SENSE (II)

The last section of the chapter on the Supramental Sense is highly interesting because it largely deals with what are called psychic powers, powers of clairvoyance, clair-audience, miracles, materialisations, things which are very dazzling to the modern mind and have been taken up as subjects for research in some of the universities in the West. We do not have institutions doing research in these subjects in the East because they do not excite the same response in the East as they do in the West. In the West they have developed the logical and scientific frame of mind which feels challenged when these miracles and things outside the purview of physical science take place. But in the East they have always been accepted as part of life, though it is known that only those who are advanced in their consciousness, who are nearer the God-level, can operate these miracles, as also those who are specially adept, who have qualified themselves by training or who are so gifted. It is taken for granted that miracles happen and they are a fact of life. In what way are they a fact of life, that is the question.

Sri Aurobindo points out that when the inner consciousness opens and the soul starts blossoming, it awakes many of the latent powers in the subliminal, in the inner mental and even the inner vital. Forces which are not easily seen or experienced in physical life, at the physical level, come into operation and we see new things happening. For instance, a man whose psychical consciousness is awakening may suddenly feel intuitions, thought readings, premonitions taking place in him.

19-A

They are not miracles but logical consequences of the powers and faculties that have come into operation. These powers are there on all the levels of the being—the mind, the life-part otherwise called the vital, the physical body and the subliminal. These forces may begin to operate from anywhere and lead to results which are called abnormal or extraordinary. But these results are not exactly as they should be. A particular force or power coming into operation from within should lead to a certain result. But normally it does not—it gets deformed, diminished, exaggerated in some ways. This is due to the interference of our own grosser parts, our ego, our desire, our likes and dislikes; all these subconsciously coat the experience and turn it into something totally different from what it should have been. This danger is very much present in the early stages when the inner ranges are opened and if the seeker has not taken pains to purify himself, to vacate these elements of impurity, elements of dilution and deflection and deviation, then there are these exaggerated consequences. He may lose his head and land in quite a different direction instead of the spiritual. That is why our ancients always made it a rule that he who seeks God shall not cultivate these powers and even if these powers manifest on their own, he shall not indulge them. They made an absolute rule—that is another exaggeration. If the seeker takes care to keep his discrimination, to eliminate beforehand the offending elements like desire and ego and ambition, and is vigilant enough to prevent these things from entering by the back door or any door, then this rule need not apply.

The manifestation of these latent powers is not omething that is unnatural, un-divine. In fact it is natural, as natural at that level, as our hearing and seeing with our physical senses are in our present state of consciousness. The point is that as soon as the psychical consciousness exerts its influence or touch upon the subliminal or the inner levels of the being, these latent powers begin to come into operation. We begin to hear what we normally would not hear with the physical ear, to see beyond the physical sight and so on. They are not something extraordinary, these do not require any degree of spirituality. All that is required is that there should be a predisposition in the person towards these occult manifestations. There are many yogis, seekers, who have not had these experiences at all. They go ahead deepening their consciousness, purifying themselves, arriving at an increasing identity with the Divine without having a single occult experience of this type. They do not see a single vision, hear a single mystic sound, but on that account you cannot say that they are not progressing. The progress is the progress of consciousness. All these may be likened to fire-works. And it is this zone, what Sri Aurobindo calls elsewhere the intermediate zone, where the seeker has to be doubly careful to see that the working of these powers is not deflected, that things are kept in their proper perspective. One does not become great spiritually by the fact of the occult powers.

Another result of the psychical opening is that the range of experience becomes illimitable. Today the range of our experience is limited to the extent of our physical senses. We may enlarge it with the help of physical instruments like the telescope, hearing devices etc. The spontaneous development of the psychic sense is different. Just as we have a physical sense, we spoke the other day of a vital sense, similarly there is what is called the psychical sense. It operates through all the five faculties; but the psychical sense does not have to use the physical organs. When the psychical sight is open one can see things through a wall, see things a thousand miles away from here. One may actually see what is happening, or the images may appear on the screen of the psychic sight. There is a psychical ether, a mental ether on which all activity is recorded. It is called *cit ākāśa* which contains the impressions or transcriptions of things that have happened on earth, that are happening and may happen. When the psychic sight opens one sees these effortlessly.

This is not confined to impressions from the earth-scene. It can as well be from the various planes of existence that overtop and surround the earth world. One may see what is happening, say on the subtle physical plane and know beforehand what it indicates, what things are preparing there to precipitate themselves in the physical universe. That is, one can know beforehand the possibility and in some cases the near-actuality of what is going to happen.

Then there are thought images caught by the psychical sight. I think, you think, and these thought-images come before the psychical vision. It is not in the form of thoughts or ideas that one understands or grasps, it is through images. The psychical discrimination points out whether the images have been originated in oneself or in another. One has to develop that art of sifting, knowing what things are going out from one and what are coming in from outside. One can see a crowd of thoughts in you, a crowd in me, but there is also such a thing as a mass of thoughts in the atmosphere, the universal atmosphere. They don't belong to anybody in particular now, though somebody may have thought them sometime back. These thoughts float in the atmosphere though the originating person may have forgotten about them.

Similarly, the psychical sense puts us in touch with the psychical parts of others as also of things. Not merely with humans, but also with material things. Those also are connected because in even the most material thing there is a psychical element. So one's psychical sense lands upon that psychical element, whether it be in a human being or in a material thing. It establishes a connection with it, enters into some sort of identity with it, and knows it. And if one knows, one can also influence something to move, to function in a particular direction. All that depends upon the strength of the will that one has. This applies not only to our physical plane but also to the other planes. The psychical sense can get into touch with things and beings and forces of the various planes of existence. The gradation of planes, the number of worlds on each plane, is a fact and as the psychical sense grows there is a greater awareness of these planes and the worlds on these planes. As knowledge increases the power given by the knowledge also increases and it is possible to acquire control over things on the other planes too.

This leads to the awakening of the mind as the sixth sense. Mind is called the sixth sense but in our usual day-to-day life the mind is content to be a slave of the five senses. But as it develops, as the pressure of the psychical consciousness tells upon the mind, the original character of the mind as the sixth sense comes to the front. One can contact others through this mind. What purpose does the contacting serve? We contact others through the physical senses, is that not enough? There are aspects of life where it is not enough, particularly in spiritual life; this contacting of sombody else through

the mental sense or the psychical sense for a spiritual
purpose is an important part of the spiritual tradition.
The Master has always this contact with the disciples.
He may or may not have physical contact, physical
means of contact. He may not write to them, but with
this inner sense or the mind as the sixth sense, there is a
continuous communication. The teacher knows what
is going on, he exerts his will.

This also helps in arriving at a mastery of oneself.
As things stand we are aware of hardly one-tenth of
ourselves. This awakening of the psychical sense or the
mental sense helps us to know ourselves more intimately
and acquire control over the movements which are
normally behind the veil. Also, the various planes of our
own being are opened up, images appear which are
seized by the inner sense—may be a word, may be a
figure with potency. Those images, those words, are
communicated to the physical mind by the inner awakened sense and they become springs, as it were, or steps to
cross over into the realm of the superconscient.

Like the physical sense, the vital sense, the psychical
sense also is but an instrument. It is not the final goal.
The psychical sense has to operate through the mind,
through the other instruments, and there is the possibility—why possibility, the certainty—of dilution. Man
being a mental being, even the psychical has to precent
itself and receive intimations through the mind, and
there is the possibility of error, of a lowering in consciousness. But this is prevented once the psychical consciousness and sense are subjected to the transformation
by the supramental force. Now, can the psychical be
transformed, you would ask. Sri Aurobindo says, yes.
The psychical also is to be subjected to the working of
the supramental consciousness and force, and when it is

so uplifted, elevated and changed in terms of the supramental it becomes the supra-psychical. When that takes place, when the supramental consciousness suffuses the psychical consciousness, one gets a spontaneous unity with the universal mind. There is unity with the universal, one acquires a universalised consciousness and a universalised sense. One is aware of both the one and the many, with the result that the fragmentariness of experience is removed. One doesn't feel one experience separate from other experiences, severely individual or aloof from others. The psychical becomes normal in its functioning. There is nothing abnormal thereafter in psychical sight, psychical hearing.

After the sense, comes the change of substance. It is not enough if there is a change of consciousness, there should be a change in the stuff of consciousness, that is, the ether on which or in which the consciousness functions. That too must be changed. The physical leads to the psychical, the psychical leads to the supramental transformation and with this the infinite consciousness acts through the universalised individual. That is, there is the unity between the individual, the universal and the transcendent. The supramental sense, the supramental consciousness does not depend upon our physical senses, though it may use the physical senses. It may use them as a starting point, but even without those physical senses, without our physical hearing or seeing or touching, the supramental consciousness can get direct knowledge and wield a spontaneous power that is wielded by such a knowledge.

There is one more point to note. Once the psychical consciousness or the psychical sense awakes, may be as a result of discipline, or may be as a result of sheer grace or the impact of powerful spiritual personality, you start

seeing things, hearing things and Sri Aurobindo says
that they look so vivid that there is almost a physical
organisation. It is almost a breakthrough into the physical scene, a materialisation which is almost physical.
Now this has intrigued me for the last 20 or 25 years,
ever since I read the book, *Autobiography of a Yogi* by
Yogananda. He describes there how his guru or his guru's
guru appeared, how beautiful buildings arose etc. They
disappeared after their purpose was over. The vividity
of the experience continued and it was as real, or perhaps
more real than things on the physical plane. How is that
so?

I had long thought that it must be happening somewhere on the subtle physical and the person thinks that
it has happened here. But in this chapter Sri Aurobindo
explains such phenomena, saying that they are materialisation in a special sense, of things that are happening
elsewhere. Our own physical contributions may enter,
but by and large they are happening somewhere and
they are projected in the earth atmosphere, so we can't
say they are not true. We can't say they are true in the
sense in which we understand it either. So if we think
that these are all imaginations we are wrong. If we think
that all these things are there organised, only we do not
see them, that also is not true. They are organised in
another world but by circumstances or by will or for
some cosmic purpose they are precipitated into the earth
atmosphere and if at that time there are other people
around the person concerned, they also may participate
in that vision. For that moment their other faculties are
suspended, they are under that spell, as it were, and they
also see those things.

All this is the result of the awakening of the inner
sense, the psychical sense, the spiritual faculties or the

latent faculties. They put us in touch with what is happening on other planes—what is happening on the physical plane itself, beyond the range normally accessible to us, what is happening elsewhere, on other planes, and the whole thing passes before the mind as on a screen. When those things happen it looks as if only those things are real and what is going on on earth is illusory, relatively false. But that again is an exaggeration. Each thing is true on its plane—the only thing that is true on all planes is the divine consciousness and the divine truth. Everything else is a formation, a manifestation—real in the setting in which it is manifest.

(From Questions & Answers)

Now, the question is, if one does not have the faculty of seeing things which are seeable when the psychical sense is awake, what should one do to see them. The answer would depend upon the person who asks it, because if he is a spiritual seeker, the answer would be, how does it help his spiritual growth to see things which he does not normally see? It may satisfy his curiosity, but does it help in the growth of his consciousness? But if one is a seeker of knowledge, wants to expand his mind, add to the fund of knowledge that he has—say a scientist—well, he has to undergo a psychological discipline to be able to exert pressure, exert his will and steadily enlarge the area of awareness, that is, enlarge his consciousness. Either we enlarge our consciousness, or by concentration, deepen the consciousness. In either case we must break through the barriers of the surface consciousness and then if we have that will, the psychical centre responds and things start blossoming.

30

SUPRAMENTAL TIME-VISION

We have arrived at the last chapter of the *Synthesis of Yoga* which we have been studying for over two years. This chapter has for its theme the Supramental Time-Sense. We have seen how the kind of knowledge yielded by the supramental sense differs from the knowledge of the physical senses. Here we come to the question of time, the experience of time and timelessness. Does this differ — knowledge or experience of time and timelessness—in the supramental consciousness, does it differ suddenly or are there steps from our mental feeling and experience to the supramental in this regard? It is a fact that as things stand, the timeless Infinite above and around, and the Infinite in time —that is, what we call time—are co-existent. We say co-existent because it has been the experience of many who have arrived at definite spiritual realisation, that *within* they are conscious of the eternal, the timeless, but on the surface they deal in terms of time. So both are accessible, even in our existing state of things.

What is our experience when our mind tries to experience this timeless Infinite? The mind is unable to keep itself in a functioning state, functioning in the normal sense, when it goes beyond a certain level. At most it can reflect the Eternal, and that it does in states of concentration like trance, samadhi. But the experience is always that the Eternal, the Infinite is above. The most that the mind can do is to reflect it; when it tries to reach it, to grasp it, the mind fails. To make the sense and feeling of the Eternal normal is not possible within

the formula of the mind. Even if the mind is enlightened, illuminated, it is not possible for the Eternal to
function as a faculty, though it may reflect itself. It is
only in the supramental consciousness that it is natural
to have the experience of the timeless Infinite, and at the
same time the Infinite in time, as a natural state and not
as something that is acquired. This includes the vision
of the three times; in Sanskrit, it is called *trikāladṛṣṭi*, in
English, a simultaneous vision of the present, the past and
the future. Naturally this cannot be achieved in one
jump. The mind has to ascend the various levels of consciousness and being. We start with our ignorant mind,
and for our ignorant mind knowledge is something which
is outside. It has to search for it, to grope for it and acquire it. But as it ascends, as rays of the higher knowledge
fall upon it, something is awakened and the mind becomes
aware that the true knowledge is within, not without.
Outer circumstances become only occasions for the
inner awakening. That is because the mind, at such
times, is in tune, if it is not one, with the universal mind.
All knowledge relevant to us, pertaining to this creation,
is there embedded in the universal mind. All truths are
perceived there though not all simultaneously for that
would cause confusion. Whatever truths one needs to
know, wants to know, reveal themselves. The rest are
all there. There is an automatic operation by which
what is needed comes to the front once one attains to
the supramental consciousness.

In the ignorant mind, that is mostly the human
mind as it is today, the Infinite in time is something that
the mind does not possess. At most, it is the time expression of the Infinite which it knows, but not the infinite
content. This is because the ignorant mind lives in a
succession of moments. Things are not stretched out

like a map to it as they are to some other mind. Moment to moment it knows, but there is a certain continuity in the background. The mind, as it is, is conscient only of what is present before it. The continuity is given by the spirit in the background.

The past is there projecting itself in the present, in this moment. This moment is not something in a vacuum. This moment has behind it a series of moments, which have produced it. So the past lives, and if we want, even our ignorant mind can recover something of it, depending on the strength of its memory. There is a limit to which the ignorant mind can go back and recover its past. But man is not content to live in the present, confined to the moment. So he goes on reasoning from cause to effect. He draws inferences and comes to certain conclusions, formulates a knowledge. This is alright as long as knowledge is confined to the realm of physical nature because there things are most rigidly organised and a particular cause normally leads to a particular effect and a particular effect normally presumes a particular cause. But as we go above or behind the physical level and come into the domain of life and mind, there is a change. There is an indefinite possible, as Sri Aurobindo calls it, a number of possibilities come into the picture. So our law—this cause leads to this effect—may not work out, because between the working of this cause into this effect any number of possibilities may intervene, may dilute, may deviate—we do not know. There is much more in a situation beyond the physical laws and the inferences based upon physical data. Even behind this life and mind, as we develop our knowledge, we may be able to get some idea of the soul and the spirit behind, introducing a totally new element which cannot be measured, defined by the reasoning mind. With the inner doors of our being opening on the subliminal or the psychical being—not psychic, but psychical—a new time-sense comes to the front. Suddenly we become aware that there are three visions possible, what Sri Aurobindo calls the retro-past vision the circum-conscient vision and the prevision into the future. The vision extends as far as we want to go back, around also—not only what we see before us, but quite outside the physical range of vision, and also into the future. But these are likely to be mixed. We may see alright, but our interpretation or even our seeing and rendering of the vision in terms of the physical understanding is liable to be interfered with by many factors. It is only an intuitive discrimination that can sift things. For that we have to go beyond the highest levels of the mind, the reasoning mind, and we have to cultivate and organise the working of intuition.

From our level of the ignorant mind, a number of sciences have been formulated—like astrology, palmistry, and so on. But these are subject to the same errors as the three visions are subject to when the mind is not purified. There is always a possibility of diminution. It is a fact, Sri Aurobindo says, that there are a number of systems of correspondence between planets and things, between this thing and that. That they are there was originally perceived by our subliminal or psychical sense, afterwards the mind came forward—the logical mind or mind of intelligence—to regularise, to systematise these perceptions. These sciences, he points out, as they are organised into branches of learning, are accurate enough as far as they refer to the past. Even visions and intimations about the past that has already happened are fairly accurate. They may be correct with what is happening at present also, but where it concerns the future it is very problematic. Because we do not have the faculties to know what are likely to be the possibilities interfering with what look to be certainties. With what is past, there is nothing to be discussed; with the present, there is an intelligent anticipation, we can look and see; but regarding the future we simply do not have the means. Even these sciences like astrology give indications, but they can never be positive or binding.

The true knowledge of the past, the present and the future can be got only when the psychical consciousness and the psychical faculties are awake. For all practical purposes we can say that these are the deeper subliminal faculties. When they are awake, the past, the present and future pass before us as images. Now images are not only visual images; there are what are called auditory images and there are other kinds which we cannot describe in our human language which is designed to express only one order of experience. But there are images and images. Sri Aurobindo sounds a warning which everyone should note. He says even when this psychical and the subliminal awake and the images cone, say of the past, all the images that come need not necessarily be the images of what has taken place. They can also be images of what tried to take place, images of what somebody wanted to take place, at different levels. They are all mixed up and when we say it must be true because it has appeared, it need not be so. Similarly in the present, there are a number of things struggling for supremacy and all these images may appear. So too in the future, the images may be of the likely possibilities. Which one is going to succeed we do not know. So at any rate for the past and the present we must have a psychical discrimination, intuitive discrimination to say that this fructified, the others tried but failed. That is why there is confusion, there

is the possibility of being mislead. In a horse race ten or
fifteen horses may run, but only one horse wins. The
whole thing is stamped in the etheric atmosphere. When
we see it, we see this horse, that horse, another horse,
but it needs an intuitive discrimination to know which
has won. As ordinary mind cannot arrive at that certainty, the certitude can be given only by intuition, a
supramentalised intuition. Even in intuition there are
grades. There is an intuition that works through the
mind, an intuition that works through the vital, an
intuition that works in a mixed mind, an intuition which
works at the top of the mind but is still subject to the
pulls of the mind, and above that there is an intuition
which functions on a pure intuitive level. The pure intuitive level, outside the range of these lower pulls,
becomes possible only when the supramental light starts
functioning on the intuitive plane.

The psychical being can, to a great extent, grasp
these truths. We do not have to wait till the supramental
consciousness is organised. The psychical being is open
to pure intimations from the universe, it is not confined
to the individual scheme, it spreads out, stretches out
into the universe so that intimations from the universal
sail into the psychical being. Even there, Sri Aurobindo
says, there is the possibility of error because the psychical
consciousness does not live in the indivisible continuity
of spirit. It is still involved in manifestation. The continuity behind does not relate itself to that, and even what
comes as intimation from the universal being is mixed,
it partakes of obscurities in the universal nature. Intuitive vision and intuitive discrimination alone can separate the obscured and the unobscured portions of truth
as it places itself before the psychical faculty. After all
these precautions are taken, when the psychical being

or the soul is able to get this knowledge, it is maintained, exercised as an abnormal power, as an acquisition, as something which functions when we are at the height of our consciousness. It is not natural. To make it natural is possible only when the supramental knowledge organises itself. There has to be a progressive intuitivisation replacing the ignorant mind. The ignorant mind is to yield to an enlightened mind, a mind that seeks knowledge from outside has to be replaced by a mind that seeks knowledge inside. And once that is there, the mind begins to get universalised, open to the working of the universal mind. It is only thereafter that it can lay itself open to the working of intuition. Even when the intuitive faculties start functioning and our purified mind reflects the intuitively grasped truth, there are mixtures. Sri Aurobindo says that these mixtures, for instance, lie first in the stress of will. Each one of us has a certain will —our mind, our heart, our vital have particular preferences, we want things to be this way or that. Now however much we may consciously keep out this element, these things enter into the situation subconsciously and prejudice the inclination of what we perceive. And there are always suggestions, not from our selves, but suggestions from the universal atmosphere. People think, we too think, all these thoughts are stored in the universal atmosphere and these suggestions constantly bang upon our mental walls. So even when the intuition reflects itself, these suggestions act and we understand and interpret without being aware that these suggestions have already gotten involved in our understanding laboratory.

Naturally it is a question of long discipline. The more the higher element enters and displaces the lower, they are slowly eliminated. But one has always to take care. Sri Aurobindo says that however much we may take precaution by way of purification and discrimination, however high we may reach, the ignorant mind has a way of projecting itself in a hundred ways and influencing and deforming the intimation or the message from the intuitive level.

Then he speaks of the actualities, the possibles and the imperatives. Even when intuition is active, there are three phases, three visions of the intuition. One is the field of actualities—what things are there already, what is there around, what was there, what is there presently. To the number of actualities present it gives its certitude, but as it turns to the present and to the future, the possible intervenes. The actuals have to battle with the possibles. Many possibilities are there out of which only some can actualise. So when it sees actuals it sees the interference or the entry of the possibles. It may not be able to say definitely; it has to go a little beyond and there there is the realm of what are called imperatives. When the intuitivised mind looks at the imperatives it knows that whatever may be the number of possibles, the imperatives are going to fulfil themselves because the imperatives in the higher region are always in tune with the eternal Will. So whatever the number of actuals, whatever the possibles that are trying to actualise themselves, seeing the imperatives, the intuitivised consciousness is able to say this is going to happen —it is a question of time.

But when the intuition, at its highest, has a grasp of all these three visions, ultimately it has to function and report to the mind. Our mind only has to understand and grasp it. It is subject to mental conditions and limitations, because our mind, after all, is not in possession of knowledge but it receives the knowledge from the intuition. The mind is still a receiving instrument, it has to be progressively uplifted from the ignorant mind to the enlightened mind, to the universal mind and to the intuitivised mind; the intuitivised mind again has so many powers, like inspiration, like revelation of truth and then there is the mind of knowledge. Our mind matures into the mind of knowledge as a result of the progressive action of the supramental consciousness, and when the mind of knowledge is formed it becomes the bridge between the human mentality and the supramental consciousness. The supramental consciousness organises itself, radiates through this mind of knowledge. And in this mind of knowledge there is an eternal consciousness of the timeless vision, the timeless feeling. All the past, the present and the future are spread out and one can see behind, around and ahead.